施璐德亚洲有限公司 编

施璐德年鉴 2021

VISION DRIVEN LIFE

CNOOD 2008 TO 2021

复旦大学出版社

图书在版编目(CIP)数据

施璐德年鉴. 2021/施璐德亚洲有限公司编. —上海：复旦大学出版社，2022.11
ISBN 978-7-309-16380-3

Ⅰ.①施…　Ⅱ.①施…　Ⅲ.①建筑企业-上海-2021-年鉴　Ⅳ.①F426.9-54

中国版本图书馆 CIP 数据核字(2022)第 153870 号

施璐德年鉴 2021
SHILUDE NIANJIAN 2021
施璐德亚洲有限公司　编
责任编辑/谢同君　李　荃

复旦大学出版社有限公司出版发行
上海市国权路 579 号　邮编：200433
网址：fupnet@ fudanpress.com　http://www.fudanpress.com
门市零售：86-21-65102580　团体订购：86-21-65104505
出版部电话：86-21-65642845
上海丽佳制版印刷有限公司

开本 787×1092　1/16　印张 19　字数 427 千
2022 年 11 月第 1 版
2022 年 11 月第 1 版第 1 次印刷

ISBN 978-7-309-16380-3/F・2909
定价：88.00 元

如有印装质量问题,请向复旦大学出版社有限公司出版部调换。
版权所有　　侵权必究

CNOOD Yearbook
(2021)

目录

1
2021 年终总结大会
The year-end summary meeting for 2021
CNOOD

12
施璐德最美逆行者
The Heroes of CNOOD in Harm's Way
CNOOD

21
上海对外经贸大学与施璐德亚洲有限公司进行产学研合作探讨
Discussion on Industry-University-Research Cooperation between Shanghai University of International Business and Economics (SUIBE) and CNOOD Asia Limited (CNOOD)
CNOOD

23
巴拿马总统视察我司参建的 Amador 邮轮码头
The Panamanian President Visited the Amador Cruise Terminal Built by CNOOD
CNOOD

26
施璐德快讯之摩洛哥栈桥钢箱梁项目
CNOOD News: The Steel Box Girder Project of the Morocco Trestle Bridge
CNOOD

34
CNOOD 高管宣布大会
Announcement Meeting of CNOOD Executives
CNOOD

39
施璐德亚洲有限公司的"第一座现场施工海外桥"
The "first on-site construction overseas bridge" undertaken by CNOOD ASIA LIMITED
CNOOD

43
云淡风轻
To Be Philosophical and Tranquil
Dennis Chi

47
共济十载，与施璐德同心携铸
A Decade with CNOOD for a Common Goal
Fay Lee

60
欢迎来到第12期IP女性人物！
Welcome to the 12th Session of IP Female Characters!
Suki Duan

76
2021，用文字证明我曾经历过
Tell My Story in 2021 with My Own Words
Maria Shaw

83
一个产生飞跃的起点
A Starting Point for a Leap Forward
Tommy Chen

88
一场疫情一场梦
The Fleeting Dream in the Pandemic
Johnson Shen

93
铿锵四人行
The Strong Foursome Team
Danni Xu

98
秘鲁二三事
Working in Peru
Zoe Cui

107
抗疫进行时，静待花开期
Waiting for the Bloom during the Pandemic
Joanna Lee

112
写在二十五岁生日这一天
On My 25th Birthday
Jodie Zhou

120
疫中随笔
Random Thoughts in Pandemic Times
Billy Gu

125

十年
A Decade
Belinda Chen

130

疫情之下
Under the Pandemic
Mira Wei

135

致孩子
To My Beloved Daughter
Jenna Hu

139

美丽的大草坪
The Beautiful Lawn
CiCi Kang

142

等待
Waiting
Sonia Le

145

项目管理和项目集群管理学习随笔
Experience Sharing on Project Management
and Project Cluster Management Learning
Chris Lee

153

生活・成长・六月的记忆
To Those Passed Years
Sophie Lau

159

暖暖
To Little Nuannuan
Nancy Qi

162

我在施璐德的这两年
My Two Years in CNOOD
Caroline Sun

167

让思绪成为随笔
When Thoughts Become Words
Kyle Wang

170
不必在乎从何时何地出发
Set Out with An Easy Heart, Whenever and Wherever
David Wang

175
感悟，巴拿马
To Those Precious Days in Panama
Michael Wang

179
不在其位，不谋其政
Not in the Place, So not concerned?
Ada Wang

185
在逆境中重生
Reborn in Dilemma
Andy Wei

190
公司的命运
Company's Destiny
Amir Tafti

197
凡事都要看开点儿
Take It Easy
Jane Yan

204
种善因，得善果
Everything Happens for A Reason
Luis Camacho Cherp

211
以人为本，吾心所向
Focusing on People Makes CNOOD the Best Place to Work
Nicolas Kipreos Almallotis

216
改善工作表现的方法
Ways to Improve Work Performance
Nicolas Kipreos Almallotis

225
谢谢你，选择我们
Thank You, for Choosing Us
Raven Song

228
我的成长回忆及"古董"奖状
Memories of the Past and My Certificates of Honor
Zhengyu Ding

238
十年之约
The Ten-Year Agreement
Cindy Fang

241
2122,我已 130 岁
By 2122, I will be 130
Allen Han

243
走自己的路
Be Yourself
Shelley Wu

246
记武汉疫情与上海疫情有感
My Thoughts on Pandemic in Wuhan and Shanghai
Liam Wu

250
疫情之下,团结之美
The Power of Unity in the Pandemic
Henry Yang

255
疫情下的我们
Our Life Under the Pandemic
Heather Zhang

259
光阴与期望
Fading Time and Our Expectations
Peipei Yao

262
志趣之路
My Way of Finding My Interest
Sherry Lee

269
随笔
Random Thoughts
Tina Xu

279
施璐德实习感想
Thoughts on My Internship at CNOOD
Yu He

286
莫向外求
Do Not Seek Outward
Tony Lau

283
施璐德实习总结
Summary of Internship in CNOOD
Xinchen Tang

291
居家的第 n 天，我还剩 15g 咖啡豆
Quarantine Day n, I Have 15g Coffee Beans Left
Siki Wan

2021 年终总结大会
The Year-End Summary Meeting for 2021

■ CNOOD

作别旧岁，共赴新程——施璐德亚洲有限公司 2021 年终总结大会暨 2022 迎新团建活动圆满结束！

2022 年 1 月 20 日，施璐德亚洲有限公司"2021 年终总结大会"在上海办公室隆重举行。此次会议历时四个小时，包括高管述职、2022 年业务计划分享、员工代表讲话、表彰先进和董事长寄语五项议程。

1. 高管述职

我司 CEO 李燕飞女士、C.E 张林先生、COO 丁林生先生和 CFO 张召环先生分别进行了述职。

CEO 李燕飞女士述职完毕后，大会迎来了一个惊喜环节——感谢李燕飞女士

Bid farewell to the old year and start a new journey — the Year-End Summary Meeting for 2021 and the team building activity for 2022 of CNOOD Asia Limited ended successfully!

On January 20, 2022, the Year-end Summary Meeting for 2021 of CNOOD Asia Limited was held at Shanghai Office. The meeting lasted for four hours, including five agendas: Executive Debriefing, Business Plan Sharing for 2022, Speech by Staff Representative, Commendation for Staff and Chairman's Message.

1. Executive debriefing

Mrs. Fay Lee (CEO of CNOOD), Mr. Lin Zhang (C.E of CNOOD), Mr. Tiger Ding (COO of CNOOD) and Mr. Zhaohuan Zhang (CFO of CNOOD) made their debriefings respectively.

After Mrs. Fay Lee, CEO of CNOOD, made her debriefing, there was a surprise

施璐德亚洲有限公司董事长池勇海博士送上纪念相框

Dr. Dennis Chi, Chairman of CNOOD Asia Limited, presents a commemorative photo frame

圆满履职2017—2021年CEO任期，施璐德亚洲有限公司董事长池勇海博士将李世民的《赐萧瑀》的诗句赠予李燕飞女士，感谢她这几年对公司的无私奉献，同时祝贺李燕飞女士续任CEO职位。

session — thanking Mrs. Fay Lee for successfully fulfilling her duty as CEO from 2017 to 2021. Dr. Dennis Chi, Chairman of CNOOD, presented the poem *To Xiao Yu* by Shimin Li to Mrs. Fay Lee to appreciate her selfless dedication to CNOOD in recent years and congratulate Mrs. Fay Lee on her reappointment as CEO.

2. 2022年业务计划分享

施璐德各主管合伙人、业务合伙人、业务储备合伙人分享了自己的2022年业务计划、业务部署，为2022年立下新年flag。

2. Business plan sharing for 2022

The managing partners, business partners, and business reserve partners of CNOOD shared their business plans and business deployment in 2022 and set up new goals for 2022.

3. 员工代表讲话   3. Speech by Staff Representative

员工代表讲话——姜洁
Speech by Staff Representative — Tina Jiang

4. 表彰先进   4. Commendation for staff

在今年的年终表彰中，诞生了一个新的奖项——忠诚奖，以表彰陪伴公司十年及以上的员工。

截至2022年1月20日，许多员工已在施璐德这个大家庭里兢兢业业工作了10年或更久。这些年来，他们与企业风雨同舟，以他们的忠诚与才智为企业的发展做出了卓越的贡献。

十余年追随公司一路走来，虽经历风雨无数，却始终不离不弃。忠诚是无价之宝，在他们的身上得到了最完美的诠释。

In the year-end commendation this year, Loyalty Award was set up to commend the staff who had worked at CNOOD for 10 years or more.

As of January 20, 2022, many of our staff have worked hard at CNOOD for 10 years or more. Over the years, they have been in the same boat with CNOOD and made outstanding contributions to the development of CNOOD with their loyalty and intelligence.

Having worked at CNOOD for over 10 years, they still stay with the company even though they experienced numerous ups and downs. Loyalty is an invaluable asset, which is perfectly interpreted by them.

春风化雨奖
Salutary Influence Award

桃李天下奖
Instructor Award

优秀党员奖
Excellent CPC Member Award

优秀员工奖
Excellent Employee Award

最佳新人奖
Best Newcomer Award

创新先锋奖
Innovation Pioneer Award

最佳团队奖
Best Team Award

施璐德有你们，真好！

5. 董事长寄语

在会上，池董事长展望了2022年公司的发展重点和方向，传达了公司2022年的战略部署，并提前向大家致以新年美好的祝福和真诚的问候。

6. CNOOD 2022 虎年迎新团建活动

2021年终总结大会结束后，1月21日，CNOOD 2022 虎年迎新团建活动于上海市青浦区工商银行青浦培训中心顺利举行！

What a nice thing to have you at CNOOD!

5. Chairman's message

At the meeting, Chairman Dennis looked ahead to the company's development focus and direction in 2022, conveyed the company's strategic deployment in 2022 and extended the best wishes and sincere greetings for the New Year in advance.

6. Team building activity of CNOOD for 2022

After the end of the Year-End Summary Meeting for 2021, the team building activity of CNOOD for 2022 was successfully held at Qingpu Training Center of Industrial and Commercial Bank of China, Qingpu District, Shanghai on January 21, 2022!

7. 娱乐时光

7. Entertainment Time

书法大家郑小云老师写"福"赠福
The calligrapher Xiaoyun Zheng writes the Chinese character "Fu" ("Happiness") to convey his best wishes

晚宴
Dinner

8. 抽奖环节 8. Lucky Draw

最后，感谢此次 CNOOD 2022 虎年迎新团建活动的承办方——采购中心总经理丁征宇和全体采购中心成员，是他们不辞劳苦地奔波忙碌、周密安排，才保证此次团建活动顺利、圆满完成。

Finally, we would like to thank Zhengyu Ding (General Manager of the Procurement Center) and all the members of the Procurement Center for organizing the team building activity of CNOOD for 2022. It was your hard work and careful arrangement that ensured the smooth and successful completion of this team building activity.

投稿人：周颖
摄影：顾天阳
时间：2022 年 1 月 21 日

Contributor: Jodie Zhou
Photographer: Billy Gu
Dete: 2022-1-21

施璐德最美逆行者
The Heroes of CNOOD in Harm's Way

■ CNOOD

随着德尔塔变异株流行，新冠肺炎疫情出现大幅反弹。全球抗疫看中国，此时国内无疑是全世界最安全、最让人安心的地方。然而，远方的使命在召唤，有这样一批施璐德人，毅然选择迎难而上。责任在肩，他们义无反顾。

2021年4月起，为保证我司海外项目顺利推进、如期交付，施璐德员工王坤、程杰、戴书伟分别前往巴拿马、秘鲁，入驻项目一线，力保项目进度。

他们中，有新晋的奶爸，有刚结婚的新郎，有来不及举办婚礼的准新郎。七尺男儿，舍小家为大家，勇挑重担，凌云壮志怀心中，浩荡乾坤担肩上！

With the spread of Delta variant, the pandemic rebounded sharply. China is the safest and most reassuring place in the world at the moment. However, the distant mission is calling us, and there are a group of CNOOD staff who resolutely choose to face the difficulties. With responsibilities on their shoulders, they have no hesitation.

In order to ensure the smooth progress and timely delivery of our overseas projects, the CNOOD employees Michael Wang, Richard Chen and Steve Dai have gone to Panama and Peru respectively to settle in the frontline of the projects and try their best to ensure the progress of the projects since April 2021.

Some of them are new dads, newly married bridegrooms and prospective bridegrooms who failed to hold weddings as scheduled. As men, they worked for the projects, which left them with little time or energy to take care of their own

正是有了这样一批批优秀的施璐德人，我们才有了今天的高速稳定发展；正是由于这样一批批奋斗的施璐德人，我们的明天才会更加光明。

在此，向你们学习，向你们致敬！

加油！青春的你们！加油，奋斗的你们！你们是施璐德最美逆行者！

1. 巴拿马阿马多尔邮轮码头项目

阿马多尔邮轮码头项目位于巴拿马运河太平洋入海口的佩里科岛，施工内容主要涵盖邮轮码头、防坡堤、港口陆域吹填、护岸等工程。该项目建成后可全天候容纳两艘长360米、运载旅客5 000人次的船只靠泊，码头前沿水深达10.5米，无惧潮汐影响。项目所在区域汇集巴拿马免税店、高级餐厅和游艇俱乐部，连岛长堤也是巴拿马一个著名的旅游风景区，码头的落成将有效带动当地旅游业冉上新台阶。

families, and bravely shouldered the heavy responsibilities. With lofty aspirations in mind, they undertook the great mission!

It is with such groups of outstanding CNOOD staff that we have achieved the rapid and stable development today. It is because of such groups of hard-working CNOOD staff that we will have a better future.

Here, we learn from you and pay tribute to you!

Keep going, the young and the striving! You are the most beautiful heroes of CNOOD in harm's way!

1. Panama Amador Cruise Terminal Project

The Amador Cruise Terminal Project is located in Perico Island, where the Panama Canal is at the estuary of the Pacific Ocean. The construction mainly covers cruise terminal, breakwater, hydraulic reclamation of port land, bank protection, etc. After the project is completed, it will be able to berth two ships with a length of 360 meters and a capacity of 5,000 passengers all day long. The water depth at the terminal apron is 10.5 meters, and it is not affected by the tide. The project area is home to duty-free stores, high-end restaurants and yacht clubs in Panama, and the long island-connecting beach is a famous tourist scenic spot in Panama. The completion of the terminal will effectively promote local tourism to a new level.

2. 项目感想（王坤）

转眼间，到巴拿马已经2月有余，这也是我在疫情期间再次踏上这片热土。出国前，就十分牵挂大宝的学习，更恋恋不舍那步履蹒跚并咿呀学语的二宝，毕竟他出生那会儿我就因为疫情原因被困巴拿马无法回国见证他的降生。可是尽管各种不舍，终究还是顶着国外肆虐的疫情，毅然决然地踏上这片熟悉的土地，追寻那尚未完成的梦想，完成那光荣而艰巨的使命。

期待项目顺利交付的那天，更期待回家后将二宝举高高的那一刻！

为疫情期间每一位深处海外坚守岗位的工程人点赞喝彩！

2. Thoughts on the project（Michael Wang）

In a flash, I have been in Panama for more than 2 months, and I stepped on this land again during the pandemic. Before going abroad, I was very concerned about the study of my first child and even more reluctant to part with my second child who just walked with a waddle. When my second child was born, I was trapped in Panama because of the pandemic and could not return to China to witness his birth. However, despite all kinds of attach ments at home, I still resolutely set foot on this familiar land to pursue my unfinished dream and complete my glorious and arduous mission despite the pandemic raging abroad.

I look forward to the day when the project is delivered smoothly, and I also look forward to the moment when I hold high my children after I go home!

Let's praise and cheer for the staff who stick to their posts overseas during the pandemic!

加油，胜利终将属于我们！

3. 秘鲁查莫罗桥和萨利特拉尔桥项目

两项目的业主方都是秘鲁交通与通信部，桥梁结构形式都是下承式钢箱系杆拱桥，其中查莫罗桥单跨160米，预制钢筋混凝土桥面板，桥头两侧连接道路长540米。萨利特拉尔桥单跨182米，钢筋混凝土桥面板，桥头两侧连接道路长880米。CNOOD为两个项目提供钢结构与钢拉杆，并负责查莫罗桥钢结构和钢拉杆的安装。

4. 项目进展

在新冠肺炎疫情全球暴发之时，全球海运运输的及时性、稳定性受到了严重影响。为确保本项目材料的及时供应，我司与英国McCalls Special Products Ltd Trading as Macalloy公司进行了多轮商务技术谈判。同时，为保证现场的施工进度不受影响，我司投入了更多的人力于此项目，并积极与总承包商展开深入沟通，优化现场施工路线，确保本项目钢结构的及时交货。

Come on! Victory will eventually belong to us!

3. The projects of Chamorro and Salitral Bridge in Peru

The owner of the two projects is the Ministry of Transport and Communications of Peru (MTC), the structure of the bridges are in the form of a down-bearing steel box tied arch bridge, the single span of Chamorro Bridge is 160 meters, with precast reinforced concrete bridge deck slabs and 540 meters of connecting road on both sides of the bridge head. The single span of Salitral Bridge is 182 meters, with precast reinforced concrete bridge deck slabs and 880 meters long connecting road on both sides of the bridge head. CNOOD supplied the steel structures and steel tie rods for both projects and was responsible for the installation of the steel structures and steel tie rods for the Chamorro Bridge.

4. Project progress

When COVID-19 broke out all over the world, the timeliness and stability of global maritime transportation were affected seriously. To ensure the timely supply of materials for this project, we conducted several rounds of business and technical negotiations with McCalls Special Products Ltd Trading as Macalloy. In order to ensure that the site construction progress was not affected, we increased the manpower

我司与总包单位交流和现场施工
Photo of communication between our company and the general contractor & site construction

2021年2月，我司第一批钢结构发出，2021年6月初，我司完成所有钢结构以及刚拉杆产品的交付，目前，相关产

in this project and actively conducted in-depth communication with the general contractor to optimize the site construction route and ensure the timely delivery of the steel structures of this project.

In February 2021, we delivered the first batch of steel structures. In early June 2021, we delivered all steel structures

品陆续到达现场。

5. 项目感想

时光荏苒，白驹过隙。不知不觉已投入秘鲁怀抱两月有余，历经城市的喧嚣与沙漠的荒芜，让我更加能体会到温家宝曾说过的那句"年轻人既要敢于仰望星空，也要学会脚踏实地"。

从合同签署以来，作为亲历者，当看着桥梁从图纸设计到交付，我心里的成就感和自豪感不禁油然而生。在领导和同事的关怀和帮助下，我期望在工程领域取得更多的进步，拥有长远的发展，追求完美，在积累中不断成长。

and steel tie rods. At present, related products are arriving at the site one after another.

5. Thoughts on the project

Time flies. Unconsciously, I have been in Peru for more than 2 months. After experiencing the hustle and bustle of the city and the desolation of the desert, I can better understand the statement of Jiabao Wen that "young people should not only dare to look up at the stars but also remain grounded."

Since the signing of the contract, I have witnessed the process from bridge design drawing to delivery. I couldn't help but feel a sense of accomplishment and pride. With the care and assistance from leaders and colleagues, I expect to make more progress in the field of engineering, have long-term development, pursue perfection and keep growing up.

虽然疫情肆虐，但我们一直遵循防疫规定，做好安全防护，请亲人朋友、公司的领导同事放心，我一定会在保护自身安全的前提下，积极推进工期进度，与项目共同成长，不负韶华。同时，我也想和我的 Aurora 说，短期的分离，是为了长久的不离不弃，谢谢你深夜里安慰的电话。

——程杰

时间很快，来秘鲁已有 5 周时间。前几年我便到过秘鲁，但此时的秘鲁给人的感觉更多的是充满不确定性，整个国家的疫情管控以及人民的自觉性与中国相较相差甚远，这或许就是为什么秘鲁每日新增感染人数居高不下的原因吧。

Although the pandemic is raging, we have always abided by the pandemic prevention regulations and provided safety protection. The relatives, friends and leaders of the staff should rest assured that while ensuring our safety, we will actively promote the construction progress, grow together with the project, and live up to the expectations of the times. At the same time, I want to say to my Aurora that short-term separation is just for long-term stay. Thank you for your comforting calls in the night.

—— Richard Cheng

Time goes by so quickly. I have been in Peru for 5 weeks. I came to Peru once a few years ago, but now, Peru is full of uncertainties. The pandemic prevention and control and the people's consciousness in Peru are far behind

很感谢公司各级领导以及同事们的关心，我在秘鲁一切安好，横跨2万多千米，来到秘鲁，投入秘鲁桥梁项目的施工组织以及秘鲁钱凯项目的前期准备工作。

在此，向各位家人和同事报以平安，在往后的秘鲁生活工作中，我将全身心地投入，不负众望。同时，我也会以百倍的小心，注意疫情防控。

与此同时，虽然秘鲁疫情态势依然十分紧张，我们要以科学、严谨的态度，组织相关人员、设备等保质、保量地完成此项工作，为我司在秘鲁的市场开发以及项目运营带来更多、更大的成效。未来几个月，项目将逐步开始现场安装工作，前方道路虽曲折，但终将被我们的专业、敬业所摊平！

——戴书伟

投稿人：王坤、程杰、戴书伟、李鹏、周颖
时间：2021年8月18日

China, which might be the reason why the number of newly infected cases in Peru remains high every day.

I am very grateful to the leaders at all levels of CNOOD and my colleagues for their concerns. I am well in Peru. After traveling more than 20,000 kilometers to Peru, I took part in the construction of the bridge projects and the preparatory work of the Chancay Project in Peru.

Here, I would like to report my safety to my family and colleagues. In my future life and work in Peru, I will devote myself wholeheartedly and live up to the expectations. At the same time, I will pay attention to the pandemic prevention and control.

Although the pandemic situation in Peru is still very tense, we should organize relevant personnel and equipment to finish the work with quality and quantity guarantee in a scientific and rigorous manner so as to bring more and greater results to our market development and project operation in Peru. In the next few months, site installation will be conducted for the project. Although the way ahead is tortuous, it will eventually be made smooth through our professionalism and dedication!

— Steve Dai

Contributor: Michael Wang, Richard Cheng, Steve Dai, Charles Lee, Jodie Zhou
Dete: 2021-8-18

上海对外经贸大学与施璐德亚洲有限公司进行产学研合作探讨

Discussion on Industry-University-Research Cooperation between Shanghai University of International Business and Economics (SUIBE) and CNOOD Asia Limited (CNOOD)

■ CNOOD

2021年7月6日上午，上海对外经贸大学工商管理学院副院长左鹏、工商管理学院副院长王朝晖教授、工商管理学院党委副书记施毅婷来访施璐德亚洲有限公司，和我司董事长池勇海博士、CEO李燕飞等人进行了亲切友好的商谈，深刻地探讨了产学研合作。双方就建立实习基地、举行定期或不定期的学术研讨会、支持和鼓励以创业竞赛为代表的校园活动等方面达成共识，坚持将社会实践与理论知识相结合，立志于让学生走进施璐德，让施璐德走进课堂。

On the morning of July 6, 2021, Peng Zuo (Vice President of School of Business Administration of SUIBE), Professor Chaohui Wang (Vice President of School of Business Administration of SUIBE) and Yiting Shi (Deputy Secretary of the Party Committee of School of Business Administration of SUIBE) visited CNOOD Asia Limited, had a cordial and friendly discussion with Dr. Dennis Chi (Chairman of CNOOD) and Fay Lee (CEO of CNOOD), and discussed the industry-university-research cooperation. The two sides reached a consensus on establishing a practice base, holding regular or irregular academic seminars, supporting and encouraging campus activities represented by entrepreneurship

同时，左鹏院长为池勇海博士颁发了聘书，聘任池博士为上海对外经贸大学客座教授。左鹏院长代表上海对外经贸大学对池博士的加入表示热烈的欢迎。

投稿人：周颖
时间：2021 年 7 月 6 日

competitions, etc., adhering to on combining social practice with theoretical knowledge, letting students approach CNOOD, and letting CNOOD approach the classroom.

Peng Zuo issued a letter of appointment to Dr. Dennis Chi and appointed him as an adjunct professor at SUIBE. On behalf of SUIBE, Peng Zuo extended a warm welcome to Dr. Dennis.

Contributor: Jodie Zhou
Dete: 2021-7-6

巴拿马总统视察我司参建的 Amador 邮轮码头
The Panamanian President Visited the Amador Cruise Terminal Built by CNOOD

■ CNOOD

2021年9月3日，巴拿马共和国总统劳伦蒂诺·科尔蒂索·科恩在巴拿马海事局局长诺里尔·阿劳兹和巴拿马旅游局局长伊万·埃斯基尔森的陪同下，参观了由施璐德亚洲有限公司参建的阿马多尔邮轮码头，为迎接2021年11月份预计到达的第一批邮轮做准备。

On September 3, 2021, Laurentino Cortizo Cohen, President of the Republic of Panama, who was accompanied by Noriel Araúz (Director of Panama Maritime Authority) and Iván Eskildsen (Director of Panama Tourism Authority), visited the Amador Cruise Terminal built by CNOOD to prepare for the first batch of cruise ships to arrive in November this year.

在视察阿马多尔邮轮码头过程中,巴拿马旅游局局长伊万·埃斯基尔森说道,"这是一个极具吸引力的码头,它的建立将为巴拿马提供一个全新的旅游地,吸引众多游客,推动巴拿马邮轮业和旅游业。"

During the visit at the Amador Cruise Terminal, Iván Eskildsen, Director of Panama Tourism Authority (ATP), said, "This is a very attractive terminal, and its establishment will provide Panama with a brand-new tourist destination to attract many tourists and promote the cruise and tourism industry in Panama."

总统视察码头现场
President visit terminal site

阿马多尔邮轮码头位于巴拿马湾内，紧邻巴拿马城南部佩里科岛东侧，南接太平洋，北侧连接巴拿马运河南口，工程坐标 8°55′N，79°31′W。该项目拟设计一座邮轮母港，可同时停靠两艘绿洲级邮轮。

此项目是中国与巴拿马在 2017 年 6 月正式建立外交关系以来，中国企业在巴拿马政府工程招标中中标的第一单！施璐德亚洲有限公司作为此项目的最大专业分包，主要负责该邮轮码头所有钢管桩的供货以及航站楼所有钢结构与幕墙的供货与安装。目前，我司王坤正带领团队在现场负责我司在该项目合同范围内的收尾工作。

投稿人：王坤、罗蓉、周颖

时间：2021 年 9 月 7 日

The Amador Cruise Terminal is located in Panama Bay, close to the east side of Perico Island in the south of Panama City, the Pacific Ocean in the south, and the south estuary of Panama Canal in the north. The coordinate of the project are 8° 55′ N and 79° 31′ W. The project plans to host a cruise home port, which can berth two oasis cruise ships simultaneously.

This project is the first bid won by the Chinese enterprises in Panamanian government project bidding since China and Panama formally established diplomatic relations in June 2017! As the largest professional subcontractor of this project, CNOOD is mainly responsible for the supply of all steel pipe piles of the cruise terminal and the supply and installation of all steel structures and curtain walls of the terminal building. At present, Michael Wang is leading the team to take charge of the finishing touches of CNOOD within the contract scope of the project.

Contributor: Michael Wang, Loreen Luo, Jodie Zhou

Dete: 2021-9-7

施璐德快讯之摩洛哥栈桥钢箱梁项目

CNOOD News: The Steel Box Girder Project of the Morocco Trestle Bridge

■ CNOOD

1. 项目简介

项目名称：阿尤恩地区新磷酸盐港口建设总承包

业主：OCP PHOSBOUCRAA
产品名称：钢箱梁
制造标准：EN1090 Class EXC3

材料标准：EN 10025-2: 2004 S355J2+N; EN 10025-3: 2004 S355N/ S355N+Z15; EN 10025-4: 2004 S355M/ S355M+Z25

1. Project introduction

Project: TURNKEY COMPLETION OF THE CONSTRUCTION OF A NEW PHOSPHATE PORT IN THE REGION OF LAAYOUNE

Owner: OCP PHOSBOUCRAA
Product: Steel Box Girder
Manufacturing standard: EN1090 Class EXC3

Material standard: EN 10025-2: 2004 S355J2+N; EN 10025-3: 2004 S355N/ S355N+Z15; EN 10025-4: 2004 S355M/ S355M+Z25

单个箱梁最大尺寸：长 44 661 mm × 宽 3 800 mm × 高 2 241 mm

单个箱梁最大吨位：83.321 吨

总吨位：24 000 吨（312 件）

2. 项目背景

摩洛哥栈桥项目全长 3.18 千米，为世界最大的磷矿公司 OCP 投资建设的综合化肥生产平台和新建码头，以满足更多的进出口散货需求，促进和加强该地区工业生态系统。

摩洛哥栈桥项目于 2019 年面向全球招标，CNOOD 团队通过专业的方案设计、完善的项目管理体系、始终坚持为

Maximum size of single box girder: Length 44 661mm × Width 3 800mm × Height 2 241mm

Maximum tonnage of single box girder: 83.321 tons

Gross tonnage: 24 000 tons (312 pieces)

2. Project background

The Morocco Trestle Bridge Project, which totals a length of 3.18 kilometers, is a comprehensive fertilizer production platform and a new terminal invested and built by OCP, the world's largest phosphate company. This project aims to meet the increasing import and export bulk cargo demands and promote and strengthen the industrial ecosystem in this area.

The Morocco Trestle Bridge Project called for bids globally in 2019. Through professional scheme design

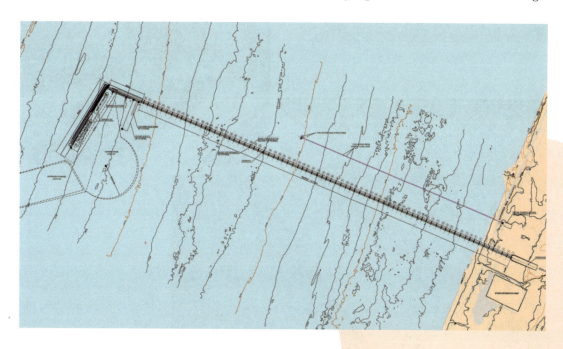

客户提供增值服务的态度，最终在业主多次审查评估后脱颖而出，分别于2019年年底及2020年年初中标供应该项目的12 000吨基建管桩以及24 000吨栈桥钢箱梁。其中12 000吨管桩已于2020年6月底交付完毕。由于新冠肺炎疫情在全球的蔓延及业主设计变更等原因，钢箱梁部分延期至2021年4月1日正式开工。

and perfect project management system, the CNOOD team always persisted in the attitude of providing value-added services to customers. After many reviews and evaluations by the owner, CNOOD finally won the bid to supply 12,000 tons of infrastructure pipe piles and 24,000 tons of trestle steel box girders in the end of 2019 and the beginning of 2020, respectively. In particular, 12,000 tons of pipe piles were delivered by the end of June 2020. Due to the global spread of COVID-19 and the design changes of the owner, the construction of the steel box girders was postponed to April 1 this year.

2019年9月业主验厂
The owner inspected the plant in September 2019

3. 项目亮点及挑战

项目规范的要求在 EN 1090 EXC3 标准的基本要求之上增加了诸多附加要求。例如，箱梁支座位置公差要求在 205 米的标准伸缩段内累计不超过 5 毫米，可谓是对超大件的精细要求。

箱梁在厂内模拟施工现场进行 2 条轴线 205 米长的整体试拼装。

钢箱梁在发货前全部两两预拼装，以确保现场顺利安装。

箱梁结构整体为密闭的箱体，内、外表面均需要做底中面三道油漆，内部防腐施工难度非常大。

疫情原因，业主无法到我方工厂进行验收，生产过程中由多方检验放行：生产车间自检，CNOOD 驻厂检验，SGS，TUV Nord，业主代表，业主在线检验等。

结构设计与生产详设相互配合，力求既达到设计要求又遵循生产合理原则。

3. Project highlights and challenges

The project specification adds many additional requirements to the basic requirements of EN 1090 EXC3. For example, the position tolerance of box girder support is required to be no more than 5 mm in the standard telescopic section of 205 m, which can be described as a fine requirement for super-large parts.

In the simulated construction site of the box girder plant, the overall trial assembly of 2 axes with a length of 205 m is carried out.

All the steel box girders are preassembled in pairs before delivery so as to ensure smooth installation on site.

The whole box girder structure is a closed box body, and the inner and outer surfaces need to be painted on the bottom, middle and surface layers. Therefore, the internal anticorrosion construction is rather difficult.

Because of the pandemic, the owner could not go to our plant for inspection and acceptance. During the production process, it was inspected and released by multiple parties: self-inspection in the production workshop, in-plant inspection of CNOOD, SGS, TUV Nord, owner's representative, owner's online inspection, etc.

The design and production details need to be coordinated well, meet the design requirements and follow the principle of reasonable production.

为业主提供必要的技术支持，与业主现场团队紧密合作，以确保顺利安装。

4. 长风破浪会有时，直挂云帆济沧海

尽管项目挑战重重，我司和项目组团队协同各方，攻坚克难，秉承着施璐德一贯服务客户、增值客户的原则，按照合同要求，通过了多家全球著名三方检验公司的检验，保质保量地完成了项目第一批的交付。

We provide necessary technical support to the owner and work closely with the owner's site team to ensure smooth installation.

4. Achieve our dreams with great efforts

Despite the challenges of the project, our company and the project team worked together with all parties to overcome the difficulties, adhering to the principle of CNOOD to serve customers and add values to them. According to the the contract, we passed the inspections by many world-known third-party inspection companies and completed the first batch delivery of the project with quality and quantity guarantee.

2021年8月31日，满载的艾姆克轮扬帆起航，乘风破浪驶向大洋彼岸的目的港。

On August 31, 2021, the loaded Eimke ship was set sail and headed for the destination port across the ocean.

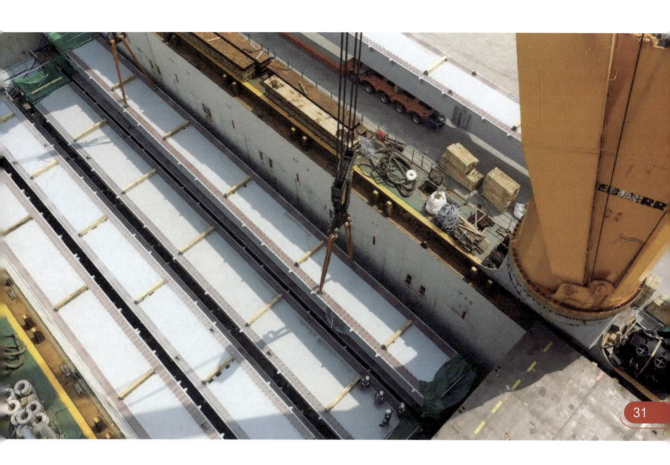

目前，项目第二批钢箱梁的加工也正在稳步推进并即将交付。公司高层将持续高度重视，项目组成员也将继续保持与各方的沟通、协调，致力于为客户递交一份满意的答卷。

中国智慧，我们在路上！

投稿人：摩洛哥项目团队
时间：2021 年 9 月 3 日

At present, the processing of the second batch of steel box girders of the project is proceeding steadily and will be delivered soon. The senior management of CNOOD will continue to pay high attention to it. The members of the project team will keep communicating and coordinating with all parties and commit themselves to satisfying customers.

With Chinese insight, we are on the way!

Contributor: Morocco Project Team
Dete: 2021-9-3

CNOOD 高管宣布大会
Announcement Meeting of CNOOD Executives

■ CNOOD

2021年9月17日下午，施璐德亚洲有限公司举行了"CNOOD 高管宣布大会"，本次会议宣布了施璐德新一任高管的任命决定。

首先，宣读高管任命书。

许秋石女士宣读了公司高管产生规则：秉承施璐德共创、共治、共享的发展理念，以贡献者为本，以公司最近五个考核年度（2016年7月1日—2021年6月30日）业务合伙人给公司创造的留存收益总和为依据，排名前十且有任职意愿的业务合伙人为候选人，通过全体员工不记名投票、差额选举的方式，最终产生 CEO 和 COO 两位当选人，由董事会任命，CFO 和 C.E 则由董事会直接任命。此次新任高管名单为：李燕飞女士为 CEO、丁林生先生为 COO、张召环先生为 CFO、张林先生为 C.E。

On the afternoon of September 17, 2021, CNOOD Asia Limited held "the Announcement Meeting of CNOOD Executives." At the meeting, the appointment decision of CNOOD's new senior executives was announced.

First of all, Mrs. Tina Xu read out the letters of appointment for the executives.

Mrs. Tina Xu read out the selection rules of the company's executives: Adhering to CNOOD's development philosophy of co-creation, co-governance and sharing, taking contributors as the foundation and basing on the total retained earnings created by business partners in the last five assessment years (July 1, 2016–June 30, 2021), two of the top ten business partners who are willing to serve as candidates are selected through secret ballot and differential election by all employees. They are appointed as CEO and COO by the board of directors, and the CFO and C.E are directly

随后，董事长颁发任命书，并与新当选的高管合影留念。

由于CFO张总因为行程问题不能亲临现场，请池总代表张总领取任命书并妥善保管。

appointed by the board of directors. The new executives were Mrs. Fay Lee (CEO), Mr. Tiger Ding (COO), Mr. Zhaohuan Zhang (CFO) and Mr. Lin Zhang (C.E).

After that, the chairman issued the letters of appointment and took a group photo with the newly elected executives.

As Mr. Zhang (CFO) was absent because of a business trip, Chairman Dennis received the letter of appointment and kept it properly on behalf of Mr. Zhang.

董事长为 CEO 颁发任命书
The chairman presents the letter of appointment to CEO

董事长为 COO 颁发任命书
The chairman presents the letter of appointment to COO

董事长为 C.E 颁发任命书
The chairman presents the letter of appointment to C.E.

高管合影
Group photo of executives

接下来，当选高管进行了表态发言。

他们梳理了未来的工作重点，介绍了未来的工作开展计划。展望未来，他们信心满满，纷纷表示，将与全体施璐德人一道努力，把公司带入发展快车道。

Next, the elected executives made their own speeches.

They sorted out the future work priorities and introduced the future work plan. Looking into the future, they were full of confidence and said that they would work together with all CNOOD staff to lead the company to the fast track of development.

CEO

COO

C.E

会议的最后，池董事长为我们描绘了施璐德未来发展的宏伟蓝图，引得在场同事心潮澎湃、热血沸腾，都想撸起袖子加油干，为早日实现公司跨越式发展贡献力量。

At the end of the meeting, Chairman Chi charted the grand blueprint of CNOOD's future development for us, which made the colleagues choked up with emotions and excitement. They all wanted to roll up their sleeves to work harder and contribute to the leapfrog development of the company as soon as possible.

池勇海（董事长）：

今天，是承上启下的日子，原高管团队圆满完成任期内工作任务、完美谢幕，并将企业发展的接力棒交到了新的团队手里。而新的团队中青结合，朝气蓬勃，蓄势待发。明天，2021年9月18日，将是施璐德新的起点，让我们在施璐德精神的指引下，勇于开拓、积极进取、艰苦奋斗、精益求精、奉献精神、勇敢担当、心怀大众、为国为民；我们要勇于突破旧我、创造新我！施璐德这个温馨的大家庭是我们一起创造出来的，让我们一起努力！

Dennis:

Today is a connecting link between the preceding and the following. The former senior management team successfully completed the tasks during their term of office and handed the baton of enterprise development to the new team. The new team is full of youthful spirit and get ready. Tomorrow is September 18, 2021, which will be a new starting point for CNOOD. Let's blaze new trails, keep progressive, work hard and keep improving, be dedicated, dare to take the responsibility, care for the public and serve the country and the people under the guidance of the CNOOD spirit. We should dare to break through the old self and create a new self! CNOOD is created by all of us. Let's work together!

投稿人：李鹏、周颖
时间：2021年9月17日

Contributor: Charles Lee, Jodie Zhou
Dete: 2021-9-17

施璐德亚洲有限公司的"第一座现场施工海外桥"

——秘鲁钢系杆拱桥桥梁顺利开工

The "First On-Site Construction Overseas Bridge" Undertaken by CNOOD ASIA LIMITED

■ CNOOD

秘鲁当地时间2021年11月6日,施璐德亚洲有限公司承建的"第一座现场施工海外桥"——秘鲁伊卡查莫罗钢系杆拱桥桥梁项目正式开启了首个桥面钢梁吊装单元的吊装。

查莫罗桥位于伊卡大区钦查省埃尔卡尔门区,是当地跨越马查多特河的主要交通道路。该桥通过1S公路及Carra EL Carmen公路与伊卡市相通,距埃尔卡门市6千米,距钦查市11千米。

受2017年厄尔尼诺的影响,查莫罗桥的桥梁结构损毁严重,给当地居民的出行和正常生活带来了极大不便,秘鲁交通部重建委员会作为业主发起了秘鲁伊卡查

On November 6, 2021, local time in Peru, the "first on-site construction overseas bridge" undertaken by CNOOD ASIA LIMITED — Peru Steel Tied Arch Bridge Project started the hoisting of the first steel beam hoisting unit on the bridge deck.

Chamorro Bridge, located in El Carmen District, Chincha Province, Ica Region, is the main road across the Machadot River. The bridge is connected to the city of Ica via highway 1S and Carra EL Carmen, 6 kilometers from El Carmen city and 11 kilometers from Chincha city.

Affected by El Nino in 2017, the structure of the Chamorro Bridge was severely damaged, which brought great

查莫罗桥
Chamorro Bridge

莫罗钢系杆拱桥桥梁项目。秘鲁钢系杆拱桥桥梁项目的高质量、高效率完工，将极大地便利当地居民的出行，也将对公司在秘鲁地区的品牌塑造产生积极影响！

在项目运行初期，我司项目组部分成员陶涛、程杰和戴书伟便毅然选择入驻项目一线，确保查莫罗桥的新建施工按计划有序推进。在疫情下，国际物流受到阻滞。为了不影响项目的预拼装，公司现场项目组成员积极地与当地运输公司进行方案探讨，制定周密的施工方案，匹配项目的节点需求。同时，考虑到安装的安全性，并且为了不影响吊装节点进度，项目组组织了300吨吊机开展吊装工作，努力做到科学安排、准备充分，全力克服疫情带来的不利影响。

投稿人：程杰、周颖、陈浩

时间：2021年11月8日

inconvenience to local residents' travel and normal life. The Reconstruction Committee of the Ministry of Transport of Peru, as the owner, initiated Peru Steel Tied Arch Bridge Project. The high-quality and efficient completion of this project will greatly facilitate the travel of local residents and will also have a positive impact on CNOOD's brand building in Peru!

At the beginnning of project operation, members of CNOOD's project team, Peter Tao, Richard Cheng and Steve Dai, resolutely decided to join the project front line to ensure the new construction of the Chamorro Bridge proceeded as planned. Due to COVID-19 pandemic, international logistics has been held up. In order not to affect the pre-assembly of the project, members of CNOOD's on-site team actively discussed the plan with the local transportation company and formulated a thorough construction plan to match the node requirements of the project. At the same time, considering the safety of installation and without affecting the progress of hoisting, the project team made arrangements for a 300-ton crane to carry out the hoisting work, making efforts to be scientific and fully-prepared to overcome the adverse impact of the epidemic!

Contributor: Richard Cheng, Jodie Zhou, Tommy Chen

Dete: 2021-11-8

云淡风轻
——人生的精彩瞬间

To Be Philosophical and Tranquil
— in Memory of Those Wonderful Moments in Life

■ Dennis Chi

　　回眸过往，云淡风轻；精彩瞬间，白驹过隙。无风无雨，无阴无晴。春有百花秋有月，夏有鸣蝉冬有雪。若无闲事挂心头，便是人间好时节。

1. 缅甸之花

　　2019年12月17日，我们踏上赴缅征程。艰苦的谈判，如期而至。最终合同延期落地，随后开始了更加艰巨的项目推进。设井点，测水位，徜徉于山水之间；请专家，答疑惑，惴惴于天灾人祸之情。

Whenever looking back upon dreariness in the past, I feel nothing but philosophical and tranquil; wonderful memories keep coming back with time passing by. Regardless of rain or sunshine, I shall stick to my own will, away from fame or gain.

Flowers in spring and moonlight in autumn,

Breeze in summer and snow in winter,

Each season brings its joy,

If you keep yourself away from the troubled mind.

1. Fruit of success in myanmar

On December 17, 2019, I started my trip to Myanmar for a tough business negotiation. We managed to extend the contract. Thus followed the project promotion which was more arduous. We

忽喜从天降，方案通过，项目推进。又遇疫情，再见洪水。身忐忑，心彷徨。还好有李总坚强的队伍，有仇工非常专业的素养，云开雾散，否去泰来，终于在 2021 年 1 月 31 日试运行成功。真是难忘的经历。每次同事离开项目，都不免感慨万千。

队伍，队伍，强大的队伍。

2. 有人辞职

疫情对公司没有影响，是假的，相反还非常大。人往高处走，水往低处流。很多人提出离职，公司都给予了支持。而且考虑到以前全员股改，公司以双倍价格回购了全部的股份，充分考虑到了大家的诉求。

施璐德是一家学习型、创业型的公司，各种思路、新模式层出不穷，各种队伍不断成长、不断成熟，有更好的平台，有更好的前程，公司只会支持，绝不会拖

set the well point and measured the water level, moving back and forth in barren hills and turbulent rivers; we consulted experts and looked for solutions, fearing and worrying about natural disasters. Great news suddenly came that our plan was approved and our project got to be promoted. Then came COVID-19 and the flood, and we were anxious and fearful all day long. Thanks to the team led by Director Lee and the professional skills of Mr. Qiu, we finally overcame these difficulties: Out of misfortune comes bliss. We achieved great success in the test run on January 31, 2021. It was such an unforgettable experience! Whenever I saw a colleague leaving the project, all sorts of feelings would well up in my mind. Team! Team! What a great team it was!

2. When someone leaves CNOOD

No one can say confidently that the pandemic has no effect on our company; on the contrary, it has influenced CNOOD hugely. Man struggles upwards and water flows downwards, as we know. Many people chose to leave the company during this tough time, and CNOOD fully supported their decisions. Considering the all-staff shareholding system, CNOOD bought their equities back with double price. The company considered everyone's demand thoroughly.

CNOOD is a learning-oriented and entrepreneurial company where everyone makes contributions to the company by putting forward new and creative

泥带水，阻碍前程。

祝愿所有离开施璐德的家人们，有更加远大更加美好的前程。

3. 细节决定成败

在缅甸光伏项目的投标中，施璐德付费请了专家指导，但没有按照招标文件的要求给予披露，导致公司付出严重代价！

这给我们提了一个醒，细节决定成败。如果在业务过程中有任何的侥幸心理，结果都可能是巨大的灾难，前车之鉴，后事之师。不可不警醒。

细节，细节，可靠的细节。

ideas and setting up new patterns. Both individuals and teams have a chance to grow. If one seeks a better future on a better platform, our platform will do nothing but give you its best wishes and biggest support. In no way will it do things sloppily or set obstacles for you deliberately.

I sincerely pray for those who have left CNOOD. Hope they get what they want in the new place and have a better future!

3. The devil lies in the details

When CNOOD paid for expert guidance in the bidding of photovoltaic projects in Myanmar, it failed to disclose it in accordance with the requirements of the bidding documents. This causes CNOOD to pay a heavy price.

We learned a lesson from it: Success lies on details. Expecting flukes in business will only lead to failures or even disasters. Lessons learned in the past can guide one in the future. We should bear it in mind.

Details, details! Details are always crucial.

4. 感谢韩总

2021年，多事之秋，内忧外患，喋喋不休。感谢韩总，在施璐德生死存亡之际，屈尊下驾，起到中流砥柱、定海神针的作用，让我们有了喘息之机，有了凤凰涅槃的机会。我们感谢以韩总为代表的，所有为施璐德的生存发展，而默默无闻、努力奋斗着的家人们，是大家的努力，让我们在时局如此艰难的状况下，还能看到明天辉煌的希望。

5. 恬淡结语

回首向来萧瑟处，归去，也无风雨也无晴。

花若盛开，蝴蝶自来。

4. Thanks to director han

The year 2021 was a tough year, with inner worries and outer dangers surrounding us. We were so head over heels, keeping ourselves alerted all the time, and CNOOD was facing a fatal challenge that it had never had before. Fortunately, Director Han came and took the whole situation under control. Under his smart and powerful leadership, we finally had a chance to take a breath and bring CNOOD back to life. I owe my thanks to everyone who strove hard for the development of CNOOD, like Director Han. It is with everyone's effort that we are still full of hope in such a difficult situation.

5. Conclusion to My Random Thoughts

Turning my head, I see the dreary beaten track.

Let me go back!

Impervious to rain or shine, I'll have my own will.

Cultivate yourself and bloom fiercely, and then butterflies will be drawn to you naturally.

池勇海
Dennis Chi

男，汉族，1970年生于湖北省仙桃市。武汉理工大学管理学硕士，硕士导师刘国新教授；复旦大学经济学博士，博士生导师洪远朋教授。2008年创立施璐德亚洲有限公司，现担任施璐德亚洲有限公司董事长。

Male, ethnic Han, was born in Xiantao, Hubei Province in1970. He received his master's degree in management from Wuhan University of Technology, where he studied under Professor Guoxin Liu and received his Ph.D. in Economics from Fudan University, where he studied under Professor Yuanpeng Hong. Dennis is now Chairman of CNOOD Asia Limited, which he founded in 2008.

共济十载，与施璐德同心携铸

A Decade with CNOOD for a Common Goal

■ Fay Lee

2022年，是我入职施璐德的十周年。从时间线来看，十年是一个里程碑，从人生维度来回顾，施璐德十年，承载了我最珍贵的职场历炼。

酝酿写这篇文章前，曾有人问我：很多人在做职场选择时，会抱着试一试的想法，也有更多人想保持职业新鲜度，会时不时更换工作，选择新环境。为什么我一入施璐德便深似海？仔细想了一下，从我进入施璐德开始，用当下比较时髦的词来说，我就"all in"了。

走进施璐德，三个关键词画饼

2010年，第一次接触施璐德，源于一次工作契机，结识了创始人，也是现在施璐德的董事长池勇海先生。初次见面，

The year 2022 marks my 10th anniversary at CNOOD. By the timeline, a decade represents a milestone; my decade with CNOOD, when reviewed as part of my life, has been closely associated with my most cherished working experiences.

Before making up my mind to write this article, I was once asked why I had maintained such a deep bond with CNOOD ever since I joined the company, while many people would take a tentative attitude in their choice of career, and others would change their jobs frequently just to avoid job burnout. After careful thinking, I realize that I have always been in a state of "all in" since the moment I joined CNOOD.

Getting to know CNOOD, three keywords to picture a dream

My first encounter with CNOOD took place in 2010, when I, by a chance related to my daily work, met Dennis

董事长在讲到公司未来发展规划时，提到了三个关键词让我印象很深刻："无边界""合伙人制度""平台式"。

经过他的描述，在我脑海中呈现了一个广阔、包容的全新型组织模式。在这个模式下，我们可以依据项目目标自主成团，随时打破，随时构建，这样的优加资源匹配模式更灵活，更有利于业务同时、快速推进，形成一个组织生态圈。

2012年，刚进入施璐德，身处当时的办公环境可能让人很难相信施璐德的未来会是这样，不得不承认，初创企业领导者的魅力和言谈举止间的魄力让人很想跟着他大干一场，凡心所向，素履以往。

事实证明，十年间，施璐德正是以这三个关键词为基础逐年推进壮大。十年后，在我写这篇文章时，组织生态圈已经顺利构建，董事长当年画的"饼"，如今已经实实在在初具成型了。

Chi, the founder of CNOOD and now its chairman. In our first meeting, I was deeply impressed by the three keywords mentioned by Dennis when he explained to me the company's plan for future development: boundaryless, partnership, and platform.

When I listened to his description, a totally new pattern of organizational structure, both extensive and inclusive, unfolded in my imagination. It is a pattern that enables us to form self-organized teams which can be dismissed or rebuilt at any time in accordance with project objects. The optimized model of matching resources is therefore more flexible and facilitates the simultaneous, rapid progress of different businesses, thus creating an organizational ecosystem.

In 2012, it was probably hard for me, sitting in the office environment of that time, to convince myself that the company which I had freshly joined would become so successful as it is now. I must admit that the personal charm of its leader and the vigor displayed in his words and actions attracted me to work with him for a great cause. I was determined to move forward against the odds toward the goal I longed for.

The fact is: CNOOD grew larger and stronger every year in the following decade, guided by these three keywords. Ten years later, as I am writing this article, its organizational ecosystem has been successfully constructed, and the big dream described by Dennis has now really come true.

以梦为马，仗剑挥手画版图

2012年5月，我刚入职没多久，公司就迎来了一个亿（美金）级的订单。由于第一次承接如此大体量的项目，每个人在项目中都要发挥职场超级单兵的特质，能够以一当十，不仅要业务熟练，还要有极强的学习能力、沟通能力和解决突发问题的能力。经过这一单，公司积蓄了不少国内外资源，行业内的影响力也迅速提升，而我也和施璐德紧紧地联结在一起，对公司的未来发展也更加笃定。

2013年开始，公司有了前期的快速积累，国内管理流程已经基本夯实：我们在个性中归纳出共性，在共性上形成统一的标准流程，促进项目执行的规范化操作，公司发展进入到升级期。

为了更好的承接项目，我开启了以母校为第一站的校园招聘，挖掘有潜力、有能力的新人进入公司；另一方面，我们也去跑海外市场，拓展业务。从最初的展会亮相，到熟悉市场后聚焦目标公司，直接进行深度商务会谈，一次次前线冲锋将公司的业务版图越做越大。写这篇文章时，我盘点了自己十年间的飞行轨迹，粗略计算走过了36个国家，而我们的项目也触

With dreams as horses, we outline our business landscape

CNOOD received an order worth more than one hundred million US dollars in May 2012, shortly after I joined the company. It was the first project of such a big value for the company that every member on the project team was required to be a "super soldier," who, in addition to being proficient at work, must possess very strong abilities to learn, communicate and solve unexpected problems. This experience helped CNOOD accumulate domestic and foreign resources, with its rapidly increasing influence within the industry. Being closely connected with CNOOD, I also became more confident about its future.

By 2013, our domestic management process had been largely consolidated owing to the company's rapid accumulation at earlier stages. Drawing on the common factors induced from individual phenomena, we were able to develop a unified standard process for promoting standardized operation in all projects. The growth of the company was greatly boosted.

To better undertake projects, I started a journey of campus recruitment with the aim of finding talented young people who would be our potential newcomers, with my alma mater as the first stage. We also sought to expand our business in overseas markets. From the first appearances at exhibitions to in-depth business talks with prospective clients after being familiar

及 69 个国家。为公司开疆拓土，挥剑驰骋的点滴经历都是宝贵印记。

那时候也正值用人际，我们从校招来的新人中选择一些好苗子，直接带到国外出差，施璐德很多新人入职的第一课不是在会议室做培训，而是拉到前线战场经历洗刷，在干中学。我们经常跟入职的新人讲，在施璐德最不缺的就是上升空间，不仅会锻炼你的职场业务技能，更会从各个方面提供学习成长的机会，帮助你修炼内核，增加身为职场人的底气。

大家心系一处，谈项目，谈规划，谈未来，不断积累的信任感和归属感让每一个人对施璐德都有了家的感觉，愿意一起守护。那种团队作战、全力奔赴的日子，十年后的今天再想起来依旧热血沸腾、热泪盈眶。

with the market, we gradually expanded our business landscape by numerous front-line efforts. I check my flight records when writing this article, and, by a rough calculation, find that I have been to 36 countries in the past ten years, while our projects could be found in 69 countries. Everything I did for CNOOD to "open up new territory" has become a most precious experience for me.

That was a time when the company was in great need of talented people. We selected a few newcomers with great potential who had been freshly recruited from campus and took them abroad on business trips. The first lesson for many new recruits at CNOOD was not a training session in a conference room, but a direct business experience in the frontline by which they could learn through practice. We often told them that they would never lack room for promotion. At CNOOD, not only would their professional skills be enhanced, but they would also be provided with multiple opportunities to learn and grow. Their core capability would be refined, adding to their self-confidence as business people.

With a common goal in mind, we would talk about projects, plans, as well as the future. The increasing sense of trust and belonging made CNOOD the home for everyone, which we are willing to protect together. The days of teamwork with all-out efforts a decade ago would always make me so excited that tears

果敢担当，责任为先

新型组织的公司，因时代潮流而发展，想要生生不息，就要抓住企业运作的首要目标——人。我们一直坚信"人"是公司的核心竞争力，培养优秀且具幸福感的施璐德人，是公司的文化理念。

大部分企业同事的工作状态是稳中有序，按照既定的工作安排保证顺利完成即可。在施璐德，每一位同事都有"人人都是CEO"的责任意识。这种意识的培养都源自我们的企业文化。

静时亦觉意思好，才遇事情便不同。这样的情况在职场实战中常有，在无事时能保持内心平静，一旦遇到问题就内心慌乱，甚至不知所措，不敢放手去做。正如《传习录》中所讲："人须在事上磨，方立得住"。经事培养出来的人，才不会纸上谈兵。这样的历炼方式，让施璐德每一位同事都敢于并能够独挑大梁。这是公司文化所体现的包容与成就，也是同事宝贵的责任意识的体现。

would well up in my eyes.

With decisiveness and courage, we undertake our responsibilities

Companies with new organizational structures move with the times. To survive, they must focus on the primary goal of business operation: people. We have always held a firm belief that "people" constitutes the core competitiveness of a company. It is the philosophy of our corporate culture to nurture CNOODers who are both excellent at their work and happy in their heart.

In most companies, people work in a steady and orderly way, and their tasks are finished once they have completed the work assigned to them. Here at CNOOD, every colleague has a sense of responsibility which can be summarized as "Everyone Is a CEO". This awareness comes from our corporate culture.

A disciple of Yangming Wang said, "I have fairly good ideas when my mind is calm; but things are different when I deal with practical business." It is, in fact, a common phenomenon in workplace: you can kccp a peaceful mind when everything goes smoothly, but when you have a problem, you start to panic, not knowing what to do. Just as Wang Yangming said in *Instructions for Practical Living*, "Only those who have tempered themselves in practical matters can stand firmly," people who have been trained in real business would not become armchair strategists. Having been cultivated in this

有一件事我印象很深刻。一位客户在一次聊天时跟我说，他工作几十年，走访过的企业不计其数，施璐德却给他留下了非常深刻的印象。我问其缘由。

他说：我印象很深刻，拜访的时候，一般都是带头人或老板给我递名片，或者是参与的人给我递名片，其他陪同的人基本默认自己只是旁观者，跟自己没关系。但是那天我到施璐德，我经过的地方，只要我点头微笑或者和我有视线对碰的人，他都会主动把名片递上来，并且会跟我进行简短交流，看看有什么需要帮忙。我觉得施璐德是一种全员都会一起使劲儿的公司，这里的每一个人都在想努力地表现自己给这个公司加分。这样的公司一定能够发展得很好。

客户给了我们项目上最核心的采购订单，不仅有了订单，他还邀请我到他们公司，以一位女性CEO的身份，分享施璐德的企业哲学/文化。那一次，我把施璐德企业文化和东方智慧带到了地球另一端。

way, every colleague at CNOOD has the courage and is able to shoulder major responsibilities independently. This is exactly the inclusiveness and fulfillment embodied in our corporate culture, and a representation of the invaluable sense of responsibility shared by all our colleagues.

I was greatly impressed when a client told me, in a casual conversation, that CNOOD left a very deep impression on him among the numerous companies he had visited during his decades-long career. I asked him why.

He answered, "I'm deeply impressed because when you visit a company, it is a common practice that a leader, a boss or someone who is involved in the project hands you their business cards, while others who are escorting basically see themselves as bystanders. When I was visiting CNOOD, however, everyone who I smiled and nodded at or had an eye contact with would give me a business card and exchange a few remarks with me to see if I need any help. I believe that CNOOD is a place where all its members will work hard together and try their best to add to its success. Such a company will certainly have a great future."

The client offered us critical purchasing orders in their project. Besides, he invited me to his company where I shared the philosophy and corporate culture of CNOOD as a female CEO. That was an occasion when I brought CNOOD's culture and oriental

这件事一直让我记忆犹新，这背后展现出的特质是施璐德人所始终秉持的责任信念：把小事当大事做，大事用细节做。正是这样的信念，让我们的企业文化生生不息，让公司蓬勃壮大。

风险与机遇并存，挑战与发展同在

创行之始，人皆视为畏途；创业之艰，即身任其事者，成败利钝亦绝无把握。尤其是在变量常存的当下，大国的腾挪虽让我们获得演化优势，却也时刻面临挑战。近两年来，全球疫情肆虐，材料频繁涨价，汇率大幅波动，海运市场疯狂，出口退税大范围取消！如此严峻的形势，我们在大刀阔斧的同时也免不得如履薄冰。

从曾经只有几个人的小公司，到现在拥有遍布全球多个国家的分/子公司、办事处、合伙人，从简单钢铁产品贸易，到为客户提供完整的、增值的解决方案，我们承接完成了诸多具有国家战略、历史里程碑、行业标志性意义的项目。

wisdom to the other side of the earth.

It is one thing that has remained fresh in my memory ever since. It reflects the characteristics that best express CNOODers' belief of responsibility: Do small things as if they were big things, and always pay attention to details when doing big things. It is this belief that gives vitality to our corporate culture and enables CNOOD to flourish.

Risks as well as opportunities, challenges as well as growth

At the beginning of our entrepreneurial journey, everyone considered it as formidable. It was such an arduous adventure that even those personally engaged in it did not have any idea whether it would succeed or fail. Especially in the current situation where everything is changing, we constantly face challenges despite our evolutionary advantages. The grave situation in recent years, including the raging global COVID-19 pandemic, frequent rise in the prices of raw materials, drastic fluctuations of exchange rates, the chaos in the ocean shipping market and the cancellation of export tax rebate on a large scale, has urged us to proceed with extreme caution while striding forward.

From a small company with only a few employees to a multinational corporation with branches / subsidiaries, offices and partners in many countries around the world, and from simple steel commodities trade to complete, value-adding solutions for clients, we have

施璐德是一个极具开拓意识的平台，不乏有难度、有挑战的项目，指派的方式格外有趣，不会限定某一团队或某一人。公司会把项目机会公开化，谁对项目感兴趣，谁想挑战突破，都可以来拿项目立军令状。我们总是鼓励大家，派发的项目一定是有挑战和难度的，可以去分析，去判断，只有把事情往前做，做到一定程度，一边做一边迭代，才能越来越接近正确的答案。

施璐德，是一家以业务为导向的企业。所以，业务发展部力求保留多元化特质，保持创业团队的活力与自驱力，以仁性为基准，以狼性为推动，结合多元化的独特属性，我们发布了针对业务发展部的工作指南、操作手册，并鼓励业务团队发起业务计划书。

在2021年试运行期间，我们共收到

undertaken and completed a number of projects with national strategic significance, which can be seen as historical milestones for both CNOOD and the industry.

CNOOD is a platform full of pioneering spirit where difficult, challenging projects are not rare. The way of assigning these projects is particularly interesting. They will not be assigned to any predetermined team or person. Instead, project opportunities are open to everyone in the company, and whoever is interested and wants to make a breakthrough can volunteer to take one of them. We always encourage our colleagues that despite the difficult and challenging nature of these projects, they can always rely on their analysis and judgment. If they keep pushing things ahead until a certain point while iterating, they can get closer and closer to the right answer.

CNOOD is a business-oriented company. Therefore, its Business Development Department strive to retain its nature of diversity to maintain the vitality and self-drive of the entrepreneurial team. With benevolence as the benchmark and "wolf quality" as the driving force, taking into consideration the unique attributes of diversity, we have issued work guidelines and work-manual for Business Development Department and encouraged the business teams to develop business plans.

We received ten business plans

十份业务计划书，经过高管会审，报批董事会后，十份业务计划书均获得了批复。这十份业务计划书，相当于十份创业计划书，而施璐德公司就是创业孵化平台，每一位有想法、有能力的实干家，在这里都会得到支持！

也正是因为这一独特性，让我们在当下的国际形势中，应对不断变化的市场与业务需求，我们唯有不遗余力持续优化、迭代，才能保持业务和团队的竞争力，实现多方向延伸，铸就施璐德的竞争力，实现立足于企业的规划和愿景。

这一系列举措能够顺利实行，都源自施璐德极具包容性和前瞻性的发展战略，以及每一位施璐德人无惧风雨、戮力同心的意志。未来仍会有更多挑战，但我们会再接再厉，遇难则强，披荆斩棘。

施璐德 CEO，不是角色，是使命

如果给 CEO 对标一个角色的话，CEO 更像是什么呢？

我想，从角色的角度来讲，如果施璐德是一艘大龙舟，CEO 更像是龙舟上的

in total during the trial run in 2021, which, after being reviewed by senior executives, were all approved by the board of directors. They are like ten plans for starting new businesses while CNOOD is like an incubator. Every person of action with excellent ideas and abilities will get support here.

It is this uniqueness that enables us to successfully respond to the changing market conditions and business needs in the current international situation. Only by continuous optimization and iteration can we maintain the competitiveness of our businesses and teams and achieve multi-directional extension, thus creating the competitiveness of CNOOD as a whole and realizing its unique planning and vision.

The successful implementation of these measures is possible because of CNOOD's highly inclusive and forward-looking development strategy, as well as the determination of all CNOODers to brave it out and make concerted efforts. There will be still more challenges in the future, and we shall redouble our efforts, become even stronger in the face of all hardships and overcome them.

CEO of CNOOD, a mission instead of a role

What is a CEO like if we are to benchmark the position against a specific role?

From the perspective of roles, if we compare CNOOD to a dragon boat,

击鼓手，是赛事期间，始终把握和保持团队节奏的那个人。他有目标意识，让龙舟手各司其职，不多做干涉，以节奏激发大家的前进动力。从企业发展的角度来说，CEO 不仅仅是种角色，更肩负着推动企业发展的使命。当职业变成事业，义务成为责任，使命感就是我作为 CEO 的动力源。

站在十年的里程碑前，回顾我的职业生涯，从最年轻的、资历最浅的业务合伙人到 2017 年公司第一任 CEO，董事长和各位同事都给予我充分的包容和支持，让我能够放开手脚，为公司的发展尽自己最大的努力。这种支撑和信任感尤为重要，与其说这十年，是我有机会为公司尽职，为客户和同事尽责，不如说是施璐德这个组织平台支持我成就梦想中的职业价值。

2021 年，连任 CEO，深感任重道远，唯有兢兢业业。在项目周期调整与出差暂缓的间隙，也让我们有机会，有时间，慢下来，做一次深度思考：面对复杂的疫情和海外业务形式，结合公司的发展历程、企业文化，我们该如何进一步优化形成契合施璐德的管理机制？

its CEO is more like the drummer who controls and keeps the pace throughout the race. The CEO must have a sense of purpose, let the rowers perform their respective duties without much interference and inspire everyone's driving force by pace-keeping. From the perspective of the development of companies, CEO is more than a role; it shoulders the mission of promoting the development of the company. When a job becomes a career and a duty becomes a responsibility, a sense of mission is my driving force as a CEO.

Standing by the milestone of a decade and looking back on my career from the youngest business partner to the first CEO of the company in 2017, I remember how the chairman and all my colleagues gave me full tolerance and support so that I was able to do my best for the development of the company. This sense of support and trust is particularly important. Instead of saying that I have been lucky enough to have the chance to serve our company, clients and colleagues in the past ten years, I would rather say that CNOOD as a platform has been always helping me achieve my career values.

In 2021, I was re-elected as the CEO. I could clearly feel the heavy responsibilities I was going to take on, and the only choice for me is to work conscientiously. During the period of project cycle adjustment and the gaps between business trips, we could have

2021年9月，施璐德新一届高管和管理团队完成任命，在推进《业务计划书》的同时，我们策划并推进了各项内部管理职能体系的完善升级，建立起了系统、全面、能匹配公司发展新阶段的管理制度。而我们也会在未来从广度、深度、高度三个角度来持续精进。

首先是广度。我们以ASIA公司为基准，调整海外分/子公司管理制度，考虑属地化特色的同时，保持步调协同，提升工作效能。其次是深度。制度的完善绝不是一马平川、朝夕之间就能达成的，还需要在实际运维中不断发现问题、总结经验、及时修正。随着制度施行，查漏补缺，广纳建议，推陈出新，持续优化，保持生命力。最后是高度。我们从过去的"无为而治"到"人性化的制度管理"，这样的跨越，更多地建立在自我的约束力和驱动力上，而非反向的制度约束和捆绑。每个人都是CEO，从CEO视角去理解、接受，共同完善新制度。

the opportunity and time to slow down for in-depth thinking: In the face of the complexity of the COVID-19 pandemic and overseas business conditions, and considering the history and corporate culture of CNOOD, what should we do to further optimize and form a management mechanism that best suits CNOOD?

In September 2021, the new senior executives and management team were appointed. While promoting the *Business Plan*, we have planned and pushed the improvement and upgrading of various internal management function systems and established a systematic, comprehensive management system that matches the new stage of the company's development. And we will continue to improve in the future from three dimensions, i.e., breadth, depth and height.

The first dimension is breadth. Taking CNOOD ASIA as the benchmark, we have adjusted the management systems of overseas subsidiaries. We take into account local characteristics while maintaining coordination and enhancing efficiency. The second dimension is depth. The perfection of the system is by no means a smooth process and cannot be achieved overnight. We need to constantly find problems, summarize experience and make timely corrections during actual operation. With the implementation of the system, we try to detect and stop all the loopholes, adopt suggestions extensively and encourage

我相信我们在当下所做的事情，对于公司未来的发展会起到扎实性的作用。我们会继续健全优化管理制度，在打造企业发展生态的大目标下笃行不怠。

最后，特此感谢承载我十年职场之路的施璐德，感谢董事长池勇海先生的栽培；感谢公司每一位同事的支持；感谢因项目结缘的每一位合作者、客户给予公司和我的信任，相信下一个十年我们会更加精进！

2022 年 1 月于上海

innovation to ensure continuous optimization and maintain vitality. The third dimension is height. Our leap from "governing by noninterference" to "humanized institutional management" is based on self-restraint and driving force rather than reverse institutional restraint and binding. Everyone is a CEO and is expected to understand and accept the new system from the perspective of a CEO. With a concerted effort, we can improve the system.

I believe that what we do now will have a firm impact on the future development of the company. We shall continue to improve and optimize the management system and persistently pursue the goal of building an ecosystem for the development of the company.

Finally, my special thanks to CNOOD, which has been supporting me over the past decade, and Dennis Chi for his great help. I would also like to thank all my colleagues for their support, and all the cooperative partners and clients who have become my friends via projects for their trust in CNOOD and me. I believe that we will be a greater company during the next decade!

Jan 2022, Shanghai

李燕飞
Fay Lee

施璐德亚洲有限公司 CEO。
自省、学习，始终坚持自我进化；
做一个值得他人信任的人，不辜负每一次信任；
做一个让人觉得温暖的人，分享每一份正能量；
坚持理想与完美主义的信仰，
不忘主观与客观结合的分析，
执着于制订计划并付诸行动，
朝着所信仰的方向不断努力，
心之所向，义无反顾。

CEO, CNOOD ASIA LIMITED.
With soul-searching and learning, she persists in self-evolution.
Be a trustworthy person, and never betray any trust;
Be a warm person, and share every positive energy.
Hold fast to the faith in ideals and perfectionism;
Never forget analyzing things from both subjective and objective angles;
Persevere in making plans and put them into implementation;
Work tirelessly toward the direction of conviction.
Never turn back once heading for something the heart gravitates.

欢迎来到第 12 期 IP 女性人物！

Welcome to the 12th Session of IP Female Characters!

■ Suki Duan

李燕飞
施璐德亚洲有限公司 CEO
施璐德智利公司董事长
重大项目（千万美金＋）总监、发起人
业务发展网络 60 个国家
职业足迹踏及 36 个国家
上海对外经贸 MBA

本期访谈你将收获：

燕飞总不仅是团队的领袖、孩子的母亲，更重要的一个角色，是她在做她真实的自己。

她用真诚、包容、谦逊、透明的心爱着这个世界，也爱着身边的人。

心中透明坦荡，内心坚定笃行，用心做好自己，一切只是时间问题。

本篇你将深入燕飞总的内心，去感受

Fay Lee
CEO, CNOOD ASIA LIMITED
Chairma, CNOOD CHILE LIMITED
Chief director and initiator of major projects (over a billion US dollars)
Business networks covering 60 countries
Career footprints in 36 countries
MBA, Shanghai University of International Business and Economics

In this interview, you will learn:

In addition to being a team leader and a mom, Fay plays an even more important role: the true version of herself.

With a heart of sincerity, inclusiveness, modesty and transparency, she loves this world and people around her.

Transparent and magnanimous in her heart, Fay always moves forward with great determination. She tries her best to be a better person and leaves the rest to time.

Now, follow us in the interview

她对这个世界、事业、人生旅程、家庭的核心理念以及思想的魅力！

人物访谈录

段芳：如果不用职业标签来概括你，你最希望自己成为哪一个电影明星、动物类型或者人物榜样？

燕飞总：我会选择"燕"。我的名字里有个"燕"，"燕飞"这个名字带着父亲对我的期望和愿景。他希望我能像燕子一样自由地飞翔，拥有更广阔的成长与发展空间。同时，它有回归的含义，无论我到哪儿，终归带着父母的那份牵挂。因为工作原因，我出差的频率很高，有人说我像是"空中飞人"，疫情前航旅纵横曾统计我的飞机记录超过了98%的人，所以，"燕"很契合我。

and explore the inner world of Fay, understand her ideas about the world, career, life journey and family and feel the charm of her thinking!

The Interview with Fay

Duan Fang (Suki): If we don't use any professional label to describe you, which movie star, animal or role model do you wish to become?

Fay Lee (Fay): I would choose "swallow" (*yan* in Chinese). My Chinese name is "Yanfei," meaning literally "a swallow flying." This is a name that carries my father's expectations of me. He wishes that I could fly freely just like a swallow, growing and developing on a bigger stage. Meanwhile, swallow has a symbolic meaning of "returning home" in Chinese culture. Wherever I go, I always remember my parents who are waiting for me at home. I travel a lot on business, and some people would call me a "road warrior." According to the records from UMETRIP before the COVID-19 pandemic, I flied more than 98% of all other passengers. So, I think "swallow" best suits me.

段芳：如果你有这样一次机会，你希望自己理想的一天怎么来度过？

燕飞总：平时的节奏比较快，对我来说，理想状态是一个相对"随心"的慢节奏。拿本次访谈来说，我今天理想的一天是早上睡一个懒觉，然后看看书，思想自由的一种状态：什么都可以想，什么都可以不想。晚上和Suki段芳老师一起做访谈，我一直觉得Suki老师在做非常有意义的事情，今天有幸能够参与，如果我们访谈的内容——我的经历，不管是职场，还是生活，对在线的朋友有一点启发，或者产生一些共鸣，我觉得今天就很值得了。我想这应该就是理想的一天。

段芳：你同时是一位妈妈，作为事业型女性，你是如何做到家庭和事业之间的融合，你做了哪些调整或努力？

燕飞总：我女儿12岁了，我十分羡慕可以有时间经常陪伴在孩子身边的妈妈。对于时间的分配，是我最难平衡的部分，每一天都在做"优先"选择题。在我有限的陪伴时间里，我努力做到有效陪伴，走入她的世界，体验她的感受。在陪伴孩子成长的过程中，我们大人往往会达到"忘我"的境界，把自己的当下与未来的期望都寄托在孩子身上。努力让孩子成为我们骄傲的同时，孩子又何尝不

Duan: If you have a chance to spend one day at your will, how are you going to spend it?

Fay: **My daily life is rather fast-paced. To me, an ideal pattern of life would be one that features slow pace and a state of "following my heart."** Taking today's interview for example, an ideal day for me is like this: getting up late in the morning and reading some books, with a mental freedom of thinking, or not thinking about anything, and doing an interview with you in the evening. I believe that you have always been doing something meaningful and I feel lucky to be part of it. If today's interview about the experiences of my career and my life would be an inspiration to our friends online or arouse empathetic responses among them, then I think it's worth it. That's what an ideal day looks like to me.

Suki: We know you are also a mom. As a career-oriented woman, what efforts or adjustments have you made to achieve the balance between your family and your work?

Fay: As the mom of a 12-year-old girl, I admire those mothers who always have the time to be with their kids. To achieve the work-family balance, the most difficult part for me is the distribution of time. I have to make choices of "what comes first" every day. In my limited amount of time to be with my daughter, I try my best to make it effective by going into her world and feeling what she feels. **As kids**

希望有一对让自己骄傲的父母。有时候，我们也可以看起来"弱"一点，甚至需要她鼓励，却一直是很努力很坚持的父母。从这个角度想，我们也可以选择活好自己的人生，她的人生，给她更多的自由空间去施展。

记忆里，职场与妈妈这两个角色，我几乎处于无缝衔接的状态。还记得，我怀孕六个月陪客户去出差，等客户下一次来中国拜访我们的时候，我已经升级做妈妈了。他说我和他出差的时候，以为我只是胖了，因为在大冬天我穿着羽绒服，不太显怀。

我的家人给了我非常大的支持，特别是我婆婆，事无巨细地照顾我们的生活，让我可以完全放手去做自己想做的事情。但无论工作多忙，我也一定安排时间与家人相处。女儿小时候，我们会一起去国外游学，她上学，我做全职妈妈，学煲汤，做点心，做菜给她吃。每年家庭"团建"（旅游）是很好的方法，就像电池需要充电一样，他们付出了一年，我也需要有表达关爱、感恩的时间。

grow up, parents who are accompanying them tend to "forget themselves" and put all their expectations on their kids. When they try to make their kids the pride of them, the kids also wish to have parents who they can be proud of. Sometimes we can look "weak" and even seek encouragement from our kids, while still being hard working and persistent. Thinking in this way, I choose to live a good life of my own first. As for the life of my daughter, I will give her much more freedom.

As I recall, I am always shifting between the roles of a mother and a businesswoman almost seamlessly. I remember going on a business trip with a client when I was six months pregnant, and by the time the client came to China again and visited us, I had already become a mom. He admitted that when I travelled on business with him, he thought I had simply put on weight, because I wore a thick down-padded anorak in the winter and it was hard to find the truth.

My family have been giving me huge support, especially my mother-in-law. She takes care of us attentively so that I can focus on my job without worrying about anything else. But no matter how busy I am, I would find time to spend with my family. When my daughter was little, I accompanied her to study abroad. I became a full-time mom as she went to school. I learned to cook soup and make desserts and prepared meals for her. The family tour every year is a good way to "recharge the batteries." I, too, need the time and opportunity to express my love and gratitude to those who have done so much for me in a whole year.

Suki: I've learned that you majored in international trade in college, and your first job after graduation was related to international trade and business. Were they the major and job you really wanted to choose at those particular stages? What impacts do they have on your life at the moment?

Fay: A right major and the necessary accumulation give us the freedom of choosing the desirable starting point. Before I started my career, I took a number of intern jobs by which I discovered the boundaries of different jobs and their "ceilings." My goal was simple and clear when looking for a job: I wanted a job that would give me room to grow by hard work. I hoped that I would be evaluated by an objective system and did not have to waste much time on interpersonal relations to secure career development.

Therefore, when I look back on my career, I realize that the business-oriented job related to international trade showed me infinite boundaries of jobs. I can keep trying in different fields from markets to products. There are no boundaries for the markets and products you want to develop, because different countries are in different stages of development cycle with different resources. Being successful

段芳：据我了解，你是从国际贸易专业毕业的，你的第一份工作选择去做了国际贸易及业务板块的工作，请问在当时学习的专业和工作是你那个阶段想要选择的吗？对你现在产生了什么影响？

燕飞总：选择专业，并做好基础积累，让我们可以自由选择自己想要的起点。在正式工作之前，我做过不少实习，从实习中，我发现了不同职业的职业边界与职业天花板。找工作的时候，我的目标其实很简单：我希望找一份工作，只要我努力，就可以有成长的空间。对我的评价体系，我希望是客观的，我不需要内耗在人际关系中去寻得职业发展的一席之地。

所以，回顾我整个职业生涯，国际贸易、业务板块的工作给了我无限的职业边界。从市场到产品，我都可以去不断尝试。不同国家的发展周期不同，资源禀赋不同，想做的产品，想去的市场，没有边界。做好既有工作（第一曲线）的同时，自然延伸出新的可能性（第二曲线），而我们就可以水到渠成地发展新的客户、新的领域、新的市场。这种无限延展的工作状态，让我尝试新事物，打破职业边界，成为自然而然的状态。

段芳：你是什么原因选择了第二份工作？你是如何来做职业选择的，以及你是如何评估新的工作的，你有哪些评估标准？

燕飞总：其实对我来说选择第二份工作没有明显的选择节点，当我们把当下的事情做到极致的时候，对面抛来橄榄枝是水到渠成的事。当我们把任何机会做到极致，就算很多机会你还没有发现，但你已经去向那个方向了。

对我个人来说，我会把工作当作终身的事业来做。如果要讨论一个评估标准，我认为广阔的职业边界尤为重要。我第一份工作更多以产品为导向，第二份工作更多是产品和服务的整合方案，以一种集成式的解决方案为业务导向，相当于在我的第一份工作上做了延伸，对我来说是比较大的吸引。而现在，我从业务导向，进一步延伸到管理导向，也是在不断扩大职业边界的过程。

段芳：你近20年的职业生涯，一共只有两份工作，很多人会不断转换行业、职能来升职加薪，你是如何在同一家公司达到你现在的职业高峰，你有什么样的原

in your present job (the first curve) will naturally bring about new possibilities (the second curve) which enable you to develop new clients, new fields, as well as new markets. This state of "infinite extension" encourages me to constantly try new things and break boundaries.

Suki: What made you choose the second job? How did you make your career choice? How do you evaluate a new job and what are the standards?

Fay: Well, actually there was no specific reason for choosing my second job. **When we have done our best in our jobs, a better offer will come naturally. If you do your best with all existing opportunities, you have already on the way toward more opportunities even before you notice them.**

Personally speaking, I see my job as a life-long career. If there's a standard, I think the broad boundaries are particularly important. My first job is product-oriented, and my second job is more about the combination of products and services, oriented around integrated solutions. It is like an extension of my first job, which is a great attraction to me. Now, I am still expanding my career boundaries as I move from business orientation to management orientation.

Suki: You have only had two jobs in nearly 20 years. Many people frequently change their jobs to get promoted and get a salary raise. How did you reach

则或秘诀?

燕飞总：在职场中，当我们不断自我提升，让我们专业能力超过职位要求时，很多时候，我们往往会选择跳槽来延伸职业边界，并且升职加薪。我想，当企业本身拥有非常完整的体系，对个人和企业来说，灵活性低。当职业技能、专业能力高于目前本身职位时，可能不得不通过跳槽实现升职加薪。

我们还可以选择全心投入，去优化一个企业平台，自己给自己设立更高职位要求。在这个过程中，勇敢去承担更多的责任，接受更高的挑战，不断提升自己，这种无边界的能力延伸对我来说是最重要的。我很幸运在第二家企业中得到这样包容的环境，并按我想要的方式去实现自己的想法，在这种情况下，个人与企业是彼此成就的关系！

段芳：作为公司的CEO，你是如何向下管理，或者向上管理，有发生过哪些艰难时刻或者令你难忘的事吗？

燕飞总：无论是向下管理，还是向

the pinnacle of your career in the same company? What is your principle or secret?

Fay: We often choose to change our jobs to extend our career boundaries for promotion and salary raise when our professional abilities exceed job requirements if we keep improving ourselves. In my opinion, people have to face a low flexibility when a company has established a very complete system. When their professional skills and abilities are higher than the requirements of their current positions, they may have to change their jobs to get a promotion or a salary raise.

We can also choose to devote ourselves to our jobs wholeheartedly to optimize the platform of the company, setting higher job requirements for ourselves. In this process, we should bravely assume more responsibilities, take on tougher challenges, and keep improving ourselves. This boundaryless extension of ability is the most important thing for me. I am lucky to get such an inclusive environment in the second company I work for in which I can realize my ideas in my own way. In this case, a company and its members are really fulfilling each other!

Suki: As the CEO of the company, how do you manage downward or upward? Were there any difficult moments or unforgettable experiences?

Fay: Whether it's downward

上管理，我都用心感受，用最真诚透明的方式。

作为CEO，最重要的一项职责，就是执行董事会决议。我还记得去年，有一项董事会决议，因为没理解，我坚持没执行，最后我们尝试了"一企多制"。当我有不同意见的时候，会充分表达我的观点，并和董事长、董事会做多次的沟通，直到我完全理解接受这项决议或者对方因为我的多次沟通而改变，亦或者，我们保留各自的观点，让时间给我们答案。因此，在我们公司，我们尝试了不同的团队管理模式，我深信，从长远来看，只要我们的建议是发自内心、充满诚意、透明的，我相信领导或者老板是能够理解我们这份心的，因为我们真心想要去把事情做得更好，真心为他去考量，不是只为了给他当下更好的感受，而是尝试从更高的视角表达对这个事情的看法。也许，在很多公司，这不一定是最好的向上管理的方法，但我始终会做真实的自己，知行合一，才能把事情做到最优的状态。

在向下管理中，我把自己定位在服务者、支持者的角色。把职业舞台的中心给他们，让他们成长与历练。我只需要在他

management or upward management, I always feel it with my heart in the most sincere and transparent way.

It is my most important duty as the CEO to implement the decisions made by the board of directors. I still remember the case last year when I insisted that a decision made by the board of directors should not be implemented because I didn't fully understand it. In the end we tried out the idea of "one company with multiple systems." When I have different opinions, I will fully express my views and communicate with the chairman and the board of directors many times until I fully understand and accept the decision or they change their mind; if neither party is persuaded, we reserve our respective views and wait for the time to give us the answer. Therefore, we have tried out different patterns of team management. I firmly believe that **in the long run, our boss will understand us if we make suggestions with full sincerity and transparency, because it's our true intention to do things better and think for his good; we attempt to express our views on a specific matter from a higher perspective instead of making him feel good for the moment.** For many companies, this is not necessarily the best way to manage upward, but I will always be true to myself and combine knowledge with practice to achieve the best state of things.

In downward management, I see myself as a server and supporter. I will

们需要的时候，帮助他们，保护他们，给他们内心的坚定。

段芳：你在施璐德工作的这段职业旅程里，共计去过36个国家，这是怎样的经历？这对你看待世界以及人生、职业产生怎样的内在变化？可以分享一两个你难忘的经历吗？

燕飞总：因为工作原因，我去过很多国家，有很多不同国家的朋友、客户、合作伙伴，这也是这份工作带给我最大的收获。很多经历和感受随着时间流逝被尘封起来了，当你问起时，脑子里还是会有很多鲜活的小故事出现。

我之前去到非洲一个国家，下飞机是武装部队接我们上车，一路护送。到了酒店，我们也是全程被武装部队包围。我很想走出那个保护圈，去体验真实的当地的样子，其中一段我尝试着走出保护圈，就有几个小朋友迎了上来，我从他们渴望的眼神明白他们想要什么，正当我准备伸手分享点什么，我瞬间被里三层外三层的小朋友围住了，场面有点失控，这时我听到了旁边武装部队的枪声（对着地面），小朋友们被惊吓，四处跑开。惊吓之余，我也特别感慨，这是我第一次距离枪声这么近！作为中国人，我们能身处在一个稳定的环境中，是多么的值得珍惜与自豪！

leave the central stage to the staff and let them grow and refine themselves. What I do is to help them, protect them and give them inner firmness when they need it.

Suki: During your career at CNOOD, you have been to totally 36 countries. What is that experience like? How does it change your ways of looking at the world, life and career? Can you share with us one or two examples of your unforgettable experiences?

Due to the nature of my job, I've been to many countries and have a lot of friends, clients and cooperative partners from these countries. It is also the biggest reward I get from the job. As time goes by, some of my experiences and feelings have been sealed in my memory; whenever I am asked about them, a few anecdotes will unfold vividly in my mind's eye.

One time I was in an African country. We were escorted by an armed force from the airport all the way to the hotel. We were guarded by armed soldiers even after we arrived at the hotel. I wanted to step out of the circle of guards to see what the local life was like. Several kids came up to me as soon as I tried to do so. I could tell what they wanted from their eager eyes. When I reached out my hand to give them something, I was suddenly surrounded by even more kids, and things began to get out of control. Then I heard a gunshot by the soldiers (fired at the ground). The kids were so scared that they all ran away immediately.

还有一次去巴拿马，由于行程紧急，我们只有一天时间往返于项目现场，我们选择了搭乘直升飞机。那是我第一次乘直升飞机，当我从直升飞机往下看，就发现整个国家都在我眼底之下，看到巴拿马城的高楼，旁边矮小破败的小房子，山顶上的牧羊人家，还有巴拿马运河，我对这个国家的感情就莫名其妙上来了，被自己所感动。到了项目现场，正值他们下雨特别频繁的季节，我还被淋了一身水。开着小艇到海上平台，必须要在海浪托着小艇往上冲时，跳上爬梯爬上海上平台。如果在海浪往下的时候跳，很可能会掉到水里。当时他们劝我不要上去，我是一个lady（女士），我拒绝了，因为这个项目是我们的baby（孩子）——产品，有我们的解决方案。当我到了上面后，我很欣慰，我们的产品呈现着不仅质量很好也很美观的这样一种状态，这是我们团队努力的结晶，我们真正在帮助他们解决当地一些问题，提升他们的效率，高质量保障产品更长的使用周期。我们很自豪，很有使命感，感觉之前为了项目所做的努力都那么值得！

Startled, I was greatly shocked because it was the first time for me to be so close to a gunshot! **As Chinese, how much should we cherish and be proud of the stable domestic environment we live in!**

And another time when I went to Panama, we had only one day to go to and from the project site because of the tight schedule, so we decided to travel by helicopter. It was my first time to fly in a helicopter. When I looked down, I could see the whole country: the tall buildings in Panama City and the dilapidated small houses next to them, the shepherds' homes on mountain tops and the Panama Canal. An inexplicable feeling for this country welled up within me, and I was moved by myself. It was a season with much rain at the time we arrived at the project site, and I even got drenched. When we went to the offshore platform in a speedboat, we were supposed to jump on the ladder as the speedboat was lifted by the waves. If we jumped when the waves were going downwards, we might fall into the sea. They tried to persuade me not to go there because it was too dangerous for a lady. However, I insisted on going because the project was like a baby to us — it was a product provided by us with our solution. I was gratified when I was on the platform: our product, both of high quality and neat design, was in a perfect state. It was the fruit of the hard work of our team. We were really helping our clients deal with their problems and improve their efficiency. We were proud

我们响应国家"一带一路"政策，以中国制造或中国智慧助力一些国家发展。通过我们的努力，整合中国资源，帮助他们更快速地发展，从基建、港口、矿山、油气等不同领域提供我们的增值解决方案，我和我的同事们都有这样的使命感与责任心。去到这么多国家，现在从工作源头去看，我们的努力承载的意义更清晰了，也让我有更包容的心境去爱甚至更爱这个世界了。

段芳：职业发展到今天，目前的职业状态是你想要的吗？什么样的公司是值得你去全力付出的？

燕飞总：是的，我很享受我当下的职业状态。

首先对于企业，企业有它的发展周期，不同的发展周期会有不同的挑战和问题。其次对于企业管理者或者创业者来说，可能因为他有比一般人更强的意志或更大的梦想，他才走到那个巅峰位置。实际上他也是一个人，他在不同阶段也会有困惑和迷茫。如果一家公司有足够包容度、自由度，让我们去成长和发挥，我们

that we had provided them with high-quality products with longer service life. We felt a strong sense of mission, knowing that all our previous efforts were worth it!

In response to the Belt and Road Initiative, we have been boosting the development of some countries with Chinese manufacturing or Chinese wisdom. Through our efforts of integrating Chinese resources, we are helping them develop more rapidly while providing our value-adding solutions in different fields such as infrastructure, ports, mines, oil and gas. My colleagues and I all share such a sense of mission and responsibility. With the experience in so many countries and reviewing our work from its origin, I now have a clearer understanding of the significance of our efforts, which enables me to love the world even more with a more inclusive mindset.

Suki: As for your career development up to now, are you in a state that you like? What is the company that you would spare no effort to work for?

Fay: Yes, I enjoy my current state very much.

First, as for any company with its development cycle, it will face different challenges and problems at different stages of the cycle. Second, as for the founder of a company, it is probably because of his stronger will or bigger dreams that he reaches the highest position. In fact, he too, as a person, will

可以全力以赴去尝试我们想做的事情，体验不同视角和角色，带来新的成长与收获，这是一件非常幸运的事。因此，无论我们身处何处，都值得全力付出，因为有些收获是公司会回馈我们的显性收获，还有一些收获是渗透在我们的能力里、经验中的隐形价值，因为过程本身就是成长与收获。显性收获是你当下值多少钱，而隐性价值则决定你未来的职业高度在哪里！

段芳：很多人说人的认知高度决定事业发展的高度，在过去这些年，你给自己在学习成长上做对了哪些重要的投资，哪些是你失败的投资，你从中最大的收获是什么？

燕飞总：我们董事长曾对我们说"我们最应该投资的是自己"！在过去这些年里我一直在做这样的实践：MBA、复旦哲学课堂，健身，旅行，包括今年加入的ITBA孵化讲师计划。无论是学习、工作，还是各种挑战，都在让我能力提升，这个经验值是一个累积的过程，也更加验证了对自己的投资是最有效的。

feel confused or perplexed at different stages. It would be lucky for us if we can exert ourselves to the full to do whatever we like, try different perspectives and roles and achieve new growth and gains in a highly inclusive company willing to give us enough freedom of development. Therefore, **no matter where we are, it is worth our all-out efforts because some gains we receive from our company are explicit, while others are implicit values embedded in our abilities and experiences. The process itself means growth and gains. Explicit gains are about how much you are worth at present, while implicit values determine your height in the future!**

Suki: Many people say that the ability of cognition determines how successful a person will be in career development. In the past few years, what right decisions have you made in self-investment? What were the failed investment? What is the biggest reward you get from them?

Fay: Our chairman told us, "The first thing we should invest in is ourselves!" In the past years, I have been busy with such practices: getting an MBA, taking classes on philosophy at Fudan University, doing workout, traveling and being part of the ITBA incubation lecturer program I joined this year. Whether in study, work, or facing various challenges, my abilities are being improved in the process of accumulating experiences, a further proof that an investment in oneself is the

在年轻的时候，我们可以不断做加法，"不挑食"，什么都可以学，尽量扩展。在这个过程中，会逐步呈现自己的知识地图。最近我也在ITBA小师老师的帮助下，整理自己的知识地图。当我们有一定的积累之后，我们可以从更高的视角去反观自己，以及预见未来的自己，选择愿意深耕细作的方向去做更有效的投入。

段芳：身为女性领导者，你和男性领导者之间有哪些领导风格的差异？女性领导者身上你认为最大的优势是什么？对于年轻的想要追求更高职位的女性，可以给她们一些女性领导力发展建议吗？

燕飞总："领导者"，无论是女性领导者，还是男性领导者，都有着一样的重要使命。看似自带光环，更带着很大挑战和期望。就像"欲戴皇冠，必承其重"，它不是与生俱来的能力，需要在成长过程中不断历练和调整，不仅在能力上，更需要心境上的持续修炼。

女性领导者的优势我认为是我们相对更具亲和力和同理心，更能站在对方立场和视角感受对方的状态，这应该就是所谓

most effective.

When we are young, we can keep doing additions. Don't be too "picky," and we can learn everything and expand our knowledge as much as possible. In this process, we will gradually form our own knowledge map. Recently, I have been sorting out my knowledge map with the help of my ITBA tutor. **When we have enough accumulation, we can review ourselves from a higher perspective and foresee what we will become in the future. Then we can choose a field in which we are willing to devote ourselves more effectively.**

Suki: As a female leader, what do you think are the differences in leadership styles between female and male leaders? What is the biggest advantage of female leaders? For young women who wish to pursue higher positions, can you give them some suggestions on developing female leadership?

Fay: Leaders, whether female or male, all have their important missions. They may look impressive, but they have to face bigger challenges and expectations. Just as the saying goes, "Heavy is the head that wears the crown." Leadership is not an innate ability. It needs continuous refinement and adjustment in the process of personal growth, not only in ability but also in one's mindset.

I think the advantage of female leaders lies in the stronger affinity and empathy, which enables us to truly

的柔性领导力。

领导者，本质上需要更多的责任担当。无论是在工作还是生活中，我们的团队、公司，都需要有人承担更多的责任。在企业里，想要追求更高职位的女性朋友，不妨让自己尝试"不在其位，谋其政，做其事"！

发展个人领导力，我认为多揽活，多"管闲事"一点。可能公司暂时没有明确的要求，但你去做了，多次尝试，提升了自己，从显性收获来看好像没有回报，但隐性价值里你得到了成长和延伸。只要机会来临，你就是唯一人选。所以大家想要有所发展的话，先让自己承担更大的责任。

段芳：你最想要拥有的人生、圆满的人生状态将会是什么样的？

燕飞总：这个问题比较感性了，对于每个人来说，很多时候会思考人生到底等于什么？很多人说，人生其实就是一种体验和经历，一场旅程，我还蛮认同这个表述。

当我们回到旅程终点，回想当下，不管如何，全情投入，也许成功，也许失败，或者正是值得纪念的状态，它们都是

understand how other people feel from their positions and perspectives. This is what we call "flexible leadership."

Leaders essentially need to shoulder greater responsibilities. No matter in work or life, in teams or companies, we all need someone to take on more responsibilities. Females who wish to pursue higher positions in companies might as well try to do things even if they are not in the position.

To develop personal leadership, I think we should always be willing to do more work and even "mind other people's business." There may not be clear requirements in your company for the time being, but you will find yourself improved after you have done it and tried many times. There might be nothing in return in the form of explicit gains, but you will achieve personal growth by increasing implicit values. When an opportunity comes, you will be the only right person for it. Therefore, if you are seeking personal development, learn to take on bigger responsibilities first.

Suki: What is the perfect life that you wish to live?

Fay: This is a rather emotional issue. Many people would spend a lot of time thinking what life truly is. **Many may say that life is an experience and a journey. I quite agree with that.**

When we get to the finish line and look back, we would be impressed by how hard we once tried, whether we

我们人生的一部分，呈现生命不同的色彩。它可能是开心、难过、成功、失败，或者是酸的、苦的、甜的、辣的，五彩缤纷，五味杂陈，有深度也有广度，那么，我的人生就是圆满的。

段芳：可以送给想要追求职业成就的女性带一句话吗？

燕飞总：我最近在看电视剧《理想之城》，"苏晓"这个角色还蛮符合当下职场女性的一种职场状态。她是极致专注，以事情为导向，没有任何杂念，集中心思做好事情。尽管电视剧情会有点夸张，但实际上或多或少表达了现实职场女性的一种状态。

我想透过这个角色分享给想要追求职业成就的女性一句话，就是去把握当下，临在当下，全力以赴，天道酬勤。一定会有贵人发现你的才华和能力，给你更好的机会；同时你自己也可以不断延伸成长，突破自我边界，更新迭代人生新的曲线和跨越新的职业巅峰！不要给自己设限，做最好的自己，去自信表达，按自己想要的方式，勇敢去做。

succeed or not. Every experience is a part of our life, each with its own color. **It could be pleasant, upsetting, successful, disappointing; or sour, bitter, sweet or spicy. A life with so many colors and flavors, both deep and broad, would be a perfect one for me.**

Suki: Can you give a piece of advice to females who are pursuing professional achievements?

Fay: Recently I have been watching the TV drama "The Ideal City." The role of Su Xiao is quite a successful representation of today's professional females. Su is extremely focused and task-oriented, without any distractions. She focuses on doing things well. Though the plot may be a little exaggerated, the story of Su captures to an extent the real life of females in workplace.

This is what I would like to share with females who wish to pursue professional achievements: always focus on and seize the present moment, spare no effort, and life will reward you for your hard work. Your talent and ability will surely be appreciated by someone who will provide you with better chances; at the same time you can continue growing, breaking boundaries, renewing your life curve and reaching new peaks in your career! Do away with self-imposed limitations, and strive to be a better version of yourself. Express your views with self-confidence, and be brave in your own way.

段芳
Suki

女性成长导师、女性领导力教练，现升级为知识女性 IP 教练。曾担任上市知名企业采购部经理；以及曾为国内知名职业女性学习成长平台商务部总监；已拥有 1 200+ 小时职业女性辅导经验，在女性成长领域、教练式女性领导力，团队沟通、识人，用人，组织人才诊断上富有经验。第一本书《崛起：女性成长七堂课》今年出版，第二本书《她觉醒》撰写中，全网影响 40 000 多位女性获得个人成长，找到人生方向。

A female growth instructor and a female leadership coach, Suki is now also an IP coach for intellectual females. Once the manager of the procurement department of a well-known listed companies and the director of commerce of a well-known professional women's learning and growth platform, she has more than 1,200 hours of experience in professional female counseling, with rich experience in female growth, coaching female leadership, team communication, personnel management and organizational talent diagnosis. Her first book, *Rise: Seven Lessons for Women's Growth*, was published this year, and now she is writing her second book, *Her Awakening*. She has influenced more than 40,000 women in achieving their personal growth and finding the direction of life.

2021，用文字证明我曾经历过
Tell My Story in 2021 with My Own Words

■ Maria Shaw

时间的脚步不会停歇，我能做到的就是留下自己成长的脚印。

1. 职场归属感

人这一生说到底都在追求两种东西，一是归属感，二是价值感。

当一个人没有了归属感，他就会心不定，就会缺乏安全感；当一个人没有价值感，无法得到认可，就会觉得无意义，进而颓废。

仔细回想起来，我们的工作、生活，还真就是这样。

2021年，我主要在执行F组项目，如BELFI管桩项目、CODELCO矿山项目。正是在执行项目的过程中，我正式融入F组。

年会后小组团建，大家驱车前往原定地点。天空中下起淅沥的小雨，仿佛预示了什么。到达地点后发现卫生环境跟网上

Time will never stop, yet I can leave my own footprints on the path of growth.

1. Keep a sense of belonging at work

Essentially speaking, what we are pursuing throughout our life are a sense of belonging and a sense of value.

Without a sense of belonging, one will be restless and insecure; without a sense of value, one will not be recognized by others, and will thus feel pointless, plunging into a state of decadence.

If we take a close look at the past, we will find that this is exactly what our work and life is like.

In 2021, I was mainly responsible for executing Team F projects, including BELFI Pipe Pile Project and CODELCO Mine Project, and joined Team F in the execution of these projects.

After the annual meeting, we drove to the location originally scheduled for team building. The drizzling rain seemed

照片相去甚远。Fay 姐征求了大家的意见，决定退掉并重新定团建地点。经历了这个小波折，Fay 姐看上去很愧疚。其实大可不必，因为接下来的活动内容实实在在地拉近了彼此的距离。大家来到我和 Siki 房间（我们房间最大），一起动手摆好沙发座椅，围坐一起，畅谈工作、生活，分享丰盛的晚餐，笑声充满整个房间，不知不觉持续到深夜。

令我印象深刻的是 Fay 姐说的一句话："我真的是想要以培养人的角度去思考，个性化制定的培养计划，希望每个人都能够按照适合的方式成长。"

加入团队后，同样是项目执行，但随着项目的深度和广度的增加，我会用更多的时间去学习和思考，责任感油然而生，会更加关注个人以及团队的成长与发展，这大概就是归属感的力量。

2. 保持运动频率

自律即自由，养成良好的运动习惯，坚持健康的饮食，保持健康的心态。这一年有偷懒、有沮丧、有怀疑，同时也有坚持、有认真、有进步。

to be an omen. The environment and hygiene of the location was so awfully different from the photos online that Fay asked for our opinions and eventually decided to cancel it and book a new location. Fay seemed to feel quite guilty of this twist. It was hardly necessary as the following activities did strengthen our bond together. Everyone came to the room of Siki and me (we had the largest room). Together we arranged the sofa seats into a circle and sat around, talking about our work and life over a grand feast. Laughter and joy filled the room. It was midnight before we knew it.

What impressed me most were Fay's words, "I truly want to think from the perspective of a trainer and make up customized training plans, so that everyone can grow in an appropriate way."

I am also responsible for project execution after joining the team. I spend more learning and thinking as the projects grow in depth and breadth. I feel a greater sense of responsibility and pay more attention to personal and team growth and development. This is probably the power of sense of belonging.

2. Keep fit

Self-discipline is freedom. We should develop good exercising habits, maintain a healthy diet, and uphold an upbeat attitude. Last year, I had moments of laziness, frustration and doubt, as well as moments of persistence, earnestness and progress.

（1）运动习惯的培养——身先动，心随行。

很多人都有个理想中的自己，想改变，但是都觉得改变很困难。可能要培养十几二十个习惯才会觉得能变得自律。但其实，关于培养习惯，只能一次培养一个，不能贪多。有一种习惯，只要找到它，坚持好它，你会发现它会帮助你完成更多好习惯的形成，这就是核心习惯。对我来说，运动就是我的核心习惯。

在快节奏的工作生活中，坚持运动的秘诀就是高效。每天起床第一件事就是穿上自己喜欢的健身服，心随身动，让自己快速进入运动状态，防止偷懒懈怠。

(1) How to develop exercising habits? Move your body first, and then follow your heart.

Many people have ideal images of themselves and want to change, but feel that it's difficult to make changes. You may have to nurture a dozen or twenty habits before you can be self-disciplined. As a matter of fact, you have to develop the habits one after another, instead of fostering them all at once. There may be a certain habit which can help you develop more good habits once you identify and stick to it. That's what I call a core habit. For me, exercising is my core habit.

In the fast-paced world today, the secret to regular exercising is staying efficient. The first thing to do after getting up every morning is to put on your favorite exercise clothes and make yourself move quickly before you can have

（2）适合自己的运动方式。

空腹晨练是不是不好？无氧和有氧怎么安排合适？锻炼45分钟以上才有效？

不要太纠结运动的方式，也不要太在意别人怎么说，也不要勉强自己，找到适合自己的运动方式才能长久坚持。把运动当成生活，而不是任务。

我喜欢每天早起空腹晨练20分钟以上，因为下班后晚饭和锻炼的时间安排对我来说是一件很困难的事情，并且早起就意味着要让自己早睡，保证良好的睡眠质量。至于晨练的项目是不固定的，可以是帕梅拉，也可以是小马哥健身操，甚至可以是非洲舞，只要自己喜欢，重点是让自己的身体动起来，短时间高效率，保持一天良好的精神状态。

a chance of slacking off.

(2) Find the form of exercise that suits you.

Is it not so good to exercise on an empty stomach? How to arrange anaerobic exercise and aerobic exercise properly? Is it only effective when we excercise for more than 45 minutes?

Don't worry too much about how you exercise. Do not care too much about what they say or force yourself. Finding the form of exercise that suits you can help you stick to it. Take exercising as part of your life instead of a task.

I like doing morning exercises for over 20 min every day as it is quite difficult for me to squeeze time for exercising after supper. That means that I have to go to bed early and get a good sleep. I don't have fixed morning exercise routines. It could be Pamela, dance workout or even African dance. Just do whatever you like. The point is to

（3）运动后能量补充。

运动过后，能量的补充也很重要。自己做一份简单的健康早餐，给接下来一天的工作提供充沛的能量。一份营养健康又不复杂的早餐，当然少不了烹饪简单又能提供优质蛋白质的鸡蛋，再配上一份拳头大小的主食，一根紫薯或者一份隔夜燕麦（我喜欢全麦）加上自己喜欢的水果，最后再来一杯"续命"美式咖啡，觉得味苦的朋友可以根据自己的口味加入适量鲜奶，还能补充蛋白质。我喜欢食物本身的味道，简单的蒸煮方便又快速。

get your body move efficiently in a short period of time and maintain a good spirit throughout the day.

(3) Replenish energy after exercise.

It's important to fuel up for energy after exercising. Make yourself a simple, healthy breakfast to fuel yourself for the day ahead. For a nutritious and simple breakfast, eggs are a convenient source for high-quality protein, which can be complemented by a fist-size purple sweet potato or a serving of overnight oatmeal (I like wholewheat) and a serving of your favorite fruit. A cup of American coffee can be a finishing touch to this breakfast. Fresh milk can be added to reduce the bitter taste and replenish protein. I love the original taste of the food, which can be retained by simple, easy and fast cooking.

（4）心态调整。

由于工作的忙碌，往往会懈怠锻炼，也会敷衍饮食，甚至选择不健康的食物，焦虑和负罪感就伴随而生，因此学会调整好心态很重要。

要学会转移和释放压力。尽量不要囤垃圾食品，想吃的时候尽量动手去做；提高工作效率，工作时间尽量不要玩手机，拒绝无效加班；一定要早睡，保证充足的睡眠才能应对运动强度叠加工作强度；根据实际情况制定力所能及的运动规划，不要制造焦虑，不强迫运动，可以适当增加日常消耗，除了运动、工作，也要给自己留够休息的时间；添置喜欢的运动装备激励自己，比如买一套漂亮的健身服，可以给自己坚持运动的动力。

要记得运动也好饮食也罢，都是生活的一部分而不是全部，它们的目的是让自己更加健康更加开心，如果它们给你制造了焦虑，记得停下来思考一下，如何能让这件事良性循环下去。

3. 跨城陪伴无须拘泥形式

我在上海工作，父母亲居住在湖北老家。因为工作关系，我很少回老家，与父母的交流仅是每月一次的短暂视频电话，简单问候，他们说一切都好，我也表示

(4) Adjust your mentality.

Busy at work, we will often slack off in exercising, pay less attention to food and even take in unhealthy food. Anxiety and guilt would subsequently creep in. Hence, it's important to adjust our mentality.

We need to learn how to deflect and release pressure. Try not to store junk food and prepare a meal yourself; improve your work efficiency, try not to play with your cell phone during the work hours to eliminate ineffective overtime; always go to bed early to ensure ample sleep, so that you can cope with working and exercising; make practical exercise plans according to personal physical conditions; do not induce anxiety or do forced exercises; increase daily energy consumption accordingly and give yourself plenty of rest time in addition to exercising and working; buy sports outfits you like to stimulate your motivation of regular exercising, such as nice fitness clothing.

Always remember that exercising and eating are just part of life, not all of life. It's to make you healthier and happier. If it induces anxiety, you should stop and think about how it can continue in a virtuous cycle.

3. Cross-town companionship

I work in Shanghai and my parents live in Hubei Province. Due to the nature of my job, I seldom get a chance to go home. We just have a short video

"嗯嗯，没事就好"。

2021年，爸爸因为股骨头坏死进行了腿部手术，术后在家复健，刚好我有假期就回家照顾他，也许是许久没有这么近距离地观察，突然发现爸爸头发已经花白，还出现了脊柱侧弯，这些不可能是一夜之间有的，为什么自己之前竟然一直没有发现，愧疚感一阵阵地涌上心头。从那以后，每周一次或者不定时地会跟爸妈视频，不拘什么话题，聊聊各自近来的生活和工作点滴。才发现原来陪伴并不一定要拘泥于形式，也并没有想象中那么困难，即使无法回家陪在他们身边，云端聊聊天能拉近彼此的距离。

仅以这些小小的片段和感悟记录这一年的收获与成长。前路漫漫，不妨关注当下，进一步有进一步的欢喜。

call every month and exchange simple greetings. They often say that everything goes well, and I will respond, "Well, cool." In 2021, my father underwent a leg surgery because of osteonecrosis of the femoral head. After that, he started postoperative rehabilitation, and I took a long leave to go to his place and look after him. Perhaps I hadn't looked at my father so closely for such a long time that I suddenly found that his hair had all turned gray and he also had scoliosis. These conditions would not develop overnight. I felt guilty. Since then, I have maintained a video call with my parents every week or on an irregular basis and talk about everything about life and work. It's not until then did I find that companionship is not limited to certain forms and is not so difficult as I thought. Though I am not being there for them at home, video chats can bring us closer.

I hereby record what I gained and how I grew over the last year with these small moments and reflections. There is a long way ahead, so we might as well focus on and enjoy the present.

肖 蒙
Maria Shaw

毕业于东华大学纺织化学与染整工程专业，2016年加入CNOOD。

Graduated from Donghua University, majoring in textile chemistry and dyeing and finishing engineering, and joined CNOOD in 2016.

一个产生飞跃的起点

A Starting Point for a Leap Forward

■ Tommy Chen

在足球场上，一支能够赢得比赛的球队不会仅仅依赖于某一个高水平的前锋，还必须同时要有过硬的中场和后防，它们共同组成一个强大的系统，分工明确，运行起来时就会无坚不摧。一个优秀团队的产生往往得益于团队内部一个个相互配合相互成就的个体，它们共同构成了一套系统，高效且高度契合的行事风格造就了成功。一个人的成就也可以是这样的道理。人的眼睛和耳朵可以获取信息，头脑负责思考，嘴巴负责表达，双手则承担执行，所有这一切共同创造了成就。成就要归功于各个优秀部分的整合，而这种整合就是一套系统。对于目前正身处于一个系统中的我来说，这种感觉尤为深刻。

今年是我在施璐德的第二年，在这一年中，公司在管理上迎来了大幅变革，无论本身的架构还是人员的归属上都有了很大改善与革新。每个部门对各自的职能和

On the football field, a winning team needs not only a high-calibre forward, but also amazing midfielders and rear defenders. These members make up a strong system with clear division of work to make the team unbreakable. An outstanding team is often born out of individuals who work and help with each other and make up an efficient and highly collaborative system leading to success. What one can achieve works similarly. The eyes that receive information, the ears that hear, the mind that thinks, the mouth that speaks and the hands that execute work together to deliver the achievements. The achievements are made because of the integration of the good parts which constitutes a system. This is especially true for me as I am currently in a system.

It was my second year at CNOOD. Last year, the company made significant changes in management as could be seen from the extensive improvement

职责进行深度地研究与明晰，同时公司里每个人的岗位职责与归属也都被一一明确，在短时间内，公司里每个人和每支队伍的状态随即都发生了很大的变化。我从中最直观的感受是每当一项新的工作任务出现时，模糊不清的职责界定少了，取而代之的是更加明确的分工，每个小个体都很清楚自己负责的范围，执行工作时都在发挥着自己的优势，各有所长且相互促进，每支队伍的精神面貌也都得到了改善，所有经历过这些变化的个体共同造就了一个更加融洽和高效率的系统。

这次公司的重新梳理为公司带去积极效应的同时，也带动着我个人对自己定位和认知的进一步明确与提升。刚入公司的前半年内，我对自己的解读以及在公司中的定位是不完全清晰的，很多时候虽然被布置了任务，每天也在输出着工作成果，但总是觉得自己缺少了一些方向感，这种

and innovation in both its own structure and staff affiliation. The functions and responsibilities of each department were profoundly studied and clarified, and the job responsibilities and affiliation of each employee were defined. These measures immediately brought about tremendous changes to the status of each member and each team in a short period of time. What I was impressed most by such changes was that there were few undefined responsibilities for each new work task. It was so well defined that every individual was aware of his/her own responsibilities and gave full play to their strengths at work. Each team took on a new spiritual look. All individuals undergoing these changes jointly make a more harmonious and efficient system.

This reorganization not only brought about positive results to the company, but also further clarified and improved my own positioning and perception. During the first six months at the company, I was not quite clear about my own role. Although I was given tasks most of the

方向感的缺失使我在定位自我发展的时候少了几分肯定，同时自己也会觉得有点力不从心。在那段时间里，我很多时候也在思考自己扮演的角色是什么、自己因何而存在于团体中、自己和所属团体的职责归根到底是什么。当参与工作任务时，虽然工作教会了我一些东西，我在工作的过程中也在学习，但如果没有一个明确的方向，所有的付出和所得都是松散且缺失章法的。随着公司开始梳理和重整管理模式，我的思维也慢慢变得清晰起来。在之前的几个月里，我随整个部门一同参与了部门岗位职责和工作范围的归类与整理，同时我也编制了个人的岗位职责并参与了一系列部门管理文件的编写。通过亲身去执行，我不仅真正地明确了自己在部门乃至公司范围里的角色设定，同时对自己所在团队的归属和职能也有了更加深刻的认识。经过在工作中的不断思考后，我的自主意识也得到了提升。在我看来，真正的

time and delivered work results every day, I felt a sense of direction missing, which resulted in my uncertainty in positioning personal development and my sense of powerlessness. During that time, I often thought about what role I played, why I was a member of the team and what the essential responsibilities of me and my team were. Although I learned from the tasks and my work, what I did and gained seemed to be loose and dispersive due to the lack of a well-defined direction. With the reorganization of corporate management, I was increasingly clear of my role. Over the past few months, I worked with others to classify and organize the job responsibilities and scope of work of the department, drew up individual job responsibilities, and participated in the

自我完善仅凭被动接受外界的安排是远远不够的，要想真正解读自我，就要自我建设，做到扮演好"主人翁"。通过一次次的修缮和打磨，我的方向感也开始变得清晰了起来。

在公司重新梳理的过程中，我所在的部门职能变得更加明确，更重要的是一种维度的提升。从公司这个最大维度的系统来讲，我们的任务简单来说就是提供支持与保障，这种支持和保障是面向公司所有的部门，作为一个职能部门，其存在的意义是协助公司这个庞大系统里的任何一个部分解决遇到的问题，通过发挥自身的优势，更高效地服务公司这个整体。在这个过程中，我感受到所有人都在不停地刷新着自我认知，同时每个人所在的团体也因此而获得了升华。各个部门通过相互配合，优势互补，共同组成了一个高效运转且互相契合的整体。

公司是一个系统，一个人也是一个系

preparation of management documents of the department. Such involvement allowed me not only to understand my role in the department and in the company, but also to gain a better idea of my affiliation and functions in the team. Through continuous reflection at work, I have improved my sense of autonomy. For me, passive acceptance of external arrangements is far from complete for true self-definition. For true self interpretation, we need to put ourselves in the process of self-construction, so that we can be the masters of ourselves. Such reflections and corrections have resulted in my increasingly clear sense of direction.

During this reorganization, the function of the department I am in became more definite. As far as the company, the maximum dimension, is concerned, our mission is to provide support and guarantee in simple terms. Such support and guarantee is for all parts of the company. A functional department is established to assist the huge system of the company to resolve problems in any part, give play to its strengths and more efficiently serve the whole. I have felt that everyone is gaining a new idea of the self, and every team is thus improving. Through mutual cooperation and advantage complementarity, all parts make an efficiently operating and mutually interacting whole.

The Company is a system, so is an

统。公司在改良自身时，里面的个体也在通过不断地变化来适应整个系统的变革，这些变化既代表着团队的进步，同时也是个体自我提升的一种表现。在亲身经历了这些变化后，我感受到一个焕然一新的模式已经诞生，一个高效且融洽的系统已经建立，这确实是一个起点，一个可以产生飞跃的起点。

individual. Every member is adapting to the improvement and reform of the company. Such adaptation represents not only the progress of the team, but also the self-improvement of individuals. Involved in such changes, I feel a refreshing model born and an efficient and harmonious system put in place. It's indeed a starting point, one for a leap forward.

陈 浩
Tommy Chen

出生于天津。硕士毕业于英国伦敦玛丽女王大学，专业为会计与金融。2020年9月加入施璐德，目前任职于投资/风控部。

Born in Tianjin, Master of Accounting and Finance from the Queen Mary University of London, joined CNOOD in September 2020.

一场疫情一场梦

The Fleeting Dream in the Pandemic

■ Johnson Shen

发完最后一封邮件，我看了眼时间，不知不觉又到了深夜，自嘲了一下居家办公的效率果然还是不如办公室。

合上了电脑，看着眼前的台灯发呆，一阵睡意袭来。

担任风控合规职能的工作已经过去半年，我忙碌于业务和管理岗位的穿插，身上的担子重了不少，承担了更多的职责和义务，也多了一个互相关心的组织。本来一切都是这样缓缓地推进了，只是疫情突然来了。

疫情的暴发，让本该忙碌的生活停了下来，隔离在家的日子把原本两点一线的日子变成原地打转。

2022年3月1日，新闻中播报上海发现了一例新冠肺炎感染者。初次听闻，我没有太过在意，而是转身继续投入工作

After I sent the last email, it was again midnight before I knew it. Working from home indeed wasn't so productive as in office.

I closed my laptop and looked at the desk lamp, abstracted. Sleepiness came over me.

Having worked in the risk control issues for over six months, I was busy handling both business and management responsibilities. As I took on more responsibilities, I found an organization that cares for each other. Everything was slowly moving ahead when COVID-19 broke out.

The sudden outbreak of the pandemic brought my supposedly busy life to a halt. Quarantined at home, I could only work from one location instead of two locations.

On March 1, 2022, a new COVID-19 infected patient was reported in Shanghai. Believing that this temporary outbreak

中。只以为这不过是一场短暂的意外，就如同前几次一样，会悄然结束。

可随之发生的变化超出了所有人的预想，疫情传播速度之快远超过所有人的想象，不到几天就侵袭整个上海，甚至外溢到周围城市。

身边的同事、朋友以肉眼可见的速度陆陆续续被隔离在家中，以至于朋友圈都有了一句笑话，"在上海，身边没有几个被隔离的朋友，说明这人的人际关系是真的不行"。就这样持续了不到几天，上海宣布实施静默管理。

我的生活也因为疫情慢了下来，每天除了工作以外多了一个抢菜。

对食物的原始追求，超越了任何物质上的满足，我们导师笑称，一群复旦金融专业的硕士、博士，每天讨论的不是金融市场的发展，也不是二级市场的波动，而是早上定了闹钟还是没抢到菜。在疫情面前，人类太渺小了，所有的一切都无法掌控在自己手中。

不同人性的体现也在此刻被放大了。有些我们以为熟悉的却变得好像不认识了，有些我们误解的却发现原来自己错了。

would quietly end as the previous outbreaks, I wasn't alarmed by it and went on with my busy work.

Yet the subsequent changes were more dramatic than anyone ever expected. It spread much faster than anyone could have imagined. Within a few days, it swept over Shanghai and spilled over to its surrounding cities.

Colleagues and friends were soon quarantined in their residential community or at home. There was a joke going viral in the WeChat Moments, "If you don't have several friends quarantined in Shanghai, it means that your interpersonal relationships really suck." Several days later, Shanghai announced lockdown policies.

My life came to a halt because of the pandemic. In addition to working, shopping for food became another job in my to-do list every day.

The primitive quest for food transcended any material gratification. Our mentor said jokingly that masters and doctors of finance from Fudan University are talking not about the development of the financial market or the fluctuation of the secondary market, but about failure to shop for the food in short supply despite setting the alarm clock. In the face of disaster, human beings are too small and unable to keep everything under control.

Humanity is magnified at this moment. What we thought we knew was not what we knew; what we thought we understood turned out not to be what we

疫情中，我们只是普通人，可如何做好一个普通人似乎都变得很难，又有多少人可以做到脚踏实地，从不困惑，不叹息，不抱怨，只是坚定地为自己的职业付出全部。在困难面前，不急不躁，不悲不喜，始终保持着冷静的态度，顽强战斗。

疫情严重之后，有人开始指责上海的管控不严，失责失效。也许大多数人最敏感的还是打乱了他们的习惯、损害了他们的利益。他们为此而不快、气愤，但这些情绪是毫无意义的。

一步步地，直到走到了全区域的静态管理，如此一来，毫无思想准备的亲朋好友们突然面临离别。母子、夫妻或情侣在分别时，还以为那是暂时的离别，有的还相约几天之后再见。可等到大家都被隔离起来才发现，这是一场漫长的等待，从刚开始确诊的人数不多，到后来越来越多，大家从惊慌到习以为常。大家都在自我隔离，都相信总有一天疫情会过去。

只是，这一次的结束，是否能给我们带来一些经验和教训呢？还是犹如过眼云

understood.

In the face of the pandemic, we are merely ordinary people. However, it seems quite difficult to be a proper ordinary person. How many of us can be down-to-earth, never confused, never sighing and never complaining, but determined to be devoted to their profession? How many of us can keep patience, shake off emotions, always stay calm and fight persistently against the difficulties?

Aware of the severity of the pandemic, everyone began to blame Shanghai for its lax control and dereliction of duty. Perhaps most people were most sensitive to things that disrupted their routines and hurt their interests. They were unhappy and angry, but these feelings were meaningless.

Gradually, static management across the region was imposed. Friends and family members faced sudden separation. When mothers and children, spouses or couples parted a few days ago, they thought it was a temporary separation, and some made plans to meet again in a few days. It was not until they were quarantined that they realized that it was a long wait. People were panic at first at the growing number of diagnosed cases, but then became accustomed to it. Everyone was quarantined at home, convinced that the pandemic would be over one day.

However, can the end of this outbreak bring us some experience and

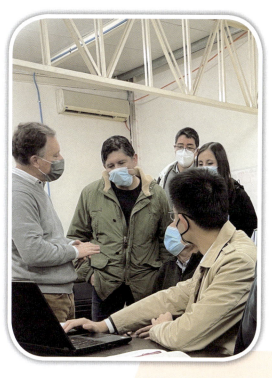

烟一般消散，直到下一次猝不及防？

思想上的转变是不是又可以给我带来些什么呢？

一阵冷意，突然醒了过来，感觉做了一个好长的梦又好像什么都想不起来。

离开书桌前，看了一眼手机中充斥着关于疫情的消息，虽然大灾大难面前总会有人性中的丑陋，但更多的是光辉。不过只有当风险到了面前，人们才会觉得这是自己的事，不然可能永远只是一个饭后谈资。

然而，运气不会永远都那么好，我们不能指望每次遇到了风险能够逢凶化吉，该是时候提高自己的"免疫力"了。

lessons? Or will we cast it aside until we are struck unexpectedly next time?

Is it possible that a change in my mind could bring me something meaningful?

A fit of cold suddenly woke me up. I felt like having a long dream, but couldn't remember what it was.

Before leaving my desk, I took a glimpse of the pandemic-related news in my cell phone. Although there will always be ugliness in humanity in the face of disasters, brilliance in humanity can be more common seen. However, it is only when facing the risks themselves that people can realize that it is their business, otherwise it may remain a topic of after-dinner conversation forever.

However, luck will not always fall upon us. We can't expect to turn ill luck into good every time. It is time to improve our "immunity".

沈佳祺
Johnson Shen

所有的相遇，都是久别重逢。不知不觉在CNOOD已经九年多了。在这样一个关怀他人、提升自我的集体中，始终能让自己充满正能量。走遍世界的角落，带着自由而无用的灵魂。

Every occasion of encounter is a reunion after a long separation. I have been working at CNOOD for more than nine years before I know it. I am always filled with positive energy in such a mutually caring and self-promoting organization. With a free and useless soul, I'm going across every corner of the world.

铿锵四人行
The Strong Foursome Team

■ Danni Xu

2021年9月，部门发展迎来了新的里程碑。部门增加风险控制功能，并新增一名成员。从此，四人行的团队成立了。

经过小半年的不懈努力，部门成员齐心协力相继完成并发布了部门操作手册汇编、部门职能及岗位说明书及部门年度考核评定机制等一系列部门文件，建立健全了相关管理制度和流程，为部门发展打下了良好的基础。

下面是风格突变的部门人员介绍：

Johnson，部门副总经理，是个幽默风趣又有点冷的男生。说他冷是因为他喜欢怀着善意怼人，怼的角度清奇，而且常

In September 2021, our department embraced a new milestone as it was renamed risk control. The foursome team was officially established.

With the unremitting concerted efforts for about half a year, our team have successively prepared and issued a series of department documents, including Collection of the Department Operation Manuals, Function and Position Description of the Department, and Annual Assessment Mechanism of the Department. The risk control management system of the company has been improved, and sound management regulations and procedures have been put in place, laying a good foundation for the development of department.

Here is an introduction to all members of our department:

Deputy General Manager Johnson is a witty, humorous and slightly cool man. He is slightly cool as he likes to pick on

常直击要害，不留情面。Johnson 习惯早起，每天八点半到公司；热爱学习，通过了 CFA 三级、CPA、司法考试、证券从业资格等一系列考试；热爱工作，每天无怨无悔地工作 18 个小时，直到脚步虚浮、双目无神。疫情期间，在其他同事居家隔离的时候，他几乎每天都出现在办公室。用他自己的话说，只有在办公室里工作效率才是最高的。Johnson 工作出色、经验丰富，似乎没有什么能难倒他。他是我们部门的定海神针，同时也是各项目组争抢的"香饽饽"。

people with good intentions and from a strange perspective, and he often hits the nail on the head. He gets up early and goes to work at 8:30 every morning. A zealous learner, he has passed the CFA Level 3, CPA, judicial exams and securities qualification. Passionate at work, he works for 18 hours a day without complaint or regret until he can barely stand and look listless. While our colleagues were quarantined at home during the outbreak of the pandemic, he went to the office almost every day. In his own words, he works most efficiently in the office. He is so good at his job and so experienced that nothing seems can stop him. He is the anchor of our department and also the sought-after member of all project teams.

Jodie，初生牛犊不怕虎。虽然入职时间不长，却已经算半个"老人"了。她经常一边吹着"彩虹屁"一边去怼副总并被副总牢牢拿捏。我曾经不止一次觉得，她想要气死Johnson然后自己当副总经理，直到有一天，她也开始气我。Jodie人长得小巧纤细但胃口很大，是公认的"干饭人"，刚吃饱饭也不忘让副总为她留两块披萨。偶尔粗心大意却不妨碍她拥有高超的技术实力。看到她做的文档、演示文件和小视频，我常常觉得大多数人简历上所谓的精通办公软件十分虚假，其中当然也包括我自己。作为公司年龄较小的同事之一，Jodie聪明、机灵有朝气，吴老师都忍不住夸赞她越来越洋气。

Jodie is a brave fledgling. Though she has joined the company for quite a short time, she has turned out to be quite "veteran". She often puts in a good word for Johnson while picking on him, but is always forced to submit to him. More than once, I thought that she picked on Johnson for his position as the Deputy General Manager until she started to pick on me as well one day. This slim girl has a huge appetite and is a recognized eater. She would ask Johnson to leave her two pieces of pizza even though she just had lunch. Her occasional carelessness did not dim her superb capabilities. Looking at her documents, powerpoint slides, and video clips, I often find proficiency in Microsoft Office on most applicants' resumes a sham. Surely, I am one of these applicants. As one of the youngest colleagues, Jodie is smart, shrewd and vigorous. Aunt Wu can't help but praise her for being increasingly international.

Tommy，一个本硕生都在国外就读的海归，多年漂泊毫不影响其根正苗红。凭自己190厘米的身高优势自然而然成为人群中的凸点。用Fay姐不恰当的比喻形容，Tommy站在旁边就好像"鹤立鸡群"一样。就连平时看起来高大挺拔的副总站在Tommy身边，硬是让我看出了"小鸟依人"的感觉。Tommy是个天津人，每次从老家回来就给我们带麻花，我特别期待年会的时候他给我们来个单口相声。Tommy对待工作严谨认真，充分发挥了不懂就问的精神。平常很赶潮流，常常用一些我看不懂的微信状态，当然每次都被我质疑然后换掉。Tommy喜欢做饭，有时会带来公司请大家品鉴，我就特别喜欢那道"土豆炖牛肉"，美味！

Tommy is a returnee who pursued both his Bachelor's Degree and Master's Degree overseas and an authentic Chinese despite years abroad. At a height of 190 cm, he is naturally a focus. Just as what Fay said, you will feel like a minnow in front of this Triton. Even Johnson who is quite tall among us looks small next to Tommy. A native of Tianjin, Tommy often brings us fried dough twist when returning to work after a trip home. I look forward to him performing stand-up comedy at the Annual Meeting Gala. Rigorous and serious about work, he is always ready to ask whenever he has a question. Up to date, he often uses WeChat icons that I don't understand, and changes them every time I question him. Enthusiastic about cooking, he occasionally brings food he cooks to the company for us to have a bite. I am particularly fond of his braised beef with potatoes. It's quite nice!

最后一名成员就是我自己了。写到这里我都想封笔了，一方面是懒，一方面是……因为当初做个人性格调查时，Johnson语重心长地对我说："Danni，你可能对自己有些误解。"所以不论我怎么写，我也不是你心中的样子，所以就不花力气啦。

曾经的我有哀伤有彷徨，觉得自己需要一个人去披荆斩棘。现在，有了团队的支持和鼓励，这条荆棘丛生的路也会走得光芒万丈。感谢所有的缘分和相遇，未来我们必须全力以赴，同时又不抱有任何希望。不管做什么事，都要当它是全世界最重要的一件事，但同时又知道这件事根本无关紧要。这才是我们长大的样子。

The last member is me. I want to stop writing at this point. For one thing, I am lazy; for another thing, Johnson said to me sincerely after the personality test, "Danni, you may have misunderstood yourself." So no matter what I write, I'm not what you think I am. I may just save the trouble.

I used to be sad and hesitant as I thought I had to blaze a trail alone. Now with the support and encouragement of the team, I believe this thorny trail will be full of moments of glory. I am grateful for all the connections and encounters. In the future, we will go all out and at the same time get rid of unrealistic dreams. No matter what you do, take it as the most important thing in the world while knowing that it doesn't matter. This is what we grow up to be.

徐丹妮
Danni Xu

2016年4月正式加入施璐德，成为施璐德大家庭的一名成员。作为一只小金牛，爱财且取之有道。渴望拥有吃喝玩乐的生活和充实的精神世界，并为此不懈努力。

In April 2016, Danni Xu officially joined CNOOD and became a member of this big family. As a Taurus, she loves money but only obtains it in a proper way. She has a desire to enjoy a life of foods and fun, and spiritual enrichment. She makes unremitting efforts for that.

秘鲁二三事

Working in Peru

■ Zoe Cui

2019年7月初拿到毕业证后，我迎来了打工人生涯中的第一份工作。专业为小语种西班牙语的我，在上海接受了为期2个多月的短暂入职培训后，于2019年9月15日落地秘鲁，正式开启了我的海外工作生涯。

在大学期间，无数次地听到老师对西语国家的描述，其中最多的就是他们的美食美景和令人遐想的神话传说。于是慢慢地开始对西语国家产生向往，想象着万一未来的某天我要是置身在某个西语国家神秘国土上的时候，我的生活会是怎样的。在落地秘鲁的那一刻，想象终于变成了现实。

我在出发前就已经和当地驻外同事取得联系，咨询了当地的气候和生活条件，了解到首都利马是世界上降雨量最少的首

After obtaining my graduation certificate in early July 2019, I started my first job in my career. Majoring in Spanish, after the induction training for about 2 months in Shanghai, on September 15, 2019, I landed in Peru, officially unfolding my overseas working life.

During my college years, I heard the teachers' descriptions of Spanish-speaking countries for countless times, among which the most delicious food, beautiful scenery and fascinating myths and legends were the most commonly mentioned. Gradually I developed a yearning for Spanish-speaking countries and imagined what my life would be if I set foot on this mystical land. My imagination finally became reality when the plane landed in Peru.

Before departure, I had contacted my local colleagues overseas and learned about the local climate and living

都，因此呈现出一面是湛蓝的海洋，一面是无垠的土丘和沙漠的神奇景观。出发前国内还是闷热潮湿，但9月份的秘鲁早已经进入深秋，一出机场阵阵凉意就扑面而来。时差调过来后就正式开始融入当地的生活。

秘鲁初印象

刚开始的生活其实并不顺利，突然被扔到了一个完全陌生的环境，虽然是自己熟悉的语言，但是当地人的正常语速实在太快，最初的几个月，内心十分抗拒单独和当地人接触，尤其是和他们电话沟通，常常是对方说完一大段话之后，我的大脑还在回想他最开始说了什么。所以在最初的一段时间，周末不上班的时候都只是在楼下的小公园溜达。因此也发现了秘鲁人对狗狗的喜爱。一户人家有两三条狗并不稀奇，不管工作日或者是周末，早起必做的一件事就是遛狗。有一次外出，看到一个小孩同时拖着7条狗，完全是"狗

conditions. I was told that Lima, the capital of Peru, has the lowest rainfall in the world, and thus presents a magical landscape composed of a deep blue ocean and endless mounds of earth and desert. It was still hot and humid in China before I left for Peru. However, Peru was in late autumn in September. I could feel the chill the moment I stepped outside of the airport. After the jet lag, I began to integrate into local life.

First impression of Peru

Life didn't start out so well. Suddenly thrown into a completely unfamiliar environment, I was quite reluctant to talk to the locals in the first few months despite my familiarity with the language as they speak too fast. Especially during phone calls, I was often still thinking about what was said at first even after a long speech was made. In the first few months, therefore, I just hung out in the small park downstairs when I didn't have to work on weekends. Hence, I noticed how much the Peruvians love dogs. It's not unusual for a family to have two or three dogs. On weekdays or weekends, walking the dogs is one of the morning rituals. Once I saw a kid dragging 7 dogs at the

楼下小公园的狗崽和它的主人们
The dogs and their owners in the small park downstairs

遛人"了。曾经有一次同事打了自己的小狗，邻居听到后竟要报警，最后费口舌做了一番解释后才得以"洗清嫌疑"。

　　除了对小动物的喜欢，秘鲁的交通也使我印象颇深。都说上海早高峰可怕，利马的早高峰也毫不逊色。在利马开车是允许鸣笛的，再加上这边大部分车辆是燃油车，所以一大早出门迎面而来的就是四面八方的鸣笛声夹杂着浓浓的车辆尾气味以及各种小巴车揽人的叫喊声（这种小巴车是私营的）。打工人的早晨初体验十分上头。

same time. For me, the dogs walking the kid might be a more accurate expression. On one occasion, a colleague beat his dog. Hearing that, a neighbor called the police. It took a lot of explaining before he was cleared of suspicion.

　　In addition to their fondness of animals, the traffic in Peru also left me with a deep impression. Shanghai's morning rush hour is horrible, and Lima's is nothing less. Honking is allowed during driving in Lima. Furthermore, most of the cars here run on fuel. So when you go out early in the morning, you will be greeted by the sound of sirens from all directions, mixed with the thick smell of exhaust fumes and the shouts of various minibuses (which are privately owned). The morning experience for a worker is truly a headache.

这个公交车后窗户是塑料膜代替的
The rear window of this bus is covered by plastic films

勇敢者的游戏

利马的气温终年比较稳定，即使在最炎热的时候也不会超过30度。冬季平均气温为15度，但因为临海，冬季雾气非常大，所以体感温度比较低。国内最冷的时候刚好是利马夏季最热的时候，每天都艳阳高照。从早上六七点开始，海边成群结队的人一个个鱼跃而下，开始冲浪。尽管利马是一座临海城市，但没有适合休闲的优美沙滩。海水温度偏低，砂石颗粒大，海浪声震耳欲聋，这些都使人们对大海的美丽望而止步，只有勇士们拿着他们的冲浪板和大海展开较量。

说完了"不太光彩"的一面，接下来说一下令人舒心的几点。

随性的生活方式

前段时间非常流行"内卷"这个词汇，用通俗的话来讲就是激烈的内部斗争。中国人遍布全球各地，不管是在多么恶劣的生存环境下都能努力开创出一片天地。大家互相比较，暗自较劲，一个要比一个拼，今天你是996，明天我就要007，争着存钱，争着发展，大城市的生活节奏快到就像被上了发条一样，根本停不下来，也不敢停下来。但是在秘鲁，可不是这样的。

The game of the brave

Lima has a stable temperature range throughout the year, with no more than 30℃ even on the hottest days and an average temperature of 15℃ in winter. Because of proximity to the sea and the foggy weather in winter, the sensible temperature is relatively low. The coldest time in China is the hottest time of summer in Lima, when the sun shines every day. From 6 or 7 a.m., crowds of people dive off the beach and start surfing. This coastal city offers no fine beaches for relaxing. The cold seawater, large grains of sand, and deafening waves discourage people from exploring the beauty of the sea. Only the brave will take on the sea with their surfboards.

With the depiction of the "unfavorable aspects", here are some encouraging aspects.

A casual lifestyle

The phase "rat race" went viral in the Internet recently. To put it simply, it means intense internal struggle. Chinese people can be found all over the world, trying to make their mark no matter how harsh the living conditions are. Everyone compares with each other, secretly and intensively. You work from 9:00 a.m. to 9:00 p.m. for six days a week. I will work around the clock for seven days a week. Everyone strives to save money and works for development. The life in big cities is so fast-paced that it's like being wound

跟南美大部分国家一样，秘鲁人生活普遍比较简单、节奏也相对较慢。他们没有储蓄的习惯，挣多少钱就用多少钱享受生活，也有大部分生活不富裕的人们，他们去超市采购也要用信用卡，就几百块的账单，收银员还会贴心地问你需不需要分期。在项目工作时刚开始接触到他们，我很费解为什么同样的活，同样的人数，中国工人可能一两天就能做好的事情，他们就要做个十天半个月。中国工人本来两个人能做的事，他们可能要四五个人才行。这一点往往被当地的中国同胞们诟病，说他们不思进取，得过且过，坐吃山空。但是有句话叫"慢工出细活"，他们的劳动成果就是对这句话最好的诠释。这大概就是"存在即合理"。

up. It's impossible to stop, and no one dares to stop. However, that's not the case in Peru.

Peruvians, like most of South American people, lead simple and slow-paced lives. They have no habit of saving money and spend every penny earned to enjoy life. There are also a majority of people who are not rich. They have to use credit cards in the supermarket for a bill of hundreds of dollars, and the cashier will thoughtfully ask you whether you need installments. When I first came to know how they worked in the project, I was quite confused at the fact that they need ten days or half a month to complete what the same number of Chinese workers can accomplish within two days. For a same task which two

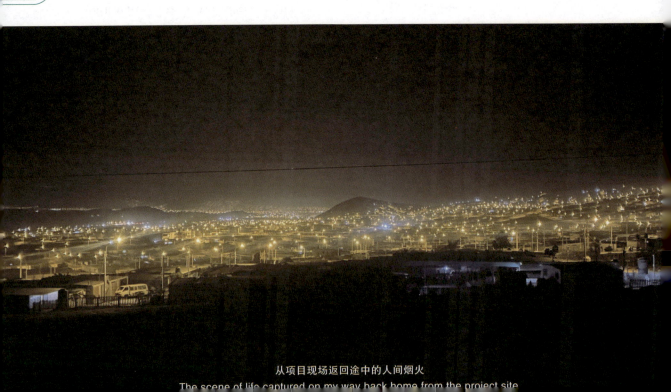

从项目现场返回途中的人间烟火
The scene of life captured on my way back home from the project site

虽然他们挣钱挣得少，储蓄也不多，但是每个周末都会和家人或者朋友小聚，在小公园的绿地上、海边、各色餐厅和咖啡厅到处都能见到他们的身影，条件好的一起聚餐吃烧烤，条件差的就在公园绿地上铺个野餐布，随便来一点音乐，他们就能随处起舞，不论男女，多少都是有跳舞天赋的。每个人脸上的笑都发自内心。等到真正地融入他们，你就会发现他们是真的在很认真地对待生活，和他们沟通起来更轻松愉悦。他们全身心地活在当下，重视家庭生活，享受着生命给予的一切。

各具特色的历史遗迹

到达秘鲁之前，我早就已经在各种书籍里面看到过他们的几大著名旅游景点。2019年到秘鲁之后，就一直心心念念想去见识一下。但因为工作的缘故，一直没有去成。最终决定在2020年的圣周假期前往位于秘库斯科的马丘比丘。当地海拔

Chinese workers can accomplish, four or five Peruvians must be hired. This is often criticized by the Chinese workers who say that the Peruvians make no attempt to make progress and muddle along. However, there is a saying going that "slow work makes good work." The result of their labor is the best illustration of that saying. That's probably "what is actual is rational".

Even though they don't earn much money or have much savings, they get together with their family and friends every weekend. They can be found in small parks, beaches, restaurants and cafes. Those who are economically affluent will have BBQ, and those who are less affluent will put a piece of cloth on the grass in the park for a picnic. When the music plays, they can dance anywhere. Both men and women have some talent for dancing. Everyone wears a genuine smile on their face. When you really get to know them, you will find that they are really serious about life, and easier and more pleasant to communicate with. They live fully in the present, value family life, and enjoy what life has to offer.

Distinctive historical sites

Before arriving in Peru, I had read about several of their famous tourist attractions in various books. Since my arrival in Peru in 2019, I had been dying to see them, but I didn't get the chance because of work. Finally, I decided to

约 2 300 米，处在热带丛林，是秘鲁境内著名的前哥伦布时期印加帝国的遗迹，也是世界新七大奇迹之一。

但遗憾的是，由于疫情影响，2020年圣周假期还未到来时，各大景点就已宣布不再对外营业，即使后来疫情有所缓解，对外开放时间也是断断续续，还有各种强制要求，我的旅行计划直到现在都还未落地。除了著名的马丘比丘之外，还有位于秘鲁和玻利维亚交界处的"的的喀喀湖"（世界上海拔最高的淡水湖）、随处可见的巴洛克式教堂、武器广场、印加古道和神奇的亚马孙雨林等。值得一提的还有他们的"神兽"：憨态可掬的羊驼和神奇长相的南美低地貘。除了美景和神奇动物外，这个国家还有数不清的各式美食（秘鲁连续 6 年蝉联全球最佳美食目的地）等待着你来探索。

visit Machu Picchu in Cusco during the Holy Week Holiday in 2020. Located about 2,300 meters above sea level in the tropical jungle, it is a famous pre-Columbian relic of the Inca Empire in Peru and one of the new Seven Wonders of the World.

Unfortunately, because of the pandemic, major scenic spots announced that they would not open for business before the Holy Week Holiday of 2020. Even after the pandemic is less severe, the opening hours are intermittent and there are various mandatory requirements. My travel plan has not been implemented yet. In addition to Machu Picchu, there are Lake Titicaca on the border of Peru and Bolivia (also the highest freshwater lake in the world), the ubiquitous Baroque churches, the Plaza de Armas, the Inca Trail and the magical Amazon rainforest. Special mention should be made of their mythical beasts: the charmingly naïve alpaca and the odd-looking tapir. Apart from the picturesque sights and fantastic animals, the country has a myriad of gourmet food to explore (Peru has topped the list of the world's best food destinations for six years in a row).

海边小餐厅
Coastal cafeteria

虽然在这个国家前后也不过才一年半，但我已经深深地喜欢上了这个国家，如果要用一种颜色来描述，我的答案是红色：热情、张扬、洒脱、永远年轻。

Although I have only been in this country for a year and a half, I have already fallen in love with it. If I had to use a color to describe it, my answer would be red: passionate, flamboyant, unrestrained and always young.

神奇动物在这里
Fantastic animals can be found here

崔佳星
Zoe Cui

95后，西班牙语专业八级，目前在秘鲁工作，希望认识到来自五湖四海、不同国家的朋友，欢迎大家来秘鲁，打开新世界的大门。

A member of the generation after 95s, passed the Test for Spanish majors — Band 8, currently working in Peru, South America, with the hope to meet friends from all over the world. Welcome everyone to Peru and open the door to a new world.

抗疫进行时，静待花开期

Waiting for the Bloom during the Pandemic

■ Joanna Lee

2022年4月奥密克戎把"魔都"折腾得疲惫不堪，为了应对这个看不到、摸不着的凶神恶煞，整个城市不得已按下了暂停键。从2020年1月第一次被封的恐慌到后来的习以为常，在烦躁和平和的循环里，我越来越意识到，应对突发公共事件，是我们这代人逃不掉的宿命。

2022年3月14日，社区发布了通知，由于疫情态势严峻，全体居民早上8点以后进入封闭管理状态。新冠肺炎疫情，肆虐已2年有余，中国也是全球控制疫情最好的地方。我也没考虑太多，仅仅准备了十天左右的物资，满怀期待解封之后恢复往日繁华的魔都。可每天面对如此多的新增病例，慢慢失去了信心，解封之日感觉遥遥无期。封控在家的日子里，每天与家人、儿子视频通话，小家伙从咿咿呀呀到蹦单词，到现在可以说出短句了，进步飞快。时常想着疫情结束后回到家人

In April 2022, Omicron has exhausted the Magic City. The city has to press the pause button to deal with this invisible menace. From the first time I was quarantined in January 2020 to the daily routine I am accustomed to now, I have been in the cycles of irritability and placidity and am increasingly aware that dealing with emergencies in the face of uncertainty is the inescapable fate of our generation.

On March 14, 2022, a notice was issued that all residents would be kept under lockdown management after 8 a.m. due to the severity of the pandemic. Considering that China is the best place in the world to contain the COVID-19 pandemic which has raged for more than two years, I didn't give much thought about this lockdown. After stocking up only about ten days of supplies, I started to envision the Magic City restoring its former prosperity after the end of the

身边，儿子是不是就可以熟练地与我们展开对话了？内心充满期待。

对于一枚吃货而言，美食最能抚慰疫情期间"受伤"的心灵。我迷上了做美食，在弥足珍贵的食材面前，只有将其价值发挥到最大化，才是对食材本身最好的尊重。

小区解封前，三棵向日葵陪伴了数日，为家里增添了点生机。但花终究还是要凋零，只能想法子，尽可能地给生活增添点情调，于是我变成了小区花园里的"采花大盗"，一些野花野草，经过修剪，插进花瓶，别有一番情调。

与此同时，作为公司杭州亚运会射箭场馆发布系统项目组的一员，项目于2022年3月14日开始施工，原定总施工周期1个半月，但还没来得及参加项目现场开工会，我们就被隔离在家中。为了不影响项目交货期，大家伙攒着一口气，克服一切困难。为了尽量减轻疫情对项目的影响，所有的办公和协调，都转到线上，

lockdown. Seeing such a large number of newly confirmed cases every day, I slowly lost my patience and felt that the lift of lockdown would be at a far distant date. Quarantined at home, I had a video call with my family and my son every day. He has grown quickly from babbling to speaking single words and phrases. I often imagine that he will be able to have fluent conservations with us after I reunite with them at the end of the outbreak. I am quite looking forward to that day.

For a foodie, food is the best way to soothe the "wounded soul" during the pandemic. I am obsessed with cooking food. With precious food ingredients, I can only maximize their value to show the best respect for the food itself.

Before the lockdown was lifted, three sunflowers kept me company for several days, adding some vitality to my home. However, the flowers withered eventually, and I had to find ways to spice up my life as much as possible. Hence, I became the "flower picker" in the community garden. These wild flowers and grass did exude their own appeal after they were trimmed and put into the vase.

As members of the Screen Project Team of Archery Stadium for the Hangzhou Asian Games, we were quarantined at home before we could attend the project kick-off meeting scheduled on March 14. The project was originally given a construction period of one month and a half. To meet the

三颗孤寂的菜宝宝,真好吃
Delicious fried rice with three lonely vegetables

嗯,真好看
How beautiful

杭州亚运会室外大屏支架吊装现场
Hoisting of support for the outdoor screen of the Hangzhou Asian Games

每周定期线上跟踪项目进展，与项目现场交流存在的问题，协调解决办法。感谢强大的5G技术，即便无法在项目现场切身参与现场管理，但可以通过前方同事云直播和云传输信息和影像资料，项目组实现了在线沟通、云管理。

通过这次疫情，我也更加体会到企业转型升级的重要性，特别是对于工程项目管理，未来向信息化、数字化、智能化方向发展将是必然趋势。

另外，这次疫情，邻居从陌生的"老邻居"迅速变成了熟悉的"新朋友"。4月初，家里的米快吃完了，三楼的小姐姐，主动把她家多余的米面送来了。一袋米，让邻居们"抱团取暖"共克时艰；一颗颗菜，让久违了的邻里关系变得越来越和谐；小小的一罐可乐，像萤火虫一样用自己微弱的光来点亮和温暖疫情下的上海。

project delivery schedule, we held our breath to overcome all difficulties. To minimize the impact of the pandemic on the project, all office operations and coordination were turned online. Project progress was tracked online regularly every week, and existing problems were communicated to project site personnel to find solutions. Thanks to the powerful 5G technology, even though I could not personally participate in the on-site management of the project, I could realize online communication and cloud management of the project through the cloud live broadcast and cloud transmission of information and video data by colleagues on the project site.

Through the pandemic, I have been increasingly aware of the importance of enterprise transformation and upgrading, especially for engineering project management. It will be an inevitable trend to develop toward informatization, digitalization and intelligence in the future.

Furthermore, this pandemic has turned unfamiliar "old neighbors" quickly into familiar "new friends." At the beginning of April, my rice was running out, and the young girl on the third floor brought me her extra rice and flour. A bag of rice keeps the neighbors together to overcome the difficulties; vegetables make the long-lost neighborhood relationship more and more harmonious; a small can of Coke lights up and warms Shanghai in the pandemic with its own weak light like a firefly.

李 敏
Joanna Lee

2020年3月正式加入施璐德，喜欢美食、旅游、拍照，坚持做好自我，求真务实。座右铭：路漫漫其修远兮，吾将上下而求索。

Joanna Lee officially joined CNOOD in March 2020. She likes food, travel and taking pictures and insists on being herself and being pragmatic. Motto: The way ahead is long and has no ending; yet high and low I'll search with my will unbending.

写在二十五岁生日这一天
On My 25th Birthday

■ Jodie Zhou

生活是种律动，需有光有影，有晴有雨，在二十五岁生日这一天，我想以最好的状态来迎接，想以不可名状的心情来记录与这世界交锋的二十多年，将生命中出现的许多值得珍惜的人和事记在我笔下，放在我心里。一路走来，遇见了很多人很多事，正是这些经历，才将我的生命装点得五彩纷呈。

父母篇

小孩期望的长大如约而至，父母的日渐衰老也悄然而至。

还记得来上海实习的前一晚，父母一边仔细地将口罩、酒精消毒液、感冒药塞满我的行李箱，一边叮嘱我要注意这些注意那些。当时觉得他们太过唠叨，我已经不是小孩子了。可现在回想起来，那些当初觉得絮叨的言语却让我感到异常温暖。父母向来是如此的，既希望我快快长大，同时又害怕我长大。而我也一样，小时候盼着长大后能够独自闯荡，如今却时常眷

Life is a journey filled with both sunny and rainy days. To celebrate my 25th birthday, I would like to take down my twenty odd years at war with the world as well as many people and things worth cherishing in my life. It's what I have been through with these people and things that make my life brilliant.

My Parents

While the expected growth of the child comes as promised, the aging of the parents also comes silently.

I still remember the night before I set out to Shanghai for my internship. My parents carefully put the facial masks, alcohol and cold medicines into my suitcase while telling me the do's and don'ts. At that time, I felt they were too nagging as I was not a kid any more. Looking back now, however, I felt unusually warm about the nag. My parents

恋父母的怀抱。

自我参加工作之后，爸妈经常会发来微信："颖宝，咱家这个天然气怎么网上缴费呀？""你抽空跟你弟聊下天，他最近学习上有点迷茫。""我在网上买的东西怎么退货呀"……小时候的我会问父母很多问题，现在却反过来了，原来，父母真的会越来越依赖你。当我久违地和父母视频通话时，看到母亲眼角的皱纹、父亲两鬓的白发才突然发现，父母真的会老，而且远比我想象得要快许多。

有人曾说："父母存在的意义不是给予孩子舒适和富裕的生活，而是当你想到你的父母时，你的内心就会充满力量，会感受到温暖，从而拥有克服困难的勇气和能力，因此获得人生真正的乐趣和自由。"小时候不懂这句话的深意，直到长大才发现，父母爱孩子是出于本能，对待父母，我所花费的心思和精力是最少的，而他们传达给我的爱意却是最为绵长与深厚的。

always want me to grow up quickly, but at the same time are afraid of my growth. So am I. I looked forward to growing up and making my own adventure independently in my childhood, but are now always attached to my parents' love.

After I started working, my parents often sent me WeChat messages. "Honey, can you tell me how to pay the gas fees online?" "Can you talk to your younger brother? He seems to be a bit confused at his studies." "How should I return the goods bought online?" When I was little, I often asked my parents a lot of questions. Now it's the other way around. Parents will indeed increasingly rely on you. When I had a video call with my parents after a long time and saw the wrinkles around the eyes of my mother and the white hair at the temples of my father, I suddenly realized that parents would grow old, much faster than I imagined.

Someone once wrote that the purpose of parents is not to give their children a comfortable and affluent life, but the power and warmth at the thought of them, so that they have the courage and ability to overcome the difficulties and thus receive the real joy and freedom of life. I didn't understand the meaning of these words until I grew up. Parents love their children instinctively. I spend the least amount of thought and energy on my parents, but they give me the most lasting and deepest love.

挚友篇

白头如新，倾盖如故，我一直相信人与人之间是存在"磁场"的，有些人不管认识多久依然亲密不起来，而有的人却在第一眼见面时就知道会与对方成为要好的朋友。人与人之间的缘分很奇妙，即使只有一面之缘，但是你就是知道她会是你日后的知己、至交、挚友。朋友不是越多越好，挚友一两个就足矣。我与她在人生的拐点相遇，我们惊叹于彼此的不同与相似，被对方的磁场所吸引。我们互相尊重、互相欣赏、互相鼓励。物换星移、寒来暑往，我们彼此相伴的时光总是平凡而温暖。

我们相识于高中，至今竟已有十载光阴。你喜欢读书、喜欢听古典音乐、喜欢看动漫，而我却总会在一旁哼着时下流行的网络红歌给你洗脑，拉着你看林正英的老电影；你总是将委屈藏于心底，坚强面对一切困境，而我却总是向你倾诉，恨不得将所有苦水一吐为快。如此说来，我们有这么多的不同之处，好似两条永远无法相交的平行线。可你却对我说，你欣赏我的包容，你说我好似海水，总为你送去或汹涌或宜人的海风，吹散你的一切阴霾。

My Friends

A person may be strange to you even after a lifelong acquaintance; a new friend met for the first time may be like an old friend. I have always believed in the magnetic field among people. You can't get close with some people no matter how long you have known them, while you know some others will be your best friends at the first sight. The interpersonal relationship is so magical that you know someone will be your future best friend when you meet for the first time. The more friends you have, the better, but one or two best friends are enough. I met her at an inflection point in our lives. We marveled at our differences and similarities and were attracted by each other's magnetic field. We respect, appreciate and encourage each other. Despite the change of seasons, the time we spend with each other is always ordinary and warm.

It has been ten years since we met in high school. You like reading books, listening to classical music and watching animations, while I always hum popular songs on the Internet to brainwash you and drag you to watch old movies starred by Ching-Ying Lam; You always keep your grievances to yourself and stay strong in the face of all difficulties, while I always get all my worries off my chest. We have so many differences that we are like two parallel lines that never meet. But you said that you appreciate my tolerance

犹记那试卷漫天飞的高三，我和你总会在每一个阳光明媚的午后，在学校操场上手挽着手散步，你说说你最近偷摸看的电视情节，我说说我学习中的趣事。虽然散步时间只有短短的十五分钟，但这足以消除一天中沉浸题海的疲惫。

一路走来，我们都见证了对方的成长。过去每当我面临许许多多的无助和难以坚持的困境，都是你陪伴在我身旁，陪我渡过一道道难关，跨越一座座山丘，然后我们再一起努力奔跑。

小龙虾同学，你可一定要记住，不要走在我前面哦，因为我可能会追不上你，也别走在我后面，因为我可能不是一个好的引路人。我希望你能走在我的旁边，这样我们就可以一路相伴，踏进彼此的人生！

搭档篇

都说人这一生大部分时间都献给了职场，陪伴在身边最久的当数同事。细细想来，和同事在一起的时间或许比跟家人在一起的时间还要长。能加入一个温暖有爱的公司，遇到一帮志同道合的同事，何尝不是一种幸运。

and I am like the sea, always sending you turbulent or pleasant sea breeze, blowing away all your haze.

I still remember that in the test papers-occupied senior year of high school, you and I always took a walk arm in arm in the school playground on every sunny afternoon. You shared the drama you secretly watched recently, and I shared the fun I had in studies. Despite lasting for only 15 min, this walk was able to eliminate the fatigue of a day immersed in test questions.

We have seen each other grow along the way. Whenever I was faced with helplessness and difficulties, you were always there for me, overcoming the difficulties, crossing the hills and running together with me.

My dear "crayfish", please remember that do not walk in front of me as I may not catch up with you, and do not walk behind me as I may not be a good guide. I hope you can walk beside me, so that we can be companions all the way and walk into each other's life!

My Partners

They say people spend most of their life time at work, and those who stick around the longest are your colleagues. If we think about it, we probably spend more time with our co-workers than with our family. It is fortunate to join a warm and caring company and meet a group of like-minded colleagues.

2021年7月份初，我加入了一个充满活力的部门。我们部门麻雀虽小，却五脏俱全。总经理Danni、副总经理Johnson带着我和Tommy这两个小跟班一路过关斩将，使得我们部门不论遇到任何事都能够有条不紊地运作。我们在工作上各司其职的同时也能做到互相帮助互相支持，共同地为我们这个小集体付出最大的努力，在生活中我们也会互相关怀，遇到烦心事也能为彼此排忧解难。曾经有一部大热美剧——《老友记》，我觉得用这个来形容我们部门也是十分恰当的，区别只在于人家是"六人行"，而我们却是不折不扣的"四人行"。

首先要介绍的就是我们部门的主心骨——Danni。Danni是我在公司认识的第一人，也是带我走上工作正轨的师父。谈及我对她的初印象，她应该就是那个经常请吃饭的姐姐吧。在我的实习阶段，Danni每天都会带着我去吃各种好吃的，而我也成功被她激发出了吃货的潜能。

她的人缘是公认的好，下午总会有三两个同事围着她聊天，有的站着，有的坐着，更有甚者是蹲在旁边，热闹非凡，而我也总是被这种热闹融洽的氛围所吸引。对我而言，Danni最有魅力的时刻贯穿每一天的日常工作。无论遇到多么棘手、多么复杂的问题，Danni总能游刃有余地一一解决，"神挡杀神，佛挡杀佛"，慌张似乎从不会出现在她的脸上。作为师父，Danni总会一步一步教我怎么去处理部门事务，即使我粗心犯错，她仍会耐心纠正，同时也会多番叮嘱，粗心千万使不

In early July 2021, I joined a vibrat team. This small department works orderly as General Manager Danni and Deputy General Manager Johnson lead Tommy and me through the difficulties, trials and hardships. While performing our respective duties at work, we help and support each other, and make the best efforts for our team together. In life, we also care for each other and solve troubles for each other. I believe the popular American drama "Friends" back in the 1990s is a perfect depiction of our department. The only difference lies in that there are six of them, but four of us.

First of all, I'd like to introduce Danni, the backbone of our department. Danni is the first person I came to know in the company and the mentor who steered me on the right track. My first impression about her was that she was the sister who often bought me meals. During my internship, Danni took me to eat all kinds of delicious food every day, and my potential of a foodie was fully unleashed.

She is known for her popularity. In the afternoon, there are always two or three colleagues chatting with her, some standing, some sitting, or even squatting beside her. I am always attracted by this lively and harmonious atmosphere. For me, Danni's most charismatic moments happen throughout her daily work days. No matter how difficult and complicated the problems are, she can always solve one by one with ease. Panic never seems to appear on her face. As my mentor, Danni

得。在我心中，Danni 不仅是我的领导，更是我的良师益友，一路为我指点迷津。

接下来要介绍的是我们部门的"定心丸"——Johnson。Johnson，一个集才华和犀利于一身的男子。我们的学霸副总通过了 CFA 三级、CPA、司法考试等一系列考试，我常暗自感叹 Johnson 脑容量高达 512GB，书读得多就是厉害。Johnson 丰富的知识库和实操经验为我们部门职责的履行提供了很好的保障。同时，Johnson 也有着极其出色的洞察力，看待事情眼光敏锐、观点犀利，具有独到的见解。作为部门的劳模，他一天的工作时长最高纪录达到 18 个小时，从他的身上，我深深感受到了"上班"与"工作"是两种截然不同的状态。一个"上班的人"，是被动型工作者；而一个"工作的人"，则对这份工作充满热爱，是主动型工作者，Johnson 生动地诠释了这一点，而这也将一直激励我砥砺前行。

最后，该介绍我们部门的身高担当——Tommy 啦。Tommy 身高 190 厘米，凭借着他的一己之力，成功拉高了我们部门的平均身高水平。Tommy 平时很安静，他总会默默地处理着自己的工作，默默完成领导交代的任务。但我每次向 Tommy 寻求帮助时，他总能条分缕析、头头是道地帮我分析，给我提供很好的指引与建议。同时，Tommy 也是公司公认的"厨

always teaches me how to deal with the affairs of the department step by step. Even when I made careless mistakes, she would patiently correct me and repeatedly tell me that carelessness should not be allowed. In my heart, Danni is not only my leader, but also my mentor, guiding me along the way.

Next, I'd like to talk about Johnson, the anchor of our department. Johnson is a man of talent and sharpness. He has passed the CFA Level 3, CPA and judicial exams. I often think he must have a brain capacity of 512GB. His rich knowledge base and practical experience provides a good guarantee for the performance of our department's responsibilities. Also an insightful man, Johnson often demonstrates a keen vision, sharp views and unique insights. This model worker had an 18-hour working record. From him I deeply feel that "having a job" and "working" are two completely different states. Those who have a job are passive workers, but the working men are active workers passionate at work. Johnson has been an amazing example inspiring me to move forward.

Finally, I'd like to talk about Tommy, the tallest member of our team. At a height of 190 cm, he has successfully raised the average height in our department. This boy always quietly completes his own work and the tasks assigned by leaders. Every time I turned to him for help, however, he could offer thorough analysis, providing me with good guidance and

房达人",他的拿手菜"土豆炖牛肉""可乐鸡翅"获得了同事们的高度评价,说到这里,我又要忍不住默默咽口水了。

我的成长离不开这些优秀的伙伴,正因为有他们,我才能一路奋勇向前、持续进步。我也相信,我们部门会在我们的协同合作下越来越好,未来一定会迈上一个更高的台阶。

对我而言,二十五岁,不仅仅是指年龄上的改变,更意味着我即将奔赴一段新的征程。"顺,不妄喜;逆,不惶馁;安,不奢逸;危,不惊惧;胸有惊雷而面如平湖者,可拜上将军。"未来,是旅途,也是战场。我将秉持着不骄不躁、不卑不亢的心态去面对一切挑战。不管是煦日暖阳,还是狂风骤雨,我都已做好充分的准备去迎接!

advice. Tommy is also a known "master chef" in the company. His specialty dishes "braised beef with potatoes" and "coca cola chicken wings" have been highly praised by our colleagues. Speaking of that, I can't help but swallow saliva.

I can't grow without these high-performing partners. It is because of them that I have been able to move forward and continue to improve. I am also convinced that our department will be better and better under our cooperation and definitely move to a higher level in the future.

For me, turning 25 is not only a change of age, but also the start of a new journey. "Don't be overjoyed under favorable circumstances; don't panic under unfavorable circumstances; don't be frightened in face of danger; those who look calm despite great astonishment in the heart can serve as a general." The future is both a journey and a battlefield. I will face all challenges in a mindful and proper manner. Whether it's the sun or the storm, I'm well prepared to embrace it.

周颖
Jodie Zhou

中南财经政法大学金融硕士，一个地道的、无辣不欢的湖北人，一个捕获到美食便能开心一天的金牛座。虽然目前"涉世未深"，但时刻相信生活充满可能，并一直保持着乐观、开朗的态度面对工作和生活！

Master of Finance from Zhongnan University of Economics and Law, a Hubei native who extremely loves spicy food, a Taurus who can have a good day when she enjoys delicious food. Although she is still "inexperienced in the world" at present, she always believes that life is full of possibilities and always maintains an optimistic and cheerful attitude towards work and life!

疫中随笔

Random Thoughts in Pandemic Times

■ Billy Gu

2021 年，我写过一篇年鉴，似乎是写给那以后可能将陷入迷茫的自己，正是写给现在的自己。

2022 年 4 月 1 日，由于奥密克戎病毒肆虐，上海正式开始全域静态管理。渴望封闭一小段时间可能会恢复，然而封控管理长达 2 个月。这次的疫情封控又是发生在自己身边，危险离得最近的一次，也是最久的一次，难免情绪有些低沉，那如何面对当下呢。

埃克哈特·托利在《当下的力量》中有说过："焦虑、紧张、不安、压力、烦恼，所有形式的恐惧，都是因为对未来过于关注而对当下关注不够所引起的。"居家许久，也的确让自己将生活节奏缓下来，思考一下当下的环境、生活，如何面对之后的挑战。这世界各处都存在着疾病带来的痛苦，并且涉及各种人士，无论是

In 2021, I wrote an essay, which, seen from now, appears to be written to my lost self that I would later become, as well as to my present self.

Omicron struck Shanghai fiercely on April 1st, 2022, resulting in Shanghai's whole-area quarantine and lockdown. The Shanghai citizens, who were in the desperate hope that it would end soon, were cooped up at home for 2 months. It is the longest time that I have been so close to danger. I can't help feeling upset. How should we face our life and the world now, and with what mentality and attitude?

As Eckhart Tolle once wrote in his book *The Power of Now* that unease, anxiety, tension, stress, worry—all forms of fear—are caused by too much future, and not enough presence. Indeed, being trapped at home has slowed down the pace of my life, enabling me to contemplate my surroundings, my life and

拥有举世瞩目的财富或者是地位的人们；抑或是身强体壮的人们，都很难避免。疾病会使强者低头，使勇者弱不禁风，疾病能影响我们的心思和意念，凭着我们个人的力量并不能抵挡疾病带来的痛楚。但疾病往往能够令人谦虚下来。

可能是疾病所带来的艰难的环境对我有益。或许我定睛看到的是其带来的患难，并未见到丝毫的益处。沉下心来，能看到一些环境给我带来的教诲。首先患难的环境，能改变个人生命的远景。平时在安稳的环境中追求安逸之外，可能很少思考事情的本质；在长期的艰难环境中，可能会对世事的认知全然变更，原先一顿平凡的火锅，在疫情当下却显得极为稀有；原先的户外散步，也成了奢侈的诉求；原本给我们带来安逸、舒适、快乐、刺激的

the way to face the challenge upcoming. Pains caused by various diseases exist every where in the world and invovle all people, whealthy or poor, strong or weak. Nobody is lucky enough to escape from it. Diseases compromise the strong and destroy the weak. Diseases can undermine our strong will and firm faith, making us unable to resist the pain that they bring if we fight alone. But plainly speaking, diseases can make people humble.

Perhaps the hardships caused by this pandemic is somehow beneficial to me. I could have noticed the positive side rather than focus on the negative side. By just taking a few minutes to observe and feel, I saw the implied meaning hidden under hardships. First of all, hardships can change one's view for life and future. We have been so accustomed to being in comfortableness, simply becoming too sluggish to think about the inward nature

事儿，却时过境迁，这让我沉思，好像一生的追求却不能一直给人带来持久的安慰和平安。

艰难的环境的确能使人谦卑，我能看到自我本性是很骄傲的，时常会对比别人，容易自负。但环境将所有拉到同一个水平线上，让我思考自身的问题。在疫情的当下，自己做得甚少。我见到我的很多朋友，在本次疫情初期最艰难的时刻就开始做志愿者，他们每天自愿去街道，不辞辛劳地为社区忙碌，还要顶着各种小区业主给他们的压力，在混乱中尽力调整秩序，我很敬佩他们。还有一些朋友，他们时刻关心着他们的邻居，一个真实的例子，有一位老奶奶是白血病患者，需要定期进行血透，但在疫情下是多么困难，我的朋友一个个电话联系医院，将她安置到医院就诊，这又深刻地感动着我，原来这世界是真的很暖，我们往往看到了太多环境的黑暗，但必然在黑暗中有那些火光，哪怕很微小，但也能温暖人心，照亮一片。我感恩那些不以善小而不为的人们，同时也思考和警醒自己是否已然失去了起初与人为善的热心。

of things. While in a long-term difficult period, our views about things could get overturned completely, when hotpot, which had used to be so easy to get, became a delicacy during the pandemic, and taking a walk leisurely in the park became something impossible to do. We could no longer have easy access, at least seen from now, to things that used to make us relaxed, comfortable, happy and excited. I couldn't help thinking that the things that can bring me peace and joy do not necessarily have to be what I've been pursuing all my life.

Hardship indeed makes people humble. I always examine myself closely, and I could see that I am a proud person in nature. I tend to compare myself with others, and it usually leads to arrogance. However, hardship always puts people on the same level, which forces me to face their true selves hidden inside. During the pandemic, I didn't do much to help, while some of my friends, to whom I show my greatest respect, became volunteers from the very beginning of the quarantine and lockdown. They've come to the community to help and tried to keep everything in order, regardless of the pressure and blames that the residents imposed on them. I have some friends who are very considerate, keeping an eye on their neighbours. One real case is that there's an old lady who has leukemia and needs hemodialysis regularly, but the quarantine has made it very inconvenient for her. Under this circumstance, my

艰难的环境还提醒我忍耐,长期处于艰难的环境对我们而言是不易的事。我们必须与一般的活动隔离,我们的计划受到干扰,工作受到限制,生活的压力不断积聚,这需要极大的忍耐。所以回想在安逸的时刻,自己是否在艰难的环境中学会忍耐而修炼,我们是否时刻准备好了面对,而不是逃避。当我们热心待人,很容易主动帮助他人。但很多人会忽视那些更不容易的被动的善行,这往往在人的温柔、谦和、忍耐、信心上得到体现。尤其是在艰难的环境中,这些被动的善行可能更容易被发现,并深深地影响着其他人。

friend contacted and consulted the hospitals one by one and finally made arrangements for the old lady to accept treatment in the hospital. I am greatly impressed by these common but noble acts. I am convinced once again that this is a warm world. We have seen and heard so many evil things going on in this world, but where there's darkness, there's light. However weak the light is, it warms people's hearts and light the way ahead. I admire and respect those who do good deeds no matter how small the deeds are, and at the same time, I always warn and remind myself not to lose my good heart and the good desire of wanting to help others.

Another thing that grows in hardship is endurance. Surely, it is not easy to endure the long-time boredom and loneliness. We are restricted from most of our daily activities, our work and plans are influenced, and our pressure accumulates day by day. That's why endurance is a useful quality. We should, in times of peace, work hard and be prepared for danger; we should face difficulties and fight instead of running away. If we are kind-hearted, we tend to help others actively, but some passive kind deeds which are even harder get overlooked. The passive philanthropy is always shown in one's gentleness, humbleness, endurance and confidence. These good qualities are easily seen in hard times. These noble people always have great impacts on others through

希望我们大家保持乐观的心态,坚守一颗正直的内心,面对环境给我们带来的冲击,相信一切都会过去,我们耐心前行,坚定地相信一切终将美好,必会迎来平安。

what they do rather than what they say.

A positive attitude and integrity are what we should have to face the challenges that the pandemic has brought us. I firmly believe the hardships will eventually be gone. All we need to do is be patient, faithful and confident, and then a time of peace will finally come.

顾天阳
Billy Gu

MBA 学历,2010 年正式加入 CNOOD 并工作至今。见证了 CNOOD 的起点以及每一次的成长,相信公司无论在什么环境下都能越来越好,发展越来越顺利。

Post graduate of MBA. I have been working at CNOOD since 2010. I have witnessed every phase of CNOOD and every improvement it makes. I believe our company will overcome the difficulties and thrive under any circumstances.

十 年

A Decade

■ Belinda Chen

2022年对于所有上海市民而言，是人生中特殊的一年，全民抗疫，众志成城。

2022年对于我与施璐德的缘分而言，也是尤为特殊的一年，十年磨一剑，今已第十年。

十年间，我有幸见证了施璐德的每一次转变，这种转变伴随着每一位同事的成长，也包括我自己。

项目突破，锲而不舍

过去的这十年，我们公司经历了从贸易到项目的转型，客户类型也随之变化，但始终有一些客户与施璐德彼此不离不弃。其中智利国家铜业公司，我从2014年开始接触，到现在为止已近九年。九年来的客户跟进，虽然遇到过各种各样的挫

2022 is a difficult year for all the Shanghai citizens, because of, of course, the pandemic. With all the citizens in Shanghai fighting hard against COVID-19, it has become a special year for them.

The year 2022 is also a special year for me for another reason: I have been deeply bonded to CNOOD for ten years. I am fortunate enough to have witnessed every major change of CNOOD, which is accompanied by the growths and improvements of every colleague, mine included.

Making breakthroughs in projects, with persistence and perseverance

Our company has experienced changes in various fields, such as trade modes and projects in the past decade. Customers varied too, but some have been supportive and remained connected closely to CNOOD. Take CODELCO

折，但我们一直没放弃。2014—2016 年，我们与智利铜业公司联系紧密，曾经多次到了直接合作的边缘却因机缘未到而错失。2017—2020 年我们通过其他工程公司间接参与智利铜业的项目，也获得了客户的高度认可。2020 年 10 月我们团队再次参与智利铜业的项目竞标，经过半年多的努力终于拿下与其直接合作的第一个钢结构项目。俗话说，万事开头难，无数次的失败其实是为了日后的成功而奠定坚实的基础。只有锲而不舍，坚持不懈，才可能有第一次的成功，进而第二次，到现在为止我们已成功拿下同一业主的多个项目合同。相信这种永不言弃的精神能让我们施璐德人走得更久更远。

(Corporacion Nacional del Cobre de Chile) for example: we have been trying sincerely to maintain a good relationship with the company since we first started cooperation in 2014; it has been nine years and we have been through so many hardships together and never turned our backs against each other. From 2014 to 2016, we had been so closely connected that we almost started to work on the same project directly, but it's such a pity that we missed the chance, because the time wasn't ripe yet. From 2017 to 2020, we finally got the chance to indirectly engage in CODELCO's projects through another engineering company, and we were highly recognized by the CODELCO. In October, 2020, our team anticipated the tender of CODELCO once again. Through more than half a year's effort, we finally got the steel structure project, which was the first project that we had worked on with CODELCO directly. As we always say, the first step is always the most difficult. Failures are only the preparations we make for our future success. Only with persistence and perseverance, can we succeed once, twice, and many more times. We have successfully signed multiple contracts with one single property owner. The spirit of never giving up will lead us further and longer.

工作生活，彼此平衡

十年来，曾经懵懵懂懂的我现在已成为两个孩子的妈妈。有人会说佩服我的勇

Finding a balance between life and work

I have grown into this strong and confident lady from the innocent little

气，因为如今社会，女性要想很好地平衡工作与生活是具有一定挑战的，二胎妈妈要想很好地平衡二者那是更加困难。就我个人而言，所谓的平衡其实都是伴随着家人的各种支持与付出、包容与妥协。二十年前，我与先生相识于高中。十年前，我们决定彼此相伴一生。我很庆幸自己遇到了这么一位能彼此信任、彼此包容、彼此成就的伴侣。而善解人意的婆婆，她就像一位超人，帮我们操持着家里的一切，照顾一家人的生活起居，任劳任怨，让我们夫妻俩能全身心投入到工作中。同时，生活与工作的平衡，也是离不开两位宝贝的支持。大宝的独立与自觉有时候让人心疼，作为一年级的小学生，学习任务基本靠自己独立完成，只有需要帮忙的时候才会来找爸爸妈妈。而作为妈妈的我，经常会因为工作而无法照顾到小朋友的情绪，甚至会因为琐事生气，但无论如何，我们都一直在包容着彼此，一起成长，维护好家庭的和谐。和谐的家庭生活为工作创造的条件可以说是无上限的，尤其是在2022年疫情影响下的居家办公期间，我们更加明白了平衡生活与工作的重要性。

girl over the past decade. Now I am a mother of two cute kids. Some may say they admire my courage, for there are more challenges for mothers rather than single ladies in today's society if we want to find balance between life and work, not to mention I am a mother of two. Personally speaking, the so called *Balance* is accompanied by the supports, efforts, tolerance and compromise that my family has given me. My husband and I met each other in high school, and ten years ago, we decided to be each other's one and only. I feel so grateful that he's such a good partner as I can rely on, understand and support, and he could do the same for me! My mother in-law is an excellent lady, who can help us arrange and organize everything in the house and take care of everyone in the family with no complaints, just like a superwoman, enabling my husband and I to devote to our work without worrying about anything. At the same time, my two babies are the key factor in balancing life and work. My elder boy always impresses me with his independence and his awareness of initiative. As a student of grade one, he always finishes

his homework independently and only turns to his parents when he needs help. But I become the immature one—I am always too devoted to my work to sense his emotions, and sometimes I even get angry over small things, but we always understand each other. We grow and improve together, and everyone is sparing no effort to keep our family united and in harmony. The good condition that a harmonious family creates for work is inestimable, which I have come to realize gradually in this pandemic—we all have to work at home, and I understand that the balance between life and work is of great significance.

学习成长,健康向上

施璐德之于我,不仅仅是一份工作、一个平台那么简单,更像是一个充满爱的大家庭。施璐德的家人们彼此陪伴、相互学习,你不成长就无法跟上大家的脚步,无形之中有一股力量督促着你不断尝试、不断学习、不断突破自己的舒适区,去挑战自己、提高自己。

过去的十年,我们收获了施璐德的成长、自身的成长、家人的成长。

未来的十年,我希望自己能有更大的突破,成就更好的自己!

Learn to grow, keep healthy

To me, CNOOD cannot be simply defined as a work or a platform. It means so much to me, a family full of love. The members in this big family help and learn from each other. Here, everyone works hard to pursue self-improvement, and you may fall behind if you don't. There's an invisible force pushing you forward, urging you to keep trying, keep learning, keep challenging and keep improving yourself by stepping out of the comfort zone.

Over the past decade, we have seen growth in CNOOD, in ourselves and in our family;

The next decade, I hope I can have more breakthroughs and expect to see a better me!

陈玲玲
Belinda Chen

2012年加入施璐德大家庭；2014—2017年一边工作一边完成上海财经大学MBA课程；2014年成为杰宝的妈妈；2020年成为杰宝和小葡萄的妈妈；积极乐观，不轻言放弃。

I have been working in CNOOD since 2012. From 2014 to 2017, I finished the MBA course of Shanghai University of Finance and Economics, while working at the same time. In 2014, I became Jiebao and little Putao's mom. I am positive and optimistic, and I never give up.

疫情之下

Under the Pandemic

■ Mira Wei

5月29日，星期天，小雨，是我在上海被隔离的第64天。2021年的6月15日我早上4点多起床，带上所有的行李箱先从慕尼黑坐ICE高速列车到法兰克福。因为疫情，慕尼黑没有到国内的直飞航班。我只能从有直飞航班的法兰克福回国。根据当时的防疫政策，使领馆给搭乘飞机回国的人员发放绿码有很严格的防疫要求。到达上海后，我要配合14天的酒店隔离管理。之后回到湖北又同样地经历了15天的酒店隔离管理。加上2022年在上海居家隔离管理，一年中我大概有四分之一多的时间都是在隔离中度过。

新冠肺炎疫情真的是改变了很多东西。越来越多的人出现发烧、咳嗽等症状。而当时我们留学生能做的就是去药店买口罩，然后寄到国内。直到后来感

May 29th, Sunday, rainy. Today is the 64th day that I have been cooped up at home. On June 15th, 2021, I got up at 4 o'clock in the morning, packed all my things, and left for Frankfurt from Munich by ICE. There's no direct flight from Munich to the Chinese mainland due to the pandemic, so I had to fly from Frankfurt. The embassy was very strict in giving the health QR code to travelers, according to the pandemic control policy there. I was put in quarantine for 14 days as soon as I arrived in Shanghai, and another 15 days of quarantine when I got back to Hubei Province. Then in 2022, I experienced another round of quarantine and lockdown in Shanghai. I was in the state of quarantine for nearly one forth of my time in one year.

This COVID-19 pandemic, has changed a lot of people's lives. People started to get sick, displaying symptoms of fevers and coughs. For students who were

染的人越来越多，网络上也开始各种信息的报道。当时大家都在议论武汉会不会封城。那天中午和同学约着下课后去学校后面中餐馆吃饭，我们都还在讨论应该不会封，毕竟武汉是一个大型城市，人流量大，这么大的一个城市要如何封得住。结果我们饭还没吃完，就看到了武汉要封城的信息。当年的非典我几乎没啥印象，直到武汉封城才意识到这次的严重性。

德国最开始暴发时，相较别的国家特别是意大利，死亡率很低。德国是个老年化很严重的国家，但是大多数的老人和子女都是分开住的。而意大利的大多数老人和子女住一起。意大利人又很热情，喜欢各种聚会。年轻人就很容易感染，然后传染给家里老人。在疫情最开始，德国甚至还能接收法国或周围的重症病人过来治疗。

2020年4月份开始的夏季学期，学

studying abroad, like me, what we could do was buying masks and sending them home to our family and friends. With more and more people getting infected, people started to get nervous and scared, and the top news on each website were about this disease. People started to wonder whether Wuhan would be locked down. I had a lunch date in the Chinese restaurant behind our school with my classmate after school. During lunch discussion, we all thought that Wuhan wouldn't be locked down, because the price would be too big, considering that Wuhan is such a big city, with super large passenger flow. But we got the official news of the Wuhan quarantine even before we could finish our lunch. I did not have a clear impression about SARS, but I actually experienced the COVID-19. I know how serious this situation is.

When the pandemic first broke out in Germany, the death rate in Germany was relatively low, comparing with that of the other countries, especially Italy. Germany is a country of serious aging problems, and most of the elderly do not live with their kids, whereas in Italy, things are quite the opposite. The Italians are enthusiastic, and they love all kinds of parties. Thus, young people could easily get infected and then pass the virus on to the elderly living with them. At the initial stage of the pandemic, Germany could even help treat the patients from France and other surrounding countries.

From April, 2020, we started to take

校也因为疫情，变成了上网课。图书馆在最初还能通过预约进去学习。但是后来因为疫情太严重，全都关闭。只有主校区的外借图书室，我们还能通过图书馆主页预定后，通过邮寄的方式拿到。各个酒吧、健身房和电影院等娱乐场所关门。但是保障居民日常生活的超市、药店、诊所都正常开放。Hamsterkauf 这个词开始在德国媒体中出现，意为"仓鼠式囤购"。但是超市里最先被买光的是我无论如何也想不到的纸巾。各式意面、番茄酱等酱料以及面粉、牛奶这我还能理解。厕纸、手纸、餐巾纸或者厨房用纸等只要和纸有关的，超市全部售空。我当时住的地方旁边是一个很大的养老院，还经常能看到老头老太太推个步行的小车，车旁挂了几桶纸。在我朋友提醒我要囤纸的时候，我没有当一回事。后来当我真正需要的时候，家附近的超市都买不到纸了。后来我终于花了4小时找到一个地方能买纸，当然每位顾客只能买一份。还好没过多久纸巾的供应都跟上了，不用再囤纸了。

online classes because of the pandemic. The library was accessible by reservation at first but soon got closed. Only the library off campus accepted borrowing reservations online and could mail the books to borrowers. All the stores, bars, gyms, cinemas and other places for entertainment were closed. Only some supermarkets, pharmacies and clinics were open to support people's daily needs. A new word *Hamsterkauf* came into being, meaning to stock up like a hamster. But I could never have imagined that toilet paper was the first item that was sold out, followed by all kinds of Italian noodles, ketchup, sauces, flour and milk. All kinds of paper, including toilet paper, tissue, napkins and even kitchen paper were all sold out! I lived next to a big Old People's Home, I could often see several old ladies pushing their shopping carts, on which there were bags of paper hanging. It did not bother me at all when my friends told me to store some toilet paper. But when I really needed them, I found that the toilet paper had been sold out in all the nearby supermarkets. It took me four hours to finally find one supermarket that had toilet paper, but with limited quota of one piece per person. The good news was that toilet paper was soon sufficient in supply again, with no one having to worry about it any more.

无论疫情多么可怕也不会影响意大利人的"热情",宿舍里的意大利同学一周内在厨房举办了4次聚会,每次十几个人,凌晨2点的时候还来敲我的门问我要不要加入他们。最后宿管群发邮件称收到了投诉信,强调了疫情期间禁止聚会,注意宿舍的休息时间。但是意大利同学依旧头铁。

疫情的影响直到2022年的夏季学期才好转。大部分的德国人已经接种完疫苗,加强针也都打完了。现在的德国,也只有在公共交通上人们会被强制要求戴口罩。我有的朋友也终于能在毕业前最后一个学期进行线下上课。不过其中的大多数都感染过了,好在之前都打过疫苗,康复之后也没有什么后遗症。

希望疫情快点过去吧。

Nothing, including the pandemic, could affect Italians' good mood and passion. The Italian students in my dormitory had four parties a week in the kitchen, with more than ten people. They even knocked at my door at 2 a.m, asking if I would like to join them. Well, the supervisor of the dorm got several complaints from other dorms and warned them not to have parties during quarantine and lockdown and that they should respect the other students. But my Italian roommates were still trying to amuse themselves.

By the summer of 2022, the situation started to get better. Most of the Germans have now been vaccinated, including the booster shot. Now face masks are only required in public places in Germany. Some of my friends get to take off-line lessons before graduation in summer. Most of them had been inffected and tested positive, but they recovered well because they had been vaccinated.

Hope the pandemic can be finished soon.

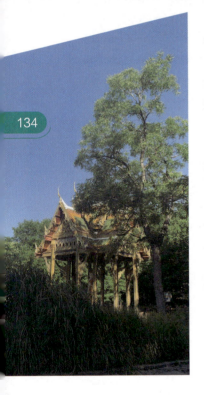

| 魏媛媛 | 湖北仙桃人，生活在上海。 |
| Mira Wei | A native of Xiantao City, Hubei Province, living in Shanghai. |

that she makes. Our house has been filled with happiness and blessedness since she was born.

养娃方知父母恩

初为人母，生活中多了很多喜悦的同时，也少不了增加的责任。有了孩子以后，更觉得时间过得飞快，我每天除了工作就是在照顾她，或者在陪玩，少了很多自己的时间。空闲时间减少了，操心的事情却增加了不少，吃喝拉撒都是操心的对象。按照现在流行的说法就是玻璃心，有了孩子以后容易玻璃心，遇到事情都要拿出手机查一查，没问题才能放心。当了一年新手爸妈，体会到其中的酸甜苦辣，也感受到那句养娃方知父母恩。有了孩子以后，对孩子都是全身心、不求回报地付出，这时候也别忘了对你毫无保留付出的父母，常回家看看。

The love of parents

As new parents, we feel so blessed, but along with these emotions come responsibilities. Time seems to have passed by a lot faster without being noticed. I am occupied with work during the day, and during the rest of the day, I am taking care of and playing with my daughter. I hardly have time of my own. Life goes on like this, with reduced freedom and increasing worries. I need to attend to her in every respect and observe whether she's eating and sleeping regularly in order to make sure she's comfortable. I have become so vulnerable, and I believe most of the moms are like

致孩子

To My Beloved Daughter

■ Jenna Hu

2021 年对我来说是特别的一年，这一年我的女儿出生了，我升级成妈妈，迈入人生新的阶段。就这样，一段全新的旅程开始了。

喜悦

一个新生命呱呱坠地，给一个家庭注入新的活力。我们家也是的，新成员的加入让家里多了很多欢声笑语。小家伙前几天刚过完周岁生日，我不禁感叹时间过得好快，她已经从刚出生时，需要小心翼翼抱她的小宝宝长成了皮实的大宝宝。在成长的过程中，孩子总能给我们惊喜。第一次抬头，第一次翻身，第一次叫爸爸妈妈，都能让我们这些新手爸妈欣喜万分。孩子出生后，家里充满了幸福和喜悦。

2021 was a year full of joy and excitement. I was granted a new role—a mom, with the birth of my daughter, and stepped in to a brand new stage of my life. A new journey has begun ever since then.

Joy

The birth of a new life always injects new vitality to a family, as is the same in mine. This little new member has brought a lot of happiness and laughter to us. How time flies! This little girl just had her one year birthday the other day. When she was born, she was so little, so cute, and so fragile that I didn't even dare to hold her too tight. Now she's turned into this strong big baby. The small baby can always surprise us: the first time she held her head up high, the first time she turned over her body, and the first time she called *Mom* and *Dad*. As parents, we are so overjoyed at every improvement

me. Whenever she's uncomfortable, I will turn to the Internet for help or for comfort. One year of parenting has shown me what a tough job it is to look after a baby! We never know the love of parents until we become parents ourselves. I love my baby girl with all my heart, without expecting anything in return, just as my parents love me. We should always remind ourselves of the love that our parents have for us, and we should go back home to be with them every once in a while.

孩子是最好的老师

孩子是最好的老师——这句话最开始是听老池说的，而且听他说了不止一次。没有孩子的时候感受不到，现在有了小孩，觉得这句话所言不虚。都说孩子一天一个样，天天在给我们制造惊喜，其实惊喜的背后是他们一直的努力。我发现小孩子特别会仔细观察，观察的时候非常专注，同时也很善于模仿，学习能力很强。超强的学习能力给我们带来一次次的惊喜。他们的努力不仅体现在脑力的发展，更表现在身体的成长。从最开始的练习抬头、翻身、爬，到后来的学站学走，都是每天不断练习，一点点进步，才能做到行动自如。就像那句话说的，你必须非常努力，才能看起来毫不费力。从孩子的身上我们可以看到，人天生是不断努力、追求进步的，我们成年人也要向我们的"小老师"学习。

Kid is the best teacher

Kid is the best teacher—I heard this from Dennis Chi, more than once. I did not know what it meant until I became a mother, and it's true. Little kids are growing everyday, and surprising us everyday. Actually, they are also practicing and trying. I noticed that my daughter loves to observe things. She is so concentrated, and she likes to imitate. She's eager to learn, and by learning and practicing, she has surprised us again and again. The same qualities are shown in the improvements of her movements. She learned how to hold up her head, turn over her body, then climb, stand and walk. She improves her skills by practicing hard everyday. As the saying goes, practice makes perfect. From my daughter, I understand that people are born to strive and struggle. We adults should learn from our kids—our little teachers!

都说孩子是上天赐予我们最好的礼物，他们也是我们前进道路上最大的动力。希望能牵着她的手，一起看尽这世间的精彩。

Kids are the best gifts, and my daughter is the biggest drive for me to move forward. I will hold her little hand tight and accompany her to explore this wonderful world!

胡静航
Jenna Hu

80后的尾巴，新晋宝妈，努力工作，用力生活。

I was born at the end of the 1980s. I am a new mom. I work hard and live my life with a true heart.

美丽的大草坪

The Beautiful Lawn

■ CiCi Kang

    静安公园的草坪四季景色别致。

    春天，小草探出脑袋，为春姑娘的到来跳起了欢快的舞蹈；樱花露出了笑脸，为春姑娘的到来尽情怒放；草坪旁边的银杏树吐出嫩芽，枝条为春姑娘的到来随风摇曳。

    夏天，下过一场暴雨，空气清新极了。草尖上挂着一颗颗晶莹剔透的雨珠，在太阳的照射下，闪闪发光。躲在树枝上的蝉，发出响亮鸣叫声，好像在说："雨后的空气真凉快啊！"

    秋天，是一个五彩缤纷的季节。小草穿上黄绿色的衣裳。红红的枫叶像一团团燃烧的火焰。金黄的银杏叶像一把把小扇子随风扇动着。枯黄的落叶给大地铺上了一层厚厚的黄色地毯。

    The view of the lawn in Jing'an Park is distinctive in four seasons.

    In the spring, the little grass pops its head out of dirt, dancing happily to welcome the arrival of Miss Spring; Cherry blossoms start to show their smiling faces, blooming fiercely with hospitality for Miss Spring; the branches of the ginkgo trees start to sprout, waving in the breeze of Miss Spring.

    In summer, nothing could be more comfortable than taking a walk after a heavy rain. The crystal clear raindrops are hanging on the tips of grass, and they are shining brightly in the sunshine. The cicadas in the tree are singing merrily, as if they were saying, " It feels so cool after the rain!"

    Autumn is a colorful season. The grass is wearing a yellow-green coat; The maple leaves are as red as the burning fire. The golden ginkgo tree leaves are like small fans waving in the autumn

冬天，温暖的阳光照在寂寞的草坪上，周围空无一人。在这宁静的时刻，一切都那么美好。

大草坪真美啊！

wind; the yellow and withered fallen leaves make a big and thick carpet for the ground.

In winter, the lawn alone is enjoying the warm sunshine, with no one else around. What a lovely and peaceful scene!

How beautiful the big lawn is!

天边的雨

天边的雨
下个不停
那雨是五彩缤纷的
是美丽的
像剪断的丝绸般一样柔顺
令人赏心悦目
那雨的颜色如彩虹般
要是我能去看上一眼它的源头
那该有多好啊
在我的梦中
我终于看见了那雨的源头
是一个在缤纷云彩边似葵花花盘的一个神秘花园
里面种满了许多颜色娇艳的紫罗兰
每一朵紫罗兰花瓣上都有几滴露珠

我仿佛来到仙境中
这就是天边的雨

The Rain from the Sky

From sky the rain,
Keeps pouring,
Colorful and graceful,
And beautiful.
Soft as satin that's been cut half,
Such a pleasant scene to see.
As beautiful as the rainbow,
How I wish,
To see its source!
In my dream at night,
Appears the source of the rain.
In a sunflower-shaped mysterious garden as white as the cloud,
Where there are charming violets,
Water drops are hanging on each petal.
In the wonderland I feel myself,
And that's where the rain is from.

康钰轩 / CiCi Kang

生于施璐德,长于施璐德,今年9岁。爱运动好幻想,是小学三年级学生,自称蚂蚁家族的蚂蚁妹妹。

A CNOOD girl. She's nine years old, loves sports and likes to fantasize. Now Cici is a Grade Three student in primary school, dreaming herself to be the Younger Miss Ant in the Ant Family.

等 待

Waiting

■ Sonia Le

2021年对我来说是个等待的一年。

"等待"这个词在我看来过于消极与被动,我不喜欢等别人也不喜欢别人等我。

但是处于自己束手无策的大环境下,除了等待或者求神拜佛寻求心理安慰也别无他法。

我习惯将事态发展掌握在自己手里,如果事情发展脱离自己的控制会让我变得焦躁不安,遗憾的是2021年总是在不停地等待。

如果等待有期限,我还能找到这场情绪旋涡的出口,如果连自己都不知道这场等待什么时候结束?

然而,机会是留给有准备的人的,如果只是麻木地等待,消极地消耗时间,那么即便我等来了那个机会,也会像流沙一

I have spent most of my time of 2021 waiting.

The word "wait" sounds too passive and negative to me. I do not like to wait for people, nor do I like to keep others waiting.

But what else can we do except waiting or praying, to have peace of mind, in this pandemic when all of us are trapped at home?

I always prefer to keep things under control. I would lose my mind if things are going beyond my control. But it's such a pity that things went so slow in 2021 and I was forced to wait.

If there's an end to the desperate waiting, I might manage to find a way out. But to my regret, I don't know when this pandemic is going to end and how long I still need to wait.

However, opportunities are for those who are prepared. If I just wait negatively and let time pass by without

样从手中流失。

在等待的时间里，找准方向，定下目标。没有方向就好像航行的船只失去舵手，做人最大的智慧就是认清自己，当一个人真正认清自己，并能正确地将自己放在对的位置上才能做好很多事。找准目标，慢慢去沉淀自己，才有成功的可能。

在等待的时间里，充实自己。活到老学到老，不故步自封，在学习中进步。巩固理论知识，学习新的政策，培养兴趣爱好，让未来更好的自己走出等待的出口。

在等待的时间里，做好情绪调节。无期限的等待很容易消耗情绪，陷入自我怀疑，甚至埋怨上天的不公。如果被拖入黑暗，出于恐惧和绝望以黑暗为食，最后与黑暗为伍，那就再也等不到那个奇迹了。常常警醒自己一定不要这样。

所以，从某种程度上来看，善于等待的才是智者。

2021年我好像一直在等待一个奇迹发生，一个不以我个人意志为转移的

doing anything, I might still let the opportunities slip away.

We should find the right direction and set a target while waiting. A man without a target is like a sailing boat without a direction. The most important thing, in my opinion, is to recognize who we are. Only when we know who we are and what place we are in, can we do the right thing. We need to set a target and refine ourselves, then we can have a chance to succeed.

While waiting, we can improve ourselves. It's never too old to learn. We should never be too satisfied with what we are now; instead, we should keep learning to improve ourselves. It is important to review the old knowledge and theories, learn new policies and develop new hobbies, so that we are prepared to face the challenges in the future.

While waiting, we should learn to control our emotions. It's frustrating and exhausting to wait endlessly, and we tend to doubt ourselves in the process and start to complain about fate. If unfortunately we are dragged into the darkness by fear and desperation, we will finally be darkness's mate, and we will never be able to see miracles happening. That's why I always warn myself not to lose control of my emotion.

Therefore, to some extent, those who are willing to wait are the real wise people.

I seemed to have been waiting for a miracle in 2021, but that's something

奇迹，我因此时常陷入焦灼状态。好在 2022 年那个奇迹出现了。

希望我们的 2022 年都有一个好的结果。

beyond my control. That's why I got depressed all the time. Fortunately, the miracle appears in 2022—things start to get better.

Hope we all end up well in 2022.

乐萍萍
Sonia Le

2016 年毕业于浙江财经大学，同年入职施璐德。喜欢去风景如画的地方旅游，喜欢品尝各式各样的地方美食，一直在努力快乐地活着。

Graduated from Zhejiang University of Finance & Economics in 2016, and started to work in CNOOD in the same year. She likes to travel to beautiful natural tourist sites and taste various local food there. She has been trying to live happily and positively.

项目管理和项目集群管理学习随笔

Experience Sharing on Project Management and Project Cluster Management Learning

■ Chris Lee

1. 前言

2020—2021 年，学习了两个项目管理协会的项目集群管理课程，分别是 AXELOS 的《成功的项目群管理》以及 Project Management Institute 的《项目集管理标准》。

以单一项目为载体，项目管理导向的培训，大多数同事已经经过 PMP 或者 IPMP 的培训。不同管理协会的课程，在管理理念、理论概念、知识体系框架等方面有着共通的方面。差异在于具体的方法论细节。

以 Project Management Institute 知识体系下的 PMP 为例，它定义"项目"是为创造独特的产品、服务或成果而进行的临时性工作，用来产生项目集所要求的输出或成果，受到确定要素的制约，如预

1. Foreword

During 2020 and 2021, I took two project cluster management courses of the Project Management Institute, *Managing Successful Programmes* from AXELOS and *The Standard for Program Management* from the Project Management Institute.

Most colleagues have taken the training courses of PMP or IPMP characterized with a single project as the carrier and project management oriented training. The courses of different management associations have common aspects in management concept, theoretical concept, knowledge system framework, etc. The difference lies in the specific methodological details.

Let's take the PMP under the knowledge system of the Project Management Institute as an example, it defines "project" as a temporary job which creates unique products, services or results to produce the

算、时间、规范、范围和质量等。

在项目管理 PMP 的知识体系中，当遇到本项目无法协调的问题，或者对于资源的协调需要组织高层支持的时候，会引申到项目集群，以及项目组合管理的范畴。

2. 项目和项目集

项目集是相互关联且被协调管理的项目、子项目集和项目集活动，以便获得分别管理所无法获得的效益。其中还有子项目集的延伸概念，即"子项目集"是为了达成主项目集重要目标子集而发起与实施的项目集。

例如，一个开发某新型汽车项目，可以作为一个项目集管理。项目集可能发起其他项目集，它们涉及新型发动机、新型变速箱、新型车机系统、新型地盘系统等方面的开发。所关联的其他项目集都将按照一致性的标准进行管理，也将作为发起项目集的组成部分进行监控和管理。

以项目集的形式管理项目、子项目集及项目集活动能确保项目集组件的战略和工作计划根据各组件的成果做出相应调

output or results required by the project set, and is subject to the constraints of certain elements, such as budget, time, specification, scope and quality.

In the knowledge system of PMP, when the problems encountered cannot be solved within one project, or the coordination of resources requires high-level support, it will be extended to the scope of project cluster and project portfolio management.

2. Projects and project sets

In a project set, project, sub project set and project set activities are interrelated and managed in a coordinated manner, so as to obtain benefits that cannot be obtained by separate management. There is also the extended concept of sub project set. A "sub project set" is a project set initiated and implemented to achieve an important target subset of the main project set.

For example, a new automobile development project can be managed as a project set. The project set may initiate other project sets, which involve the development of new engines, new gearboxes, new vehicle engine systems, new site systems, etc. Other associated project sets will be managed according to the consistency standard and will also be monitored and managed as part of the initiating project set.

Managing the project, sub project set and project set activities in the form of project set can ensure that the

整，或者按照发起组织的方向或战略做出相应变更，从而加强效益交付。

项目集实施的目的主要是向发起人组织或发起组织的组成部分交付效益。项目集可通过多种方式交付效益，如增强现有能力，促进变革，建立或维护资产，提供新产品和新服务，创造产生价值或保有价值的新机会。上述效益将作为成果交付给发起组织，该成果为组织与项目集预期的受益人或相关方提供实用功能。

项目集的预期效益主要通过组件项目和子项目集交付，它们的目的是产生输出和成果。项目集的组成部分通过其互补目标相联系，这些目标都对效益的交付有所贡献。

项目和项目集之间的一个主要区别在于，项目集效益交付战略可能需要优化调整，因为项目集各个组成部分的成果都是分别实现的。项目集效益交付的最佳机制起初可能模糊不清，并不确定。项目集各组成部分的交付成果有助于项目集预期效益的交付，必要时，需要细化项目集及其

strategy and work plan of the project set components are adjusted according to the results of each component, or changed according to the direction or strategy of the initiating organization, so as to enhance benefit delivery.

The purpose of project set implementation is mainly to deliver benefits to the sponsor organization or components of the sponsor organization. A project set can deliver benefits in a variety of ways, such as enhancing existing capabilities, promoting change, building or maintaining assets, providing new products and services, and creating new opportunities to generate or retain value. The above benefits will be delivered to the sponsoring organization as products, which provides practical functions for the intended beneficiaries or interested parties of the organization and the project set.

The expected benefits of the project set are mainly delivered through component projects and sub project sets, which are designed to produce outputs and results. The components of the project set are linked through their complementary objectives, which contribute to the delivery of benefits.

A major difference between a project and a project set is that the benefit delivery strategy of the project set may need to be optimized and adjusted, because the results of each component of the project set are achieved separately. The best mechanism for delivering project

组成部分的战略。项目集可能需要适应其组成部分的成果和输出，修改其战略或计划，因此，项目集各组成部分可能需要采用迭代、非时序的方式达成。

在这里需要指出一个概念，那就是项目集管理的目标目的是产生输出和成果，产生效益。如果组件项目或项目集不会促进共同目标或互补目标的实现，或者并不会一同为共同效益的交付做出贡献，或者仅通过支持、技术或相关方等共同资源相关联，那么对于这样的多项目管理，则使用项目组合管理往往比使用项目集管理更好。项目组合管理的相关内容，在后续学习到了之后，和大家继续分享及交流。

3. 案例

对于执行周期长，涉及利益相关方（供应商、合作伙伴、客户、业主等）较多，需要较多团队成员加入，工作环节较多等特点的项目，可以引入项目集，乃至项目集群管理的理念，以更好地实现项目目标，实现组织的收益等使命和愿景。

set benefits may initially be ambiguous and uncertain. The delivery of each component of the project set contributes to the delivery of the expected benefits of the project set. If necessary, the strategy of the project set and its components need to be refined. The project set may need to adapt to the results and outputs of its components and modify its strategy or plan. Therefore, each component of the project set may need to be achieved in an iterative and non-sequential manner.

We need to mention a concept. The goal of project set management is to produce output, results and benefits. If component projects or project sets do not contribute to the achievement of common goals or complementary goals, or do not contribute to the delivery of common benefits together, or are only related through common resources such as support, technology or interested parties, for such multi-project management, using portfolio management is often better than using project set management. We will continue to share and exchange the relevant contents of project portfolio management after the follow-up learning.

3. Cases

For projects with long implementation cycles, involving more relevant parties (suppliers, partners, customers, owners, etc.) and requiring more team members and more links, the concept of project set and even project cluster management can be introduced to

例如，某基础设施建设项目，其工作分解结构涉及的前端设计、结构设计、原材料采购材料和供应、产品生产和供应、物流运输方案、财务融资方案等环节。考虑工作的体量，每一项分解结构均可作为一个项目来管理运作。

对于其中的设计工作、材料采购、生产制造，作为三个单独的项目进行管理，那么作为贯穿三个项目管理的一个重要信息流，原材料的选型选择这一工作，在三个项目中有不同的考虑侧重点。

better achieve the project objectives and realize the organization's revenue goal and other missions and visions.

For example, For a infrastructure construction project, its work breakdown structure involves front-end design, structural design, raw material procurement and supply, product production and supply, logistics and transportation scheme, financing scheme, etc. Considering the volume of work, each breakdown structure can be managed and operated as a project.

The design work, material procurement and manufacturing are managed as three separate projects. As an important information flow through the three project management, the selection of raw materials involves different considerations in the three projects.

（1）对于设计工作，以符合项目技术环境、项目的合规性，符合设计要求等为材料选型的主要考虑方向。在符合要求的情况下，设计会进行优化迭代，以节约材料，降低成本。

（2）对于原材料采购工作，往往会优先考虑实际的采购供应情况。如果材料的选型更为集中，或者更加有利于本国制造实际的选型，那么对原材料的采购议价、供应周期、整体的成本控制更为有利。

（3）在生产制造环节，制造厂则会在原材料的及时供应，缺少材料时的临时供应灵活性，以及对于生产制造的便捷性等方面均有诉求。

在作为单一项目管理，其收益点有潜在的难以协调协同的时候，以整体的项目集管理思维，从多个维度，综合考虑，提出最优解决方案。

（1）在设计阶段，与材料供应商沟通并交换意见，对于材料选型的方案，在制定设计规范时给予合理的考虑。

（2）制定采购方案时，可以和设计方进行充分沟通，预估预判后续的使用量，并和原材料生产厂商就所需要的潜在用量

(1) For the design work, the main consideration in material selection is to conform to the projects technical environment, project site compliance and design requirements. When the requirements are met, the design will carry out optimization iteration to save materials and reduce costs.

(2) For the procurement of raw materials, the actual procurement and supply are often given priority. If the selection of materials is more centralized or more conducive to the actual selection of domestic manufacturing, it will be more beneficial to the purchase negotiation of raw materials, supply cycle and overall cost control.

(3) In the production and manufacturing process, the manufacturer will demand the timely supply of raw materials, the flexibility of temporary supply in case of lack of materials, and the convenience of production and manufacturing.

When, during single project management, it is potentially difficult to coordinate the revenue points, the optimal solution is proposed from multiple dimensions with the overall project set management in mind.

(1) At the design stage, communicate and exchange opinions with material suppliers, and give reasonable consideration to the scheme of material selection when formulating design specifications.

(2) When formulating the procurement plan, we can fully communicate with the designer, estimate the subsequent

达成产能和供应的预先协议。

（3）基于实际的制造经验，可以提供综合的替代方案，从制造方法和质量检验等多方面给予综合方案，以便工程师做方案的判定。

仅以此为简单举例说明。在我们的日常项目管理实际活动中，可以及时地总结归纳好的经验并记录下来作为组织的资产，为项目团队以及组织的收益服务。

4. 结束语

在项目管理的理念基础上，引入项目集管理的理念和方法，可以更好地促进各个工作分解结构之间的协同，更好地实现项目集的目标和收益。

项目集经理为了优化对组织的效益交付而对战略进行调整，对于项目集经理的经验、专业性、综合沟通能力、综合判断能力、与公司高层战略之间的理解力和执行领悟力等方面都提出了更高维度的要求。

随着更深入地学习，在更多的项目集

usage and reach a pre-agreement on the capacity and supply with the raw material manufacturers based on the required potential usage.

(3) Based on the actual manufacturing experience, a comprehensive alternative scheme can be provided from the aspects of manufacturing method and quality inspection, so that engineers can judge the scheme.

These are just simple cases. In our daily project management activities, we can summarize good experience in time and record it as the assets of the organization to serve the project team and the income of the organization.

4. Conclusion

On the basis of the concept of project management, the introduction of the concept and method of project set management can better promote the collaboration between the work breakdown structures and better achieve the objectives and benefits of the project set.

In order to optimize the benefit delivery to the organization, the project set manager adjusts the strategy and puts forward higher requirements for the experience, professionalism, comprehensive communication ability, comprehensive judgment ability of the project set manager, as well as the manger's understanding and implementation of the company's high-level strategy.

With more in-depth study, we will

管理思维和方法论方面，与大家进行进一步的沟通。共同学习，创造价值，实现公司的战略目标、使命以及愿景。

further communicate with each other in terms of project set management thinking and methodology. We will learn together, create value, and realize the company's strategic objectives, mission and vision.

李云龙
Chris Lee

中共党员，毕业于东华大学机械工程学院，机械制造及其自动化硕士。加入施璐德8年。获得项目及项目集管理 MSP、PMP、IPMP 认证。

A member of the Communist Party of China, graduated from School of Mechanical and Engineering, Donghua University, with a Master's degree in Machine Manufacturing and Automation. I have been in the CNOOD family for eight years. I have certificates in MSP®, PMP®, and IPMP.

生活·成长·六月的记忆

To Those Passed Years

■ Sophie Lau

2018 年 6 月

这一年的 6 月，与 CNOOD 初相识。

在结束了自有记忆以来便与之抗衡的校园生活后，正式地进入 CNOOD。刚进入 CNOOD 的我们，即使参与了很多前辈的培训，但是突然面对一堆陌生的文件，还是有很多疑问：什么是 WPS、什么叫第三方见证、PWPS 是啥等。幸运的是，没过多久，我们便有机会带着疑问与新奇，和大部队一起去到了华澄。

在华澄，有太多的第一次经历：第一次以 CNOOD 名义发邮件；第一次见证了直缝管从钢板到钢管的全流程；第一次见证了真正的 WPS 焊评；第一次整理交工文件；第一次在工厂被蚊子咬得满身包；第一次和工厂直接协调……这些，都构成了我对项目执行的初印象。

June, 2018

It was in that June when I joined CNOOD.

After finally finishing those long and boring school years, which I had been struggling against throughout my memory, I officially stepped into CNOOD. Having received much training from my seniors, when facing piles of documents that were so unfamiliar to me, I was still confused: What does WPS stand for? What does Third Party Witness mean? And what on earth is PWPS? Fortunately, the newcomers like me had a chance to go to Huacheng with the team, with our questions and curiosity.

I experienced so many things for the first in Huacheng: The first time to send email in the name of CNOOD; the first time to witness the whole process of straight seam pipe turning from a steel plate into a steel pipe; the first time to witness WPS wielding evaluation; the first time to

这一年的夏天，让我对自己未来的工作内容有了最初的轮廓和了解。

2019 年 6 月

这一年的 6 月，很凉爽。

我们来到了坐落在海滨城市营口鲅鱼圈区的北钢。在结束北钢一天的工作，吃完晚餐后，和小伙伴开始了日常对话。

A：我们从这里走回宾馆吧。
B：好啊。
C：真的吗？好吧，减肥！

于是，宽直的马路上便多了两个大长腿和一个小短腿的身影。顺便走出了我人生中最高的步行速度。

鲅鱼圈的樱桃便宜又好吃，路上经过水果摊，顺便拎上点；旁边小卖铺，再买根东北老冰棍，边走边吃。有点像儿时放学回家的路，大家一起聊天，各种生活琐事，项目趣事，无所顾忌。几乎覆盖鲅鱼圈一半以上的道路，总是能够在这种有的没的的聊天中不知不觉走完。

鲅鱼圈夏天的晚上，没有南方的潮湿和闷热，海风吹过，分外凉爽。

arrange handover documents; the first time to have mosquito bites all over my body in the factory; the first time to negotiate with the factory directly...All those memories formed the first impression that I had for the implementation of projects. That summer, I came to know my work contents and the outline of my future work.

June, 2019

That June was pretty cool.

In June, we went to North Steel located in Bayuquan District, Yingkou city- a coastal city. After a whole day's work, my partners and I always had dinner together, and after dinner, there's always daily discussion like this.

A: Let's walk back to our hotel!
B: Good idea!
C: Seriously? Fine! Anyway, it's a good way to lose weight.

Then the beautiful setting sun projected the shadows of two long-leg boys and one short-leg girl. It was the time when I walked the fast in my life.

The cherries in Bayuquan District always tasted so sweet, and they were so cheap. We would always buy some on our way back to the hotel. The Northeast ice drops bought in the store beside the fruit stand gave us so many pleasant memories. It felt like going back to my school life, walking with my schoolmates and chatting. On the way, we talked about our daily lives and interesting things about the projects, without thinking about the things that bothered us. We were walking and talking so happily that we didn't even realize that we had crossed almost half of the district. That summer in Bayuquan, unlike in southern cities, was so cool, with the breezes coming from the sea.

2020 年 6 月

这一年的 6 月，很欢喜。

新冠肺炎的暴发，让原本还在和检验员开玩笑说年后谁最后过来要遭到惩罚的我们，全部都被困在了家里。

然而，这时候，国外项目的交期依旧很紧急，项目组也在各方面努力地协调复工。而我，坐上了南下的列车，车站除了工作人员，几乎没有乘客，这也让我享受到了专列的待遇，整个车厢除了乘务员，只有我一个人，到现在那种感觉记忆犹新，对病毒的恐惧，对停摆世界的好奇，对终于可以去到工厂的欣喜，三种感觉交织在一起。

结束隔离后的我们终于相聚在工厂。面对紧迫的交期，几乎每天都在紧张地催进度，看检验，做报告。而除了这日常的工作，还多了每天的例行对话。

A 说：××确诊了？
B 说：离我们多远？
C 说：我们不会被隔离吧？
也正因为这种问题每天的循环出现，我们似乎对于病毒的恐惧感越来越小。随

June, 2020

That June was full of joy.

The COVID-19 pandemic broke out. We were joking with our examiners that whoever came to the company last would be punished, but we were all trapped at home. No one was allowed to go anywhere.

However, the projects overseas still needed to be finished on time, so the project team was trying to negotiate about the working time. When I stepped on the train going south, I was shocked — there was no passenger but the staff of the train station, and I was the only passenger on the train! Even until now, I could still remember how it felt like. I felt a complicated and mixed feeling of the fear for the disease, the curiosity for the static world and the excitement of being able to step out and work.

After quarantine, my colleagues and I finally got to meet in the factory. Facing the deadline of the projects, we were busy pushing, checking and making reports. And besides these daily work, our daily discussion continued.

A: ×× is tested positive?
B: How far is he?
C: Will they put us in quarantine?

This kind of conversation went on day by day, thus making us less and less scared

着国家控制政策的实施，疫情慢慢被扼制，工厂逐渐复工。

终于，伴随着 6 月的到来，项目顺利交付完成，这是半年以来，最让人欣喜的事。

2021 年 6 月

这一年的 6 月，在上海。

在 4 月底结束北钢之旅回到上海后，终于可以在上海度过夏天了。

连续两年在北钢的夏天，已经让我忘记了上海夏天的闷热和连绵不断的小雨。宁愿待在办公楼一天不动，也不愿为了午饭还要出门感受烈日或细雨。

办公室的生活，对我而言，有更多需要学习的东西。上海的生活，于我而言，也已经积攒了很多需要做的事情，这一年的 6 月，很忙碌。

2022 年 6 月

这一年的 6 月，刚刚到来，而我应该还在上海。

从 3 月开始，便因为疫情被困家中，体会到了从未有过的居家感（做饭真的好烦啊）。

生活的片段总是时不时在大脑中出

about the disease. Thanks to the control measures and policies, the disease was finally under control, and our factory could start to work normally again.

To our delight, we managed to handover the project with the arrival of June. It was the most exciting thing that happened in the year.

June, 2021

That June, I was in Shanghai.

When I finished the trip to North Steel at the end of April, I went back to Shanghai, thinking that I could finally spend the summer there.

I had spent two summers in North Steel, Yingkou City, and I almost forgot about the humid weather and soft rain in Shanghai. When I finally got back, I would rather stay in the office building without going anywhere, than be tortured by the hot sun or the cold rain just for a bite of lunch.

There's so much for me to learn in the office, of course. And there are still many things waiting for me to do in Shanghai. It was quite a busy summer.

June, 2022

June has just arrived, and I am still in Shanghai.

Since March, I have been trapped at home, of course, because of the quarantine and lockdown policy. I have never actually felt what it is like to be at home (I mean, cooking is really a tough job!)

But these daily scenes always come

现，有工作，有生活，有开心，有懊恼，很多小事情，都稀松平常，却记忆深刻。

如果可以，我希望这些记忆永远不忘，在老年时光里，可以和小伙伴再一次提及，那应该是很自豪和开心的吧。

每一年的6月，总是与自己斗争的一个月，会为过去的一年懊恼或欣喜，也会为新的一年慢慢计划。

2022年6月，可以走上街头，再一次感受上海的熙熙攘攘，灯红酒绿。
山河无恙，国泰民安，大家的小生活都可以慢慢继续。

back to my mind, about work and life, happy and unhappy. Small as the things are, they are unforgettable.

If I may, I hope I could keep all these memories, so that when I get old, I can share them with my friends. That must be so much fun!

I have spent every June struggling and striving for life. I may be regretful or happy when I look back at the passed year, but I always make better plans for the new year.

This June, I can walk on the street again to feel the prosperity of Shanghai.

I hope the hardships could be gone, and everyone has a happy and healthy life, and of course, I hope our country can be prosperous, so that our sweet and warm lives could go on and on...

刘 婷
Sophie Lau

毕业于上海大学，2018年6月加入CNOOD。爱玩又爱宅家，一个具有双面性格，永远感觉在路上的女孩。

I graduated from Shanghai University and joined CNOOD in June, 2018. I love having fun outside, and I enjoy staying at home too. I have double sides, and I am on the way of chasing my dreams all the time.

暖 暖

To Little Nuannuan

■ Nancy Qi

我给予你生命,你也赐予我新的身份与认知。

当得知我孕育了一个小生命时,心情激动又紧张。

去学习所有的孕期知识,去添置所有必需的非必需的母婴用品。

从一开始期待你的心跳,到你的每一次胎动都让人欣喜。

为你播放胎教音乐,给你讲爸爸妈妈的故事。

畅想着有你的未来!

随着你的呱呱坠地,世界好像都变了模样,生活变得忙碌但多彩。

我学会了所有一切新手妈妈的技能,努力做一名合格的妈妈。

无论在何时何地,内心多了那一份牵挂。

想见证你的每一点成长,陪伴你的每个第一次……

当你学会笑、抬头、翻身、爬行、咿

I gave you life, and you granted me a new identity and cognition in return.

When I first knew that you were coming, I was both excited and nervous.

I tried to learn everything about pregnancy and to buy everything that we might need after your birth.

I felt your heartbeats and counted your kicks in my belly.

I played prenatal music for you and told you the stories of your parents-to-be.

I pictured your future in my mind.

Your first cry made my world colorful.

Life got busy but full of happiness.

As a new mom, I am trying to master all the skills to be a good mom.

And I think about you whenever and wherever I am.

I want to witness your every improvement and be there with you for your every first...

When you first learned to smile,

呀学语、蹒跚学步；

当你生病，当你害怕，当你饿了困了；

当你开心，当你嬉笑，当你依偎在我的怀里，喊出一声"妈妈"，所有的一切都值得。

当你"卑微"地拉着我的手求牵牵，求抱抱；

当你在我怀里，你会拒绝所有其他人的抱抱；

当你学会主动嘟嘴亲亲，主动抱抱，我觉得你就是暖暖本暖。

两个多月的隔离，我们有了更多互相陪伴的时间，也让你有了更多黏着我的机会。

其实也不太清楚，是你需要我，还是我需要你。

期待疫情过去，我们带你去很多你没去过的地方，你一定会新奇又开心。

期待你慢慢长大，未来变成你喜欢的模样，勇敢追求自己的梦想。

让我们一起以时间为笔，以爱为墨，在时间长河里书写你的成长。

hold up your head, turn over your body, crawl, speak and walk,

When you get sick, scared, hungry and sleepy,

When you are happy, when you giggle, and when you cling in my arms, when you first called me *Mom*, you made my day.

When you were *begging* me to hold you and hug you,

When my cuddle is the only thing you want,

When you pout your lips trying to kiss me and when you reach your arms to hug me, just like your name, you warm my life.

Two months of quarantine enables us to spend more time with each other, and you have become clingier.

As a matter of fact, I don't know whether you need me more or I need you more.

When the pandemic is finally over, I will take you to many places that you've never been to. Your little head will be filled with curiosity and joy.

Take your pace, and grow up happily. Be someone you wish to be, and pursue your dreams bravely.

Let's take time as the brush and love as the ink, and write your story in the book called time.

齐晓燕
Nancy Qi

小暖宝的妈妈。本科毕业于上海大学材料工程专业，硕士毕业于上海财经大学工商管理专业，2015年加入CNOOD。

Mother of little Nuannuan. Graduated from Material Engineering, Shanghai University, received MBA from Shanghai University of Finance and Economics, joined CNOOD in 2015.

我在施璐德的这两年
My Two Years in CNOOD

■ Caroline Sun

　　江河逐流去，岁月千万里，2020 年 6 月我从学校收拾了行囊，带着我的理想和抱负、青涩与冲动，奔向了施璐德这个大家庭。我想我是幸运的，能幸运地遇到一群可爱的人，一群充满信念的伙伴，一群值得我用一生去学习的前辈老师。

　　2020 年 8 月，我开启了人生第一次出差旅程，当时的我是忐忑不安的，甚至还有些可笑，每天担心如何去沟通，自己应该怎么做，怎么样才能最好，如何做才是正确的等，至今我还有一个疑问，是不是所有新进职场的人都会如此焦虑。我很感谢这个机会，让我完成了从学校向职场的蜕变，我开始真正意识到了人生走向了一个新的开端。

　　毫无疑问，所有的开端都会伴随着一些过去标签的打破。而"天真"，是我打破的第一个标签，打破这个标签成为了我

　　Time passes by like the river, flowing away day and night. In June, 2020, I packed up all my things, as well as my dreams and ambition, and my innocence and impulse, and left for CNOOD from school. I am lucky, I assume, to have met such a group of cute colleagues who are so wise and faithful. There are so many things I need to learn from them.

　　In August, 2020, I started my first business travel. I was anxious somehow, which now seems hilarious. I was worried about how to communicate with my clients, what to do and how to do things well. I still wonder now if all the new staff feel the same way. I really appreciate this chance, which helped me quickly adapt to the business world. I started to realize that my life had opened up a new stage for me.

　　There is no doubt that every new start is accompanied by abandoning the old things. And *innocence* was the

工作的基石。我开始明白三思而后行的重要性，学会去理解，去求证，而不是只是须有表面的"道听途说"。我打破的第二个标签是"舒适圈"，"舒适圈"是近几年提出来的一个热词，似乎当代年轻人都很在意自己是不是在舒适圈内，是否能打破舒适圈也成了独立社会人的标杆之一。同样，我也渴望打破舒适圈，早在刚进公司的第一天，看着大家能游刃有余地用英文与客户交流，专业及时地回复客户邮件，高效地穿梭在不同的工作任务和会议中，我就期望着能成为和大家一样优秀的人。

2020年12月，我出差去了蓬莱，这一次少了忐忑，多了笃定，在前辈们的熏陶下我开始系统地整理项目管理方法，比起第一次出差只能看见原材料，这一次我更能全面系统地了解我们的项目与产品，直观地看到了从下料卷圆到焊接防腐的整个产品生产过程，这使程序文件们更加生动了。蓬莱的项目倾注了大家很多心血，在现场，大家不断遇到问题，讨论问题，解决问题。在团队的共同努力下，项目每天都在推进。过程中确实遇到很多难题，但是大家迎难而上的决心和踏实认真的工作态度使高山逐渐变为平地。我感叹于大家的精神与工作效率，或者说这也是一种生活态度：即便满布荆棘，依旧能满园芬

first thing I abandoned. This was fundamental to my work. I started to know the importance of *thinking twice*, which requires me to understand and test first before making a conclusion, rather than accept blindly what others say. The second thing I abandoned was the *comfort zone*, which has become a hot word recently. Young people nowadays seem to care a lot about if they have successfully stepped out their comfort zone, for stepping out is one of the characteristics of being independent. I want to leave my comfort zone too, and I have had this idea since the first day I came to this company. I was so impressed by the passion that my seniors had for work, who were busy communicating with their clients in English and replying to emails on time with their professional skills. See them busy handling all kinds of difficult tasks, I knew I want to be one of them.

In December, 2020, I went to Penglai for business. I was less anxious and more confident. Under the influences of my competent seniors, I gradually learned to manage my projects systematically. This time I got to know our projects and products more comprehensively and systematically, compared to the first time when I could only see the raw materials. I could see the whole production process directly shown in the documents, from blanking and rolling to wielding and corrosion prevention, which makes the documents easier to understand. We went all out to carry out the Penglai project.

芳。工作之余，蓬莱的海鸟让人印象深刻，每天都成群地盘旋在海上，当投出一根火腿肠时，迎来的便是无数海鸟的"袭击"，场面壮观，令人惊叹不已。项目管理其实是一个很细节的过程，不仅仅是对各个工序产品质量的管理，还需要对工厂进行管理，对客户进行维护，这就显得大家的沟通尤为重要，而沟通也是有其技巧存在的，这一点我还在不断学习中。

2021年8月，我带着《走出非洲》这本书迈向了下一个项目地。与原先设想的不同，本以为是一本有如《次第花开》一样有关修行的书本，却不想是一本动人缱绻的书，主人公对非洲的热爱体现在每一个字里行间，在农场里，在草原上狮群的奔跑中，甚至在枪声响后的枯草的摇曳下。作者的文字充满了克制，可以说这是一本流水账也不为过，但是读完却让人怅然若失，这不禁让我联想，我今日的点滴，在往后的人生中回想起来是否也能觉得历久弥香？或许这就是人生的意义，一个人的生命应当这样度过：当他回首往事的时候，他不因虚度年华而悔恨，也不因

When we encountered problems on site, we would discuss them and finally worked out a solution. The project was finished day by day with our efforts. There were a lot of difficulties indeed, but everyone was so professional and hard working. This attitude and spirit could even rock the mountain. I was impressed by everyone's passion and efficiency, which reflected an attitude towards life: roses bloom among thorns. Besides working, another thing that impressed me about Penglai was its seabirds. They are flying above the sea everyday. By throwing one hot-dog, you will awed by a remarkable scene of *seabirds attack*. Project management is a rather detailed work, in which we need to control the product quality of every process, manage the factory and maintain the clients. Thus communication, becomes rather important. There are special skills in communication, and I am still learning.

In August, 2021, I marched to the next project site with a book called *Out of Africa* in my bag. I thought this book was about Buddhism and meditation like the book *Cidi Huakai* (*Flowers Bloom Successively*), but to my surprise, this book was full of passion. The writer's love for Africa was evident between the lines. He loves the farms, the running lions, even the dry grassland after gunshots. The writer was rather restrained in his expressions—you may call it a general journal. But you'll find yourself lost in it when you finish reading the whole book.

碌碌无为而羞愧。

随着和大家越来越深地相处，我愈发觉得施璐德是一个充满爱又充满正能量的集体。在我工作上遇到困难时，总会有人及时为我解答疑惑；在我身处低谷内心迷茫时，也会有人告诉我：所谓黑暗只是因为黎明就在前方。两年来，每一位同事的鞭策、鼓励与帮助，都让我觉得无比珍贵。

感恩施璐德，能给我成长的时间与成长的机会，这个集体勤奋踏实，工作高效，遇到困难决不退缩，所有人都在为内心的目标不断努力奋斗，创新尝试，总结进步，每个同事都有自己的独特优势却又不骄不躁。这样的氛围更使得我不断反省自身，身边的每一个人都成为了我需要学习的老师榜样！

封控已解除，期望能早日一起迎接复工后的上海，一起工作成长！期待每一位施璐德人都能健康地在这个大家庭里继续创造和实现自己的价值，在人生这条道路上熠熠生辉！

I couldn't help thinking whether my life story could be so charming and long-lasting. Maybe this is the meaning of life, and a man's life should be spent this way: *he must live it so as to feel no torturing regrets for wasted years, and to never know the burning shame of a mean and petty past.*

The more time I spend with my colleagues, the more I feel CNOOD is a family full of love and positive energy. Whenever I meet with difficulties, there's always someone helping me; and whenever I am lost and feeling down, there's always someone telling me that dawn is right ahead. During the two years, all the encouragement and help from my dear colleagues have been so precious for me.

I owe my greatest thanks to CNOOD, which has given me a chance to grow. In this big family, everyone is hard-working, efficient and courageous in face of difficulties, and everyone is working hard for their dreams. We keep trying and making progress. Everyone is unique but humble. I keep examining myself all the time, and try to learn from everyone around me!

The quarantine has ended, and we are looking forward to seeing Shanghai recover rapidly, when everyone can work together again. I hope everyone in CNOOD can make progress, find their personal meaning here and achieve their goals!

孙璐婵
Caroline Sun

中共党员，上海应用技术大学工学硕士，于2020年6月加入施璐德。座右铭：时光荏苒，愿历久弥香。

A member of the Communist Party of China, Master of Engineering from Shanghai Institute of Technology, joined CNOOD in June, 2020. Motto: Charm of life never fades away with time going by.

让思绪成为随笔

When Thoughts Become Words

■ Kyle Wang

问：纯设计项目和 EPC 项目中的设计工作最大区别是什么？

答：纯设计项目中的设计工作或者设计管理工作主要是依据建设工程法律法规，从方案设计到施工图设计，以及与本专业设计相关的其他专业之间的协调配合。所以说设计项目满足功能要求、行业规范等规定，符合业主要求即可。而 EPC 项目则需要在此基础上，优化设计方案，促进设计与施工之间深度融合，有利于后期现场施工和控制成本。

望着窗外，我回忆着当时 IPMP 面试考试的场景。一场突袭的疫情，打破了生活的平静，但对于我个人而言平静也是一

Q: What is the biggest difference between pure design project and EPC project?

A: The design work or design management work in a pure design project is mainly based on the construction engineering laws and regulations, which involves coordination and cooperation with other relative disciplines, from scheme design to construction drawing design. Therefore, the design project only need to meet the functional requirements, industrial specifications and other regulations, as well as the owner's requirements. On this basis, EPC project needs to further optimize the design scheme to promote the deep integration between design and construction, which is conducive to site construction and cost control later.

Looking out of the window, I am lost and drawn back to the moment when I was interviewed for the IPMP

种很好的生活状态。趁繁华的都市、喧嚣的街道寂静下来的时候，我索性将有关项目管理的知识重温一遍，以便能够帮助自己更加深入地探索项目管理。

和遥远的路途相比，一粒沙看似微不足道，却决定着路途中花费的时间和精力，影响着行走的力度，这也就是我们平常所说细节的力量。在施璐德，我作为一名设计技术协调者，感受最深的是，在处理相关界面管理工作的时候，需要高度注重细节。比方说各专业之间的界面管理不仅影响设计的质量还有可能影响整个项目的进度，其中界面管理中的细节工作一定要处理得当。当不同供应商同时进行深化设计的时候，由于不是利益共同体，这些界面问题就会相互影响。面对这方面的细节问题也要提前做好相应计划。

对于服务商技术方案的选择，这不仅影响着生产制造，也会影响现场施工。先进的国内技术方案不仅能够体现能效更强，还能够缩短施工周期，更能够节约制造成本。合适的国标材料选择性的替代方案，也能够缩短制造工期。我们要将各项资源整合在一起，向业主展示来自中国的优势：我们有先进的技术方案，成熟的生产工艺和高效的现场施工。

certificate. With the COVID-19 hitting us so suddenly in Shanghai, our peaceful lives were interrupted. But to me, peaceful live means a relatively good state of life. When the prosperous city and noisy streets finally become quiet, I get to go over all the knowledge about project management, so that I can explore it in-depth.

Compared with the long and rough journey, a sand seems too small to notice, but it gets to decide how much time and energy you consume, and it affects the speed you walk. That's what we always talk about—the power of detail. As a design technology coordinator at CNOOD, I need to pay extra attention to details when I am handling work related to interface management. The interface management in different specialties can not only influence the quality of the design, but also the whole project, making it very important to pay attention to details. When doing in-depth design for different suppliers, the interface problems would affect one another, because different suppliers focus on different interests. Therefore, we need to make corresponding plans in advance.

The choice of the design plan of the server provider's technology not only influences our production, but also our manufacturing on site. The advanced domestic plans can not only show how effective we are, but also shorten the estimated time and save costs. We should integrate all the resources and show our clients our advantages: we have advanced

项目管理是一条漫漫长路，所有的经验都是靠逐个项目的积累与沉淀，并不存在"迅速上手"的方法论。路曼曼其修远兮，吾将上下而求索。

technology plan, mature producing skills and effective on-site manufacturing.

There's a long way to go in exploring project management. All our experience is accumulated from each project. There's no such thing as a short cut. The way ahead is long and has no ending, yet high and low I'll search with my will unbending.

汪 凯
Kyle Wang

少言是我的一个特点，但绝不是孤僻；认真是我的习惯，马虎我不太喜欢；有余晖的傍晚偶尔踢场足球，追风也在等日落。

I might be reticent but in no way am I unsocial. I love to devote and I despise carelessness. I play football occasionally at dusk. I enjoy the breeze as well as the sunset.

不必在乎从何时何地出发

Set Out with An Easy Heart, Whenever and Wherever

■ David Wang

从 2021 年 6 月，我正式开始拓展数字化相关的业务。

接近一年的时间，虽只是小有成绩，但内心充盈。借年鉴，分享几个小故事，谈谈个人的成长。

故事一："最多的一天见了 9 个不同客户"

面对新的业务，第一时间我给自己定下的目标：聚焦省内的数字化转型重点区域和行业，花两个月的时间跑一遍。时间紧，任务重，所以每天的计划都排得满满当当，也就有了印象中最多的一天见了 9 个客户，说了 9 套不同的解决方案。

见"9 个客户的这一天"很痛苦。长途跋涉是小痛苦，9 个客户需要 9 套方案那才是大痛苦：毕竟每个部门的数字化转

I started to expand digital-related business from June last year.

It has been one year, and though my achievements are countable, I am still content and joyful. In this essay, I would like to share some stories about my growth and improvement.

Story one: I visited 9 director in a single day

About the new business, I set a goal for myself: focus on the key digital transformation-related areas and industries in the province and visit them one by one within two months. With so little time and so big a task, I had to arrange my whole day with work. That's when I met 9 directors in a single day and displayed them 9 different plans respectively.

It was a miserable day, more mentally than physically. Despite the long travels, I needed to prepare 9 plans and

型工作重心和任务是不一样的。还好在见客户之前，做了一些功课，了解了其部门的规划，这才接得上9个客户的话。

但这一天又很痛快，仔细地分析总结每个部门的想法和需求，看似不一样，但其实大同小异，能够发现其中的一些共性；另外，和不同部门的交流，也能够产生很多新的业务思路和想法，不断改进方案。从那天以后，业务思路大的方向也就能够慢慢捋顺、明确下来，至少不会跑偏。见其他部门的领导，也更自信了，业务的交流也更顺畅了。

战略上如果锁定了目标客户和方向，战术上的执行不仅要"广撒网"，也要不断变化与调整。

故事二："不到一个月，拿下了一个国家级工程项目"

经过几个月的不懈努力，我们非常幸运地拿下了第19届亚运会场馆的数字化项目。这个项目从2022年1月开始拜访业主到确定入围，花了不到一个月的时间。

突破口在哪里？像亚运会场馆建设，这样国家级别的项目，业主的想法比较简单：需要一支专业且有运动场馆建设经验的团队来实施。明白了这一点，拿下这个项目机会的信心也就增加了一大半。当把刚刚结束的北京冬季奥运会方案给业主汇

demonstrat them to the 9 directors: after all, different departments have different focuses and tasks. I was fully prepared before I visited the 9 directors and did some research on their departments, and that's why I could have conversations with them smoothly.

It was also a great day. After analyzing the requirements and demands which may seem different, I found something in common existing in them. Communicating with different departments helped me to come up with new ideas and improve my plans. Ever since that day, my direction had been gradually clear. Talking with those directors had made me more confident, and I can now perform better in business communication.

If we have targeted the clients and set our direction at the strategic level, we need to not only perform widely, but also make changes and adjustments when necessary.

Story two: I got a state-level project within one month

After months of hard work, We successfully got the digital project of the 19th Asian Games stadium. It took only one month, from visiting the client to getting the project.

Where did the breakthrough lie? For a state-level project like the construction of the stadium for the Asian Games, the client's requirements are simple: the construction team needs to be professional and has relevant experience. This gave

报的时候，业主眼前一亮；更重要的，牢牢掌控整个项目的节奏与细节，环环相扣。业主有任何的需求，我们都是及时响应：好几个凌晨4点从上海出发，8点准时与业主交流改进方案，快速解决问题，给业主留下了很好的印象。也正因坚持不懈地努力，才把几个大厂远远甩在了身后，后来居上，我们顺利地拿下了国家级工程项目。

一旦锁定项目机会点，全力以赴给客户创造最好的价值，让其无法拒绝。

me great confidence. When I presented the plan that I made for the 2022 Beijing Olympics Winter Games to the clients, they were impressed. The next and most important thing was that we were able to control every detail in every step of the project. We could respond to any requirements of the clients: there were many times that I left from Shanghai at 4 a.m and presented the plan to the client at 8 a.m, which impressed the client a lot. Our perseverance and profession are our advantages over other big factories, helping us get this state-level project.

Once you get a chance, try your best to convince the client that your service is of great value, which the client will never say no to.

故事三:"吃着碗里的,看着锅里的,种着田里的"

现阶段的项目,无论大小,我基本都是自己设计规划的,也是一站式的全程跟踪。哪怕客户起初的订单仅仅是视频会议,我都会拜访客户。因为只有和客户面对面交流,你才能较为准确地抓住客户真正的需求;客户的需求是可挖掘、可延伸的。很多时候,可能客户自己都不知道行业中已经有了这么好的方案,这不新的项目机会点又悄然形成了。所以,吃着碗里的,看着锅里的,种着田里的,能做深做透一个客户,让客户觉得你是充分可信任的,那么业务就是相对可持续的,这一点我还在不断探索和提升中。

Story three: be of help to the client and make in-depth plans

The existing projects, big or small, are all designed and planned by myself, and I follow up the whole process. I would visit my client in person however small the project is. Only by communicating with the clients face to face can we know what their real desires are; besides, we should always keep it in mind that the clients' demands can be deepened and extended. The clients don't even realize that there is such a good plan, and by exploring, you can surprise them by giving them more plans. Therefore, do what you do well, think about what else you can do, and just go ahead to do it. Help the clients know what they really want and make them think you are reliable, and your project will be long-lasting. I am still exploring this field.

总结：要做中长期的业务规划，长久的生意才是王道

不必在乎从何时何地出发，抓住任何一个机会点，去做、去尝试，就有希望。全力以赴，结果都不会太差。

Conclusion: Make middle and long term plans, for a long-lasting business is what matters

There's no need to think about when and where to start. Just seize the chance, do it, keep trying, and hope will be with you. Try your best, and things will work out for you.

汪耘拓
David Wang

90 后，浙江杭州人。毕业于美国伊利诺伊大学厄巴纳-香槟分校，曾在华为公司欧洲区任职，现为施璐德亚洲有限公司业务合伙人。

born in the 1990s, a native of Hangzhou City, Zhejiang Province. He graduated from University of Illinois at Urbana - Champaign and once worked in Huawei European district. Now he is a business partner of CNOOD.

感悟，巴拿马

To Those Precious Days in Panama

■ Michael Wang

时光飞逝，岁月如梭！自巴拿马邮轮码头项目启动至今，已近4年，回想起自己在这1 400多个日日夜夜里奋斗的身影，细数自己在这段历程当中留下的每个脚印，犹如昨日重现，历历在目！

通过巴拿马邮轮码头项目的历练，也使我从单纯的质量技术人员迅速向项目管理者过渡和转变，许多事情也不曾经历过，但敢于接收别人的质疑、乐于接受别人的批评与建议并虚心请教学习，细心观察、用心感悟，方能在每一次的蜕变中悄然成长。

在巴拿马的800多个日日夜夜，见证着每一次的朝阳初升，目睹着每一起的潮涨潮落；感受着太平洋吹拂的暖风阵阵，赤道海岸线上涛声依旧。每每仰视天空，遥看浩瀚星辰，感悟生命万物之渺小；每每俯身大地，大家众志成城，方知力量团结之伟大。在这片远离故乡的热土上，你

Time flies like a fleeing show! It has been four years since the Panama cruise terminal project started. The 1,400 days and nights that I've spent here and every footprint that I've left here are so fresh to me, just like yesterday!

By engaging in the Panama cruise terminal project, I have successfully turned to the project management field from the quality technology field. Because there are more things for me to experience, I am willing to accept other people's questioning, judgments and suggestions, and I am humble enough to learn, to observe and to think. Only in this way can I make progress.

During my stay here, I have watched every sunrise and sunset and every ebb and flow; I've been bathing in the humid wind from the west Pacific Ocean and listening to the tides on the coasts of equator. Every time I look up into the starry sky, I am impressed by its

可以看到每一位辛勤的劳动者们忙碌的身影，挥汗如雨，你也可以看到他们质朴的笑脸，憨态可掬；你可以看到项目会场每一位分包商的唇枪舌剑、铁齿铜牙，你也可以看到施工现场大伙们的紧锣密鼓、热火朝天。在这里，我们虽然说着不同国家的语言，但揣着共同的梦想；在这里，我们虽然从事不同的专业，但却拥有着共同的目标。

月是故乡分外明，每逢佳节倍思亲。每当华灯初上，月明星稀之时，心头总是牵挂着远在万里之外的亲人，燃起无尽的思念。作为两个孩子的父亲，我错过了他们太多的成长，缺失了他们太多快乐的瞬间；每每这样，只有默默注视着他们成长的照片，将寂寞与思念深埋在心底，沉浸在工作的孤独当中，享受着成功带来的快乐。

在巴拿马的 800 多个日日夜夜，经历过酷暑当头，经历过狂风暴雨，经历过披星戴月，经历过病毒肆虐，每每处于项目艰难困境，方知创业维艰；每每完成项目关键节点，总会欣喜若狂。每一个项目节点成功的背后，都凝聚着团队的默默付出；每一次精彩难忘的瞬间，都饱含着大家无数的心酸与泪水。世界上没有一份工作不辛苦，更没有一处人

grandness and sigh about how small we are. When I see how united people are, sticking their feet on the ground, I know the strength of teamwork. On this far land away from home, you can see the diligent people working hard day and night, and you can see their simple and beautiful smiles, too. You can also see the contractors negotiating fiercely and my colleagues working passionately. Here, we speak different languages but we have the same dream; here, we are specialized in different fields but we have the same goal.

Bright is the moon over my hometown, and I think of my beloved and family and friends on festival occasions. When it's dark and the whole city is lit up, and when the stars are shining over my head, I start to get homesick. As a father of two kids, I have missed too many important moments. I should have spent more time with them and fulfill my responsibility as a father. Every time I think of them, I could only stare at their pictures, keeping my deep love in my heart. Then I bury myself into work again, distracting myself with the joy of success.

I worked under the hot sun and the rainstorms and worked from dawn to midnight during the pandemic. Whenever I meet with difficulties in handling the project, I know deeply how hard it is to keep such a big business running; every time we manage to solve the key problems, we feel overjoyed. Every success is accompanied by the hard work

事不复杂,无论当下我们正在经历着什么,都要调整心态,乐观向上,迎着阳光,温暖前行。

在这里,留下了无数个难以忘怀的身影,烙下了每一个奋斗成长的足迹,让我在这每一方寸之间品味着人生百态,笑看云卷云舒。引路靠贵人,走路靠自己,成长靠经历,愿你骨子里有倔强,信念里有坚强,努力不一定成功,但一定能够成长,将来的你,一定会感谢现在努力拼搏的自己。奋斗前行的你,值得为自己每一个拼搏的精彩瞬间而喝彩加油!

of the team, and all our hard work and tears have paid off. There's no easy job in this world, as there's no simple way to get on well with people. Whatever we are going through at the moment, we have to adjust out mindset. Be positive and march toward the bright future.

My busy working figures and my footprints are witnessed here. Those struggling moments are so unforgettable. I have experienced and tasted all kinds of life here, and I can still hold a simple heart. With the wise leading the way, you have to explore by yourself, and you grow with those experiences you have accumulated. I hope we are strong in the mind and firm in the faith. We don't have to succeed every time we try, but we sure should learn from failures. We will be thankful to ourselves for working so hard today. Everyone who strives for dreams deserves the applause for the efforts paid!

| 王 坤　Michael Wang | 2009年本科毕业于南昌航空大学，毕业之后一直在外企工作，2018年加入施璐德。
Graduated from Nanchang Hangkong University and had been working in a foreign enterprise. In 2018, I joined CNOOD. |

不在其位，不谋其政

Not in the Place, So not concerned?

■ Ada Wang

"这些发票不能用""这个报销不能报""这笔款还不能付"……这些"不近人情的话"，是我日常工作中时常说到的。因为有些工作上不同意见，会让有些同事误解。偶尔也会问自己，领导们都审批签字了，是不是多管闲事？

一次我在家里说："还是别多管闲事了，'不在其位，不谋其政'那是孔子说的！"家里的那位"杠精"听了就问我："'不在其位，不谋其政'是什么意思？"我说："不在那个职位上，就不要考虑它相关的事情啊。""呵呵，不对！"家里的那位"杠精"又开始与我"杠"上了。我理直气壮地说："专家学者都是这么解释的，《论语》全解的书也是这样的解释，你还可以去百度啊！"

"These invoices are invalid!" "These expenses cannot be reimbursed!" "The payment is still not available!"...Those cold and hard words are so common during my work life. Different jobs lead to misunderstandings. Sometimes I ask myself too—the leaders have approved already—do I interfere too much by giving them extra work?

Once I said at home, "Don't be officious, as Confucius said, 'Not in the place, so I'm not concerned'!" My husband, who loves to dissect little things, asked me, "What do you mean by 'Not in the place, so I'm not concerned'?" I replied, "You are not in the place or position, so do not concern about or interfere with the things in that field." "Well. You are wrong," he started to argue. I said confidently, "That's how the scholars explain, as well as the annotations on *Analects of Confucius*. You can look up its meaning online!"

"杠精"说："如果专家学者解释错了，孔子也没法来否定他们；如果我解释对了，孔子也没法来给我肯定，不管对错，我们还是可以讨论一下。"我笑而不语。

"杠精"继续大论："读书分三种情况：读者的思想认知低于作者、读者的思想认知与作者差不多和读者的思想认知高于作者。只有读者的思想认知与作者差不多，才能读懂作者的意思。如果读者的思想认知低于作者，那读到的都是读者自己思想认知的投影，也就是'一千个读者就有一千个哈姆莱特'这个意思。如果读者的思想认知高于作者，那就能说出作者的思想优点与不足。"

"解释《论语》有几个难点：一是时代年限相差太大，同一个字的意思已经不同了；二是字体从大篆、小篆、隶书、楷书的演变，有的字已不能一一对应；三是成书过程内容会有增减；四是《论语》的内容是春秋时代，用的是春秋笔法、微言大义。"

"所以解释《论语》是很难的。我们最好是先了解孔子生活的社会背景、他的人生经历等等，再了解整部《论语》思想内容，再来解释某一句意思。比如：'不在其位，不谋其政'。这一句解释为：不在这个职位上，不要考虑这职位相关的

My husband said, "Confucius won't be there to correct them even if the scholars are wrong, as he won't be here to recognize my explanation if I am right. So, right or wrong, it won't hurt if we just discuss it." I showed a smile.

He continued, "Three situations can occur in the process of reading: The reader's cognition level is lower, the same as and higher than that of the writer. The writer's work only makes sense when their cognition is at the same level. If the reader's cognition level is lower, he'll be influenced by the writer. There are a thousand Hamlets in a thousand people's eyes. If the reader's cognition level is higher, then he'll be able to know the advantages and shortages of the writer's thinking."

"There are several difficulties in explaining the *Analects of Confucius*. First, the time span. Some words have lost their original meanings. Second, in the process of transformation from big-seal style and small-seal style to clerical and regular scripts, some words were lost. Third, there are additions and reductions in editing the book. Fourth, *Analects of Confucius* was edited in the Spring and Autumn Period, when people use short words to express great emotions and ambitions."

"Therefore, it is difficult to explain the *Analects of Confucius*. We'd better first learn about the background of the society where Confucius lived, as well as his life experiences before we try to analyze the whole book or even a certain sentence.

事。就是把'位'这个字用现代汉字的意思来解释了,'位'即职位、岗位、位置。按照这样的意思来翻译就是:孔子说,我不在这个当官的职位上,不要去考虑这些为政的事了。呵呵,这样看起来,孔子就像是一个事不关己,高高挂起的小人,哪像一个圣贤君子?"

他继续说道:再来看看《论语·为政》。

或谓孔子曰:"子奚不为政?"子曰:"《书》云:'孝乎惟孝,友于兄弟,施于有政。'是亦为政,奚其为为政?"

意思就是有人问孔子:"你怎么不为政当官啊?"孔子说:"《尚书》记载:'对父母孝,对兄弟敬悌,践行实施就是从政,这也是为政,要怎样做才算为政呢?"

"从这里的对话可以看出,为政与有没有职位官位没有关系啊,按现在的解释'不在其位,不谋其政',是不是矛盾了呢?"

我听了似乎有些道理,直接问:"那你觉得怎么解释呢?"他得意地笑笑,接着说:"这个'位'不是职位、岗位的意思,是'位次'的意思,就事物的发展过程的次序,就像《周易》的乾卦。

For example, on 'Not in the place, so I'm not concerned', here you interpret the word *place* as *position*, as in a post at work. So it can simply be understood as: 'I am not an official in this field, so I won't bother worrying about whatever happens about it.' Now, don't you think our great Saint has turned into some selfish little man?"

Now let's look at the *Analects of Confucius · On Politics*:

Confucius was once asked, "Why not be an official and do something that matters?" He replied, "As is written in *The Book of Documents*, 'One be obedient to his parents, and be faithful to his brothers, this is what matters.' Why does one have to be an official to do great things?"

The sentence can be interpreted as: Someone asked Confucius why he did not want to be an official so that he could so something great. Confucius answered that being obedient to parents and faithful to the brothers is also a great thing, so why did he have to be an official to do such great things?

From the above we can see that the word *position* doesn't have to be about politics. So won't it be inappropriate that we interpret it with our way of thinking?"

Well, that seemed to make sense. So I asked directly, "How do you interpret it then?" He put on a smug smile and continued, "The word *place* here doesn't mean job position. It means status, as in the different status in which things develop. As it is written in *The Book of*

初九：潜龙勿用。

九二：见龙在田，利见大人。

九三：君子终日乾乾，夕惕若厉，无咎。

九四：或跃在渊，无咎。

九五：飞龙在天，利见大人。

上九：亢龙有悔。

用九：见群龙无首，吉。

潜龙、见龙在田……到飞龙在天、亢龙有悔、群龙无首这样发展的阶段叫位次，或者称'位'，不同的位次，有相应的措施。"

"再来看原文'不在其位，不谋其政'，前一句的话：《论语·泰伯》，子曰：'笃信好学，守死善道，危邦不入，乱邦不居。天下有道则见，无道则隐。邦有道，贫且贱焉，耻也；邦无道，富且贵焉，耻也。'"

Changes · Qian Divination:

Chujiu: The dragon is hidden in the deep water. Do not conduct big actions impulsively.

Jiu'er: The dragon is in the field. You will be able to meet a great man.

Jiusan: A noble man works hard in the day and examines himself during the night. Though he's in a difficult situation, he will always be safe.

Jiusi: The dragon is either in the sky or in deep water. As long as you move according to the actual situation, you won't make mistakes.

Jiuwu: The dragon is flying high up in the sky. You will be able to meet a great man.

Shangjiu: The dragon is in high position and should be cautious not to fall.

Yongjiu: Dragons are leaping in the sky, with their heads blocked by clouds. This means a great situation.

Here, different stages when the dragon is in the deep water, in the field...in the sky, in the high position and when the dragons' heads are blocked by the clouds are what I mentioned above, the different status. We take different measures in different status."

"Now let's go back to our text 'Not in the place, so I'm not concerned' whose previous sentences are 'be strong-willed and study hard, guard the noble idea in ruling and behaving. Do not enter a country that is in chaos, and do not live in a country that is in a mess. If the world

"危邦、乱邦、有道、无道，都是社会发展的不同阶段，孔子采取相应的措施是不入、不居、见、隐。因此根据前后文的意思来解释：社会发展不在相应的阶段，不考虑相应的管理政策。原文是古代的否定句式，如用肯定句来表达：在其位，谋其政。也就是：国家社会发展到哪个阶段，就采取相应的管理措施。"

听了他的这段言论，觉得他说得很有理的。大到管理一个国家，小到管理一个公司，是不是也这样呢？公司发展到哪个阶段，就采取相应的管理措施。比如公司发展初期，很多事项没有经验，制度还不够全面，那就要灵活调节；公司发展成熟了，事情都有规律性了，制度也全面了，就要按规章流程执行。当我们的思想境界跟不上 Dennis 时，多读一些 Dennis 推荐的书；当我们对制度流程掌握了，思想境界也提高了，我之前那些"不近人情的话"也就多余了。

is in order, then be an official; if the world is in disorder, then stay secluded and cultivate yourself. If the world is prosperous but you are cheap and poor, shame on you; if the world is messy and poor but you are rich and mean, shame on you too.'"

"In chaos, in a mess, or in order and in disorder, we call them different social stages of the country. The suggestions that Confucius gave respectively are: do not enter, do not live in, be an officiale and be secluded. Therefore, we can understand our sentence as: do not adopt the corresponding policies if our society is not in that status of development. If we turn the negative sentence into an affirmative sentence, we will get: in the place, take the corresponding measures. That is, adopt the policies according to the social stages."

His words made sense and I was impressed. The same theory can be applied into managing a company, can't it? For example, if a company is in its initial stage, lacking enough experience and comprehensive regulations, we should be flexible; when the company gets mature in its management and regulations, we should stick to those regulations. When our cognition level is lower than Dennis, we should read more books recommended by Dennis; when we are sophisticated with the regulations and processes, our cognition will be improved as well. Then my cold and hard words that I mentioned earlier will be naturally

哈哈，这位"杠精"解释不一定对，但至少让我有点启发思考！

understood.

What my husband said is not necessarily true, but I benefit a lot from those words.

王月平
Ada Wang

2014年加入CNOOD财务部，温柔而坚定，知足而上进。不要为小事遮住视线，我们还有更大的世界！

Joined the Finance Department of CNOOD in 2014. I am gentle and strong-willed; I am content but eager to improve. Do not let small things block our sights, because there's a bigger world ahead!

在逆境中重生

Reborn in Dilemma

■ Andy Wei

从未曾想过，已过而立之年的我，在参与工作 10 年之后，有机会居家长达 80 多天。这三年，疫情对生活和经济的影响在此不作评说，网络上已有专家从不同视角对疫情下的不同行业、不同地区的真知灼见。

年龄越大，有些故事越是看不得，比如独居的老人、无家可归的"城市流浪者"、愁白了头发的小老板等。网络上出现这些文章或视频时，往往只会匆匆扫一眼标题而不敢去看、去听、去感同身受。若是前些年，想必我也会通过转发、分享及点评来表达自己的呼吁，仔细想来，我把这种转变称呼为"懦弱的成熟"，人，终究活成了自己讨厌的样子。

疫情里的人和事，在芸芸众生之中不

I had never imagined that I would one day stay at home for over 80 days at my age, after ten years' working. There's no need to talk about the influences that the pandemic has on our life and economy. It has been three years and there have been a lot of comments and opinions from experts in different industries of different areas.

My heart gets softer as I get older. The essays about old people who are living alone, urban vagrants and hard-working businessmen who are struggling to support his staff and his family could always arouse my empathy. Sometimes I dare not to read them thoroughly. Instead, I only read the titles. My heart would ache if I read, hear and feel. When I was younger, I would re-post, share and comment to show my support. But now, as I grow maturer, I get weaker. I become the kind of person I used to despise.

This experience of the pandemic

过是沧海之一粟，无波澜壮举，不过对个人和家庭而言却是值得铭记一生的沉重，有些人走了，还会回来，有些人走了，就是走了。

鲁迅先生曾说"人类的悲欢并不相通"，在疫情暴发期间，经济不说、政治不评，他人的故事也无法做到感同身受、悲欢共通。那么除了核酸检测、抗原检测和"抢菜"外，总该记录一些有意义的事，在此，我给大家分享一下我和我的小家。

首先，由衷地感谢公司和老板，作为一家私企，在这特殊的时期里，并没有任何降薪、停薪甚至裁员的举措，让我可以聚焦于生活中的琐碎的事情与烦恼，而不是努力地去活着，就像前些时日与父母亲通话那样。

is only one of the many unforgettable experiences in life, but it means a lot to many families. Someone recovered after being infected, but some lives are forever lost.

Mr. Lu Xun once said that on one in the world share the same happiness and sorrow. In this spring when the pandemic prevails, I am not going to talk about economy, politics or other people's stories, since we can't share the same happiness and sorrow. Our daily lives are filled with doing nucleic acid tests, fighting agaist disease and buying vegetables. But there must be something I can share with you— my dear family and I.

First, I'd like to give my thanks to the boss and CNOOD, for not cutting or suspending our salary, or even cutting down the number of the employees, though it is tough for the company as well. Therefore, I get to pay attention to the trivial things in life without worrying about making a living. I made a phone call with my parents the other day:

我问:"如果疫情不是现在而是10年前发生的,你们怎么办?"

父母回答:"怎么办,那能怎么办呢?"

由于疫情原因,父母的小店也已经关闭两个多月了,但我们并没有过多心忧,既然损失无法避免,那就保重好身体吧,只要活着,就有希望。究其原因,不是自己心态有多好,境界有多高,而是损失并未到达不可承受之重罢了;若是10年前,整个家庭的所有支出都指望着父母的小店时,他们连生一次病都不敢,何况被隔离两三个月呢?无法想象那时我们又会是怎样的心态。

"世间事,除了生死,哪一件不是闲事"(仓央嘉措),我想我们能坐在家里抱怨因疫情导致的不便时,也应该对公司心怀感恩,因为只有一定的经济基础,才会让我们关心除了生死之外的"闲事"。公司知遇之恩,不胜感激,无以为报,唯有做好自己,疫情期间也要履行好自己的职责,为公司尽一份力,以免良心有愧。

疫情弊端,不再多提,衷心希望早日无疫,回归正常生活。某种层面上来说,除了封控造成的损失和不便外,我也必须感谢这次长时间隔离,是它给了我充足的时间,让我能陪伴我的家人,让我见证和陪伴了小暖宝在此期间的成长,虽活动范

I asked, "What if the disease had broken out ten years ago? How will you make a living?"

"Well, there's nothing we can do."

My parents' store has been closed for more than two months, but it doesn't bother us at all. Now that there's nothing we can do, let's stay healthy. Nothing is more important than life. It's not because of how well-refined I am or how optimistic I am; it's just because the loss is within our tolerance. If this disease had happened ten years ago, when all the expenses came from this little store, my parents would feel frustrated of they fall ill, not to mention if they have to close the store for two or three months. It's hard to imagine what mindset we would have had then.

Everything in the world is small, except life and death -Tsangyang Gyatso. While we are sitting at home complaining about the inconveniences that the pandemic has brought for us, we should be thankful to our company, which enables us to maintain a decent life and have spare time to care about other small things except life and death. I am so grateful for the company's support. There's nothing else I could do but fulfill my duty well and make contribution to the company.

Mention no more the negatives sides of the pandemic. I hope it could be over soon and the world can go back to normal. To some extent, I am grateful that I get to spend such a long time with my family and accompany my little baby.

围受限，但父母就是她的整个世界，爱，没有受限。

看着她，蹒跚学步；
听着她，咿呀学语；
你抱着她，她牵着你；
你爱她，她也爱你。

虽然她还不会讲话，但是一个动作，一个眼神，一声哼唧就足以让我明白她的意思；为她精心准备的晚餐，只要她喜欢吃，就会充满成就感；从不网购的我，会愿意花时间在网上搜寻挑选给她的儿童节礼物；关心她的吃喝拉撒睡，陪她捉猫抓狗追蝴蝶；当她在我的指挥下参与互动时，就会兴奋地邀请全家来观看。

最后，特别感谢我的妻子，在疫情期间，包办了家庭所有采办，同时在小暖宝成长期间，通过视频记录并整理了她的成长过程，她的可爱、调皮与乖巧，让我可以保留这份回忆。也请我的妻子原谅我在生活上的"充耳不闻与屡教不改"，以及情感上的"移情别恋"。我能做的就是：执子之手，与子偕老。

希望我们的小家可以长长久久幸福，也希望大家都越来越好，愿好。

Though there's no where to go because of the quarantine, we are her world, and there's no quarantine in love.

I can see her struggling to walk;
I can hear her practicing speaking;
I hold her, and she grabs my finger;
I love her, and she loves me.

Though she can't talk yet, she makes me understand her with one gesture, one look and one sound. I would prepare dinner for her, and if she likes it, I would be so proud. I would choose a gift online for her on children's Day, though I never liked shopping online. I attend to her every need and accompany her to play games; when she gets involved in interactions under my instructions, she would invite the whole family to appreciate her performance.

Finally, I would like to give my sincere thanks to my wife, who was responsible for all the housework including buying daily necessities. More importantly, she recorded every precious moment of my baby girl so that her loveliness, her being naughty and cute could be treasured forever. I have been indifferent and stubborn in life, but my wife has given my enough patience. I have transferred the love for her to my daughter, and I am grateful that she allows it. I'll always be with her and this family.

I wish the best for my family. Hope there are more happy moments to come. Hope everyone can be happy.

魏 坤
Andy Wei

在施璐德亚洲工作超十年老员工,新晋奶爸。爱国、爱党、爱群众、爱公司、爱家庭。

I am an old employee and have been working at CNOOD for more than ten years. I am also a new father. I love our country, our Party, our people, our company and my family.

公司的命运
——根据个性制定策略

Company's Destiny
—Strategy Based on Character

■ Amir Tafti

2022年5月，上海的疫情已经得到基本控制。上海都承受了"严重的个人和经济损失"。

虽然本次封控对上海经济影响巨大，但很明显，上海经济的长期乐观趋势没有改变。尽管如此，大部分的公司，尤其是私营企业陷入了极具挑战性的局面，这就需要采取一种特殊考虑和战略。

作为一名拥有多年企业经验的工作者，在目前这种封控背景下，我有大把的时间就多种不同主题进行思考。在此，我想带领各位讨论一个新的主题，即"我们公司的命运将如何？"希望本文能够为您和我们的公司带来有益的思考。

In May 2022, Shanghai has basically brought COVID under control, it has been at "very significant personal and economic costs".

Although this pandemic & lockdown had an enormous impact on Shanghai's economy, it is clear that the long-term positive trend of Shanghai's economy has not changed. Despite this, most of the companies, especially private sectors fall to such challenging situations that they need special considerations and strategies.

As one person with years of work experience, during the current lockdown, I had so much free time to think about different topics, so this time I would like to pull you toward one new subject, "how can we define our company's destiny?" Hope this article can bring some useful thinking for you and our company.

Introduction

During my working years till now, I have visited many different companies and firms and conducted countless negotiations, surely more than one thousand. I also had in-depth discussions with people at different posts, including shareholders, founders, board members, executives and employees (company's team).

I found that most of them have one common target: "How we can grow quickly?" One strange thing is that many of them have the same understanding of company's growth: "to multiple company's revenue".

They look for such methods or solutions for company's growth and never think logically about company's future. Some of them even look for special strategies to maximize the company's revenue.

Many companies adopt such kind of thinking. I witnessed it that many companies grow so fast that after some years they are faced with too many problems to survive. Some of them even disappeared as fast they had grown. Although most of these companies had strategies or duplicated other companies strategies they focused too much on fast growth as their goal. This is why most of them did not end well.

引言

自我工作到现在，我拜访了许多不同的公司，与他们进行了不计其数的谈判与磋商，具体多少次我记不太清楚了，但是肯定有上千次了。我与各个职位的人士都有过深度交谈，包括股东、创始人、董事会成员、总裁以及公司员工（公司团队）。

我发现大多数人们都有一个共同的目标：我们如何才能快速成长？奇怪的是，我发现，对于公司成长，不少人都有着相同的理解，即增加公司收入。

他们痴迷于寻求为公司增收的方法来实现公司的成长，全然忘记了去理性地思考公司的未来。甚至有人以为追求特殊的方法来实现公司利润最大化。

有这种思想的公司不在少数。我曾多次目睹许多公司飞速增长，可随之而来的是这种增长下的诸多弊端，一些公司甚至已经不复存在了。尽管大部分的公司会自己制定策略或复制其他公司的模式，但是他们都不约而同地将为公司增收定为目标，因此导致了公司的气数不尽如人意。

快速增长实则危机四伏

待公司稳固之后，公司利润逐渐增长，团队（股东们）就开始思索着如何促进公司快速增长了。但如果增长过快，公司就会遇到一些意外状况和挑战，大多数情况下，团队并不能找到符合逻辑的经营策略来解决这些问题。

有一点很清晰，当公司开始成长，机会便会随之增加，但阻碍也会相应变多，每一项新的业务对公司来说都会带来潜在的威胁。公司过快增长不仅会给公司带来许多挑战，而且还会造成巨大损失。

过快增长会带来许多问题，有一些问题需要公司采取一些控制和管理措施来加以解决：

（1）在面对日益增长的市场和业务时，会出现现金流紧缩问题。
（2）会造成经营低效率，因为公司快速扩张会花费大量时间、资金和其他资源。
（3）为公司团队（股东）和员工制造一些问题，因为员工往往没有针对新市场进行培训。
（4）增长过快的话，公司大部分情况下都无法对现有市场做出快速反应。
（5）快速增长期间，公司团队无法获取新市场的精准信息，无从应对新客户。

Dangers of fast growth

After establishing a company and once the company's business becomes profitable, the team (specially shareholders) begin to think about how they can grow. But if growth comes too fast, surely the company will run into some unexpected problems and challenges. Most of time, it is difficult to find logical and operational solutions for them.

It is clear that when a company grows, opportunities increase, but on the other hand, obstacles also increase, and each new business act as a threat for company. Fast growth not only brings many challenges for the company but may also cause huge losses.

Fast growth creates many problems, and some of them are main problems that need the company's team to control and manage.

(1) Face a cash flow crunch as it deals with increased markets and businesses.
(2) Create operational inefficiency because the fast expansion will cost company's time, money and other resources.
(3) Create some problems for the team and employees because of the lack of enough training for new markets.
(4) With fast growth, most of time, the company cannot respond quickly enough to existing markets.
(5) During fast growth, the company's team does not have accurately enough information related to the new markets and don't know how to deal with new clients.

制定策略，勾勒公司未来

对任何一家公司来说，无论是快速增长还是正常增长的公司，都有必要制定策略，因为如此可以对公司的未来形成导向作用。事实上，制定策略的同时，一种有效的系统可以随之产生，可以较好地描述公司政策、流程和步骤，对公司目标的实现产生辅助作用，从而实现其目标。

制定策略是公司团队去思考公司的目标，也有助于理解公司目前和将来的运作模式。当时所有这些都被考虑到时，就有助于公司实现快速增长。

制定公司的策略需要做出特别的计划，有以下几方面的原因。

（1）战略规划可以提供一个系统的和科学的方法来解决和发展公司的策略。

（2）值得注意的是，战略性规划的过程是一个分析的过程。

Formulate strategy to shape company's future

For any company, no matter fast growing or not, the formulation of a strategy is necessary, because it shapes a company's future. In fact, a strategy will lead to a system with a combination of policies, processes and procedures that are employed to help a company operate according to its missions and achieve its goals.

Formulating a strategy gives the company's team an opportunity to consider the company's goals as well as understand the behavioral patterns of the company in present & future conditions. When all these factors are considered, it can help the company achieve fast growth.

The formulation of a company's strategy requires special planning. There are several reasons.

(1) Strategic planning provides a systematic and scientific method formulate and refine the company's strategy.

(2) It should be noted that the strategic planning process is an analytical process.

（3）仅仅有这种分析性过程并不能为公司制定有效战略，因此有必要与公司理念相结合。

（4）除了制定有效策略，必须要先形成战略化思维。

（5）这一规划过程有助于公司系统的形成，变得更加精确和清晰，使公司整个团队都易于理解。

根据个性制定战略

个人、公司、企业甚至国家都有自己的个性特征，这些特征相对稳定。但我们团队的特性是什么？事实上我们问的是：他们会感到无聊吗？他们会听取别人想法吗。他们能够准确评估一个主体吗？他们情绪化、易激动吗？他们依赖于别人的认同吗？他们愿意改变吗？他们会多久对话题做出反应？或者其他问题。

我们应该明白企业的感官和个性，与公司其他人和谐共存。因此，我们应该使用这一天赋形成以企业为基础的个人特征。

为了生存和发展，公司需要依靠以个人特性制定的策略。总之，公司的发展需要着眼于系统，这套系统由公司团队创建，集中于两个原则：合作与学习。没有这两点，则公司没有提升与发展的可能。

(3) However, this analytical process alone cannot define effective strategy, and it is necessary to be combined with the ideas of the company.

(4) In addition to developing effective strategies, it's necessary that a kind of strategic thinking must first be formed.

(5) This planning process helps to shape the company's system so that it becomes more accurate and clear and the whole team has a correct understanding about it.

Formulate Strategy based on Character

People, companies, firms and even countries all have characters that are relatively stable. But what do we mean by a team's character? In fact, we ask: Will they feel bored? How much do they listen to others? How well are they capable of evaluating one subject accurately? How emotional and excited are they? How much do they need other people's approval? How interested are they to change? How long does it take to react to a topic? Et cetera.

We should understand the sense and characters of the company and get along harmoniously with others. So, we should use this gift to form our own personalities based on the company's characters.

To survive and develop, the company needs to formulate a strategy based on individual personalities. To summarize: a company's development needs to focus on a system which is created by the company team and which follows two principles: Cooperation and Learning. Without

结论

公司的命运在很大程度上取决于塑造公司未来的战略,并且这个战略根据公司的特性而制定。

现在,在我们生活的世界里,决定人和公司特征的最重要的原则一方面是"合作原则",另一方面就是"学习"。

现在我们是时候要求公司的团队,将学习、创新、竞争、效率和合作等因素结合起来,并努力将这些品质转化为团队的品质。

凭借这样的品质,公司能够制定适当的战略来塑造公司的命运。

我认为这就是名言所说的:性格决定命运。

these two, there will be no progress and development for the company.

Conclusion

A company's destiny highly depends on the strategy which shapes the company's future, and this strategy is based on the characters of the company's team.

Right now, in the world we live in, the most important principle that defines the characters of people and companies is the principle of cooperation. Another principle is learning.

Now it is time that we ask the company's team to integrate factors such as learning, innovation, competition, effectiveness and cooperation and turn these qualities into the team's characters.

With such characters, companies can formulate proper strategies to shape the company's destiny.

Just as the famous proverb goes: "Character is Destiny."

阿米尔
Amir Tafti

拥有飞机工程学士学位，在工业领域，有38年的特殊工作经验。回顾过去的岁月，我发现，因为某些原因，自己是一个幸运的人。我在一个专门的办公室工作了20年，负责审核不同项目，从普通员工到高层经理，我学到了很多可以积累大量相关经验的东西。这份工作是我成长为合格人才的一个很好的具有挑战性的平台。

现在我已经58岁了，我很高兴能作为一个施璐德团队的一员，尽我最大的努力将我的经验和知识传授给我的同事，创造一个更好的竞争环境。

I am Amir with a bachelor's degree in aircraft engineering and around 38 years of special work experiences. When I take a look at my past years, I find myself as one lucky person for some reasons. For 20 years I worked in one special office to review different projects. From an ordinary employee to a top-level-manger, I learned a lot and collected a huge amount of related experience. The job, has provided a good and challenging platform for me to grow into a qualified worker.

Now 58 years old, it is my pleasure to join the CNOOD team and do my best to transfer my experience and knowledge to my colleagues to create a better competitive environment.

凡事都要看开点儿
Take It Easy

■ Jane Yan

有天早上,哥哥很严肃地说要跟我聊一聊。

"妈妈,我觉得你有一点做得不好,我没有犯错误,你老是冤枉我,我很难过。"

"比如你昨天晚上做得就很不好,我刚打开平板电脑,你就说我怎么又在玩儿游戏。"

可他明明就是在玩游戏!

他难过?
每天衣来伸手饭来张口,读绘本时,我除了肢体表演还得声情并茂;做游戏时,我既要体力充沛还得当牛做马。

休闲娱乐不是扛着机关枪四处扫射,就是拎着水枪把家里搞得"水漫金山",还可以有事没事玩玩弟弟!

Early in the morning the other day, my elder son said seriously that he wanted to talk to me.

"Mom, I think there's something I'd like to point out about you. You always criticize me when I have not made mistakes at all. I am sad about it.

For example, you did it again last night. You accused me of playing computer games, but I had just turned on my laptop!"

Well, he WAS playing computer games then!

How could he say he's sad?

He's been taken so good care of, with easy food and fancy clothes. When I read story books I actually perform the stories for him, and when we play games together I act as a horse!

When he's having fun, he would either shoot around with his water gun or split water everywhere! From time to time, he can play with his little brother!

现在难过这事，也这么卷了吗！

该难过的，难道不是你亲妈我吗？

刚生完老二的我，原本的计划是，把哥哥往幼儿园里一送，弟弟往外婆怀里一送，老母亲还时不时能出去透个小气儿，逛吃逛吃。结果疫情来得太突然，于是乎我刚出月子又入"月子"，而且是全上海人民一起"坐月子"。大神兽被学校退货，小神兽嗷嗷待哺，更让我不能活的是，当爹的还被封在单位，让本不富裕的人手雪上加霜。

果然，人无远虑必有近忧，美梦猝不及防一地稀碎，碎得我真恨不得躺在玻璃碴子上就地死一死。

然而，现实怎么可能允许我躺平。无论内心如何崩溃，还是被迫支棱起来，开始又当妈又当爹。

所以我的封控生活过得相当充实。

白天带着哥哥这个"失学儿童"搞艺术（乱写乱画）、搞运动（上蹿下跳），偶尔搞搞学习（抱着弟弟给他读绘本），还时不时搞搞角色扮演，当然我的角色一般都是被奥特曼打的怪兽、被警察抓的小偷、被孙悟空打的妖怪，诸如此类。

为了见缝插针搞事业，在和哥哥斗智

Who gives you the right to be sad? Shouldn't I be the sad one?

I had planned to enjoy my life after giving birth to my younger son, by sending the elder one to kindergarten and the younger to my mom, so that I could go out once in a while to relax. But the pandemic hit us so suddenly that I had to sit home for another one or two months, and this time with all the Shanghai citizens! The elder one has to take online lessons at home, and the little one requires my love and attention all the time. What makes the situation more desperate is that their dad was trapped in the company! Life immediately became tough.

It's true that he who does not think of the future is certain to have immediate worries. I was struck by this reality and could not see a slice of hope at all!

However, life doesn't allow me to give in. No matter how desperate I feel, I have to be strong. I act as both a mom and a dad.

Therefore, my life during lockdown is very content.

In the day, I would join my son who has "dropped out of" school in art creation (drawing pictures), sports (jumping up and down), study (reading story books for him with his brother in my arms) and role playing—I always act as the beast that gets beaten, the thief who gets caught by the police and the monster who gets killed by Monkey King.

Besides, I need to set aside some

斗勇中锻炼得眼疾手快，但也还是不可避免地在准备一气呵成时被迫中止，感觉就像是一台运行的计算机被强行关机，下次启动再重新加载。

晚上"主攻"弟弟这个宝宝本宝，哄睡喂奶换尿布，贴心服务一条龙。

同时，身为一个合格的家庭对外联络员，各个 APP 无缝切换卡点抢菜，外加各团购群里流窜，这都是决定一家老小生活品质的必备技能。

所以我的隔离生活也过得相当规律：白天鸡飞狗跳，晚上睁眼睡觉。

time for my work. I've learned to be very quick and acute while playing with the elder but I still got interrupted when I am about to finish my work. I am like a computer that's forced to be shut down, and when I restart, I have to reload again.

At night, I am fully focused on the little one, including putting him to sleep, feeding him and changing diapers. I can manage the whole process smoothly.

At the same time, as a qualified contact person to the outside world in this family, I can log in different apps to buy vegetables and check all the chatting groups. I have acquired all the necessary skills for living a quality life.

So my quarantine life is rather regular: Make a mess in the day, and sleep with my eyes open at night.

终于有一次，在我叽里呱啦一顿吐槽——人心不齐队伍难带，而老王发来一大段看似慷慨激昂实则隔靴搔痒的宣言，无非就是鼓励我多喝热水，坚持就是胜利的时候，我在屏幕这头忍不住翻了个白眼，对于这个毫无诚意的选手，想了想还是该浅怼一下以示尊重，于是我哐哐敲了几个大字：我不需要鸡汤，我要参汤！

按理说一整天忙忙叨叨的，也没太多时间给我emo。

但14天又14天以及不知道接下来还有多少天的时候，是个人都会有点儿情绪吧。毕竟连家门都不能出，士气真的很难长盛不衰。

为了防止我的唉声叹气影响家庭氛围，我又在家里每天循环播放着励志歌曲，以期振奋精神，顺便打打鸡血。

你看，我哪是能顶半边天，简直是能顶整片天！

不仅没被长枪短炮鸡飞狗跳的生活打倒，还扛起了独立女性的大旗！

当然，我这flag能立起来，就不得不说说我背后的女人，也就是我妈。

每一个当了妈但偶尔还想做回孩子的女性背后，都有一个强大的后援团，我妈无疑是我后援团的顶梁柱。她因为带大了哥哥又帮我带弟弟，而和我爸长期分隔两地。都说老伴儿老伴儿，因为我，把他

Finally, once when I was complaining about how difficult it was to lead a team, Wang sent me a text which looked passionate but was full of words of empty meaning—it didn't help at all. In his text he encouraged me to drink more hot water and said that I should have faith in myself. I rolled my eyes and replied, to show my respect to him: No more chicken soup! I need ginsen soup to build up my body!

I am busy all day, so surely there's no time left for me to feel depressed.

But fourtnight after another fourtnight, I do not know for how many days I still have to stay at home. Anyone will be depressed in my place! After all, it's so hard to keep your spirit high if you stay home this whole time!

To prevent my pessimistic emotion from affecting my family, I have to play some exciting music to keep my spirit high and to encourage myself.

Women can hold up half of the sky? No! I can hold up the whole sky!

I did not get defeated by the mess that life has caused, further more, I am a good example of ladies being independent!

Certainly I am what I am, because of someone I have to mention here—my mom.

Every new mom actually, once in a while, be her mom's little girl again. My mom always provides me with strong support. She helped take care of my elder son and now my younger, so she

俩变成了两半儿。我有个弟弟，工作以后他在杭州我在上海。年轻的时候觉得没什么，可是现在苦了我妈，想兼顾却又很难兼顾，虽然一直跟我在一起，心里对儿子的记挂只多不少。不过她最记挂的，还是她九十多岁的老父亲。之前即使路途遥远，每年也要回去几趟，现在因为疫情，尽孝都成了奢侈。

就算为了我妈，我也不能怂。不然立 flag 一时爽，打脸啪啪响，怎么对得起几分钟前还斗志昂扬的自己。

还好，我不是全村的希望，不用非得要求自己做得多么完美。

但我好歹算是全家的希望，嗯，之一。搞好小家，不能说为祖国建设添砖加瓦，也勉强算不拖国泰民安的后腿。

这段时间很多人都过得不容易，似乎看不清楚未来，但意外又无处不在。偶尔我也会看到一些让我心情不那么好的新闻，但总不能一直在悲观的情绪里不出来。

所以，我总时不时搞点事情让日子嗨起来。生命不就在于折腾，说不定折腾着、折腾着，未来就来了。

对孩子来说也是，想要能面对复杂应对变化，那就把他们养得强大，那我自己就得更强大，积极乐观能扛事儿。他们才会相信你的相信，热爱你的热爱。

has been apart from my dad for a long time already. A couple is thus separated because of me. I have a younger brother who lives in Hangzhou now. As I grow older, I feel stronger that I want to take care of my mom, but now that she's with me, she's the one taking care of me. She sometimes misses her son, but she misses her ninety-year-old father more. She used to visit him many times every year, but now it seems so difficult to do because of the pandemic.

I can't give in, even for my mother's sake. I can't be independent this minute and clingy the next.

Fortunately, I don't have too much pressure. So I am allowed to be imperfect.

But still, I am the hope of the family, well, one of the hopes. I will take care of my family, so that I am closer to the target of "A Harmonious Family, A Prosperous Country."

Life has been tough for a lot of people lately. The future is hard to see, and accidents are just everywhere. Sometimes I see frustrating news, but I adjusted myself not to be too negative.

Therefore, I always find changes to make things interesting. Life is about making surprises; maybe one day a bright future will be the biggest surprise.

For the kids, if I want them to be strong enough to face the changes and challenges, I'll have to raise them this way: First I'll have to be strong myself, be positive and brave. Then they'll look up to me and make me their best example.

生活嘛，哪有事事如意，只有看开。看开想开，日子才能过得开心。

人嘛，最重要的就是开心。

某天我推门进来，就看到哥哥正在看他喜欢的书，像模像样，肉乎乎的弟弟挨着他，也在看，也像模像样。

老大闹心、老二费心，都挺烦人的。

可是这样，也挺可爱。

春天迟到，但终将盛开。

They'll finally believe what I believe and love what I love.

Life isn't always full of flowers and cakes. Take it easy, and life will still be sweet.

The most important thing in life is to be happy.

Just like the other day, when I opened the door of the bedroom, I saw my elder son reading his favorite book carefully, and his brother, the little chubby boy was sitting closely next to him, reading too.

The elder is naughty and the younger is energy consuming. They might seem annoying.

But they are the best thing that's ever happened to me.

The spring might be late, but the flowers will eventually bloom.

"妈妈，你听 外面是汽车发动机的声音 真好！"

闫京亚 Jane Yan	山西人，工科女，毕业于上海大学，入职施璐德 8 年。心有点儿大但逻辑自洽，理性工作、佛系养娃，努力变成更好的自己。目前的愿望是把生活折腾成想要的模样。 A native of Shanxi Province. A science lover. Graduated from Shanghai University and joined CNOOD 8 years ago. She is a bit careless but has her logic. She treats her work seriously and raises her kids free-willed. She is trying to become a better person and hopes to live the life she wants.

种善因，得善果
Everything Happens for A Reason

■ Luis Camacho Cherp

在好朋友的鼓励下，带着助人助己踏上新征程的愿望，开始了马德里创业之旅。

最初的想法并不仅仅局限于西班牙，还要覆盖欧洲、北非，以及拉丁美洲这些在文化和语言方面有优势的天然市场，并以战略性区位将其作为亚洲与其他地区之间连接的桥梁。

即使在如此艰难的时期，即使受到新冠肺炎疫情以及各种限制影响，依旧充满热情并努力工作，这是一次巨大的挑战，是一次冒险，更是一次激动人心的创业和享受之旅，带着一个在开始时并不明确的目标，带着一个我个人小小的愿景。Dennis 一步一步地帮助我拓宽了视野，并不断鼓励我大胆思考。

我的资源和素养的主要来源是创造

Encouraged by that friend who had produced such a good feeling in me, eager to help and to start a new adventure, the process of developing the company in Madrid began.

The first idea was not to be limited to Spain but to have ramifications in Europe, North Africa and the natural market, by culture and language, which is Latin America, serving as a connection point between Asia and the rest of the locations because of its strategic position.

Plenty of illusion and hard work ahead, in a difficult time due to COVID-19 and restrictions, a great challenge, an adventure, an exciting journey to undertake and enjoy, with a goal... not very well defined at the beginning and a small vision on my part, Dennis gradually helped me to broaden my perspectives and continues to encourage me to think big.

The resources and training I have

力和想象力，因此，最初我时常与那些具备出色管理技能且能够帮助我激发这些想法和创意的朋友共同探讨交流，在此我要特别感谢的是 Javier Tabernero 和 Alberto Croso 两位朋友，他们是陪伴我度过这次冒险之旅最初艰难时期的伙伴，在我们共同的努力下孕育了我们的"孩子"（CNOOD EUROPA），创业的想法始于 2020 年 10 月，经过 5 个月的筹备后，于 2021 年 3 月在马德里筹备创立。

这一切都离不开集团这个大家庭的帮助和支持，尤其是母公司 CNOOD ASIA，每一个进展都离不开母公司的参与，这才让这次创业得以实现。

创业这条路走来极为艰辛，最初是从内部开始讨论，经过了反复思考、大量工作、设想、会议，经过了日复一日周复一周的筹划，经过了对大大小小计划的考量以及通过会议、电话、聊天进行不断的沟通和交流，还经过了 CNOOD 大家庭每个成员的帮助，在这里要感谢 Dennis、Johnson、Lu、David、Danni、Ahuan、Loreen、William、Peter、Fay、Sonia、Aurora、Belinda、Pat、Ben 还有其他让我难以忘怀的人，还有来自拉丁美洲的朋友 Nicolás、Mario 等。

任何时候，经历过程远比实现最终的目标更重要。

经过备至呵护和蹒跚学步后，"孩子"迈出了第一步，在一年后，也就是 2022 年 3 月，Dennis 到访马德里办公室，目前正在参与合适、舒适、有吸引力、协调且带有 CNOOD 标志的办公室创意过程的设

are based mainly on creativity and imagination; therefore, I had to surround myself initially with people of great management skills who helped to direct these ideas. I want to make a special mention to Javier Tabernero and Alberto Croso, fellow travelers at the beginning of this adventure, attending the birth of the "baby" (CNOOD EUROPE), which had been gestated in October 2020 and after a pregnancy of 5 months, was born in Madrid in March 2021.

All this, through the assistance and support of the whole family, the mother CNOOD ASIA, all its components had assisted at all times to make this birth possible.

The path started from home, with a creative process, a lot of work, imagination, conferences, trying to design day by day, week by week, imagining big and small plans, meeting as much as possible by conference, calls, chats, many of the family members of CNOOD with intention to help, always available: Dennis, Johnson, Lu, David, Danni, Ahuan, Loreen, William, Peter, Fay, Sonia, Aurora, Belinda, Pat, Ben... and so many others that I don't want to forget, as well as our brothers and sisters from Latin America: Nicolás, Mario, etc.

Enjoy the journey at all times, which is more important than the final goal.

Having started the journey and been at home protected, the "baby" has to start walking, to take its first steps, just a year later, on March 2022. With the visit of Dennis, the choice of the office in Madrid

计，这是一个为整个CNOOD大家庭提供的空间，为每一个来到马德里的成员提供的空间，更是一个让人忘掉过去满怀热情展望未来的后疫情时代空间。

办公室联合设计师备注说明（玛尔塔·加西亚·伊格莱西亚斯）

在看过Dennis和Luis选择的办公室的一些照片后，在第一次参观时，对于大量的自然采光，我感到非常惊喜，我们用了最好的"材料"来创造空间，将一半墙壁设计为地板到天花板的窗户，沿着墙壁前行，可以抵达一个覆盖植被的开放空间。

最初的创意是创造一个工作空间，但经过在家中的长期办公并思考利弊得失后，我们想要找到一个可以带给人一种家一样感觉的办公空间，相比传统的冷冰冰的功能性办公室，可以让人感觉更温暖舒适。所以我们选择了原木色和芥末色这种温暖的颜色和材料，这也是CNOOD特有的颜色之一，我们还在办公室的不同地方放置了天然植物。

一个像家里客厅一样舒适的并配有少量其他元素的休息区，构成了一个可以让每个人都感受到舒适的空间。

我们已经在前行，虽然我们可能会像孩子一样跌倒，但我们会以更大的力量和热情在跌倒后重新站起来。

takes place, being currently involved in the creative process of designing the right space, comfortable, attractive, balanced, identified with CNOOD, a space for the whole CNOOD family, for any member who comes to Madrid, a post COVID-19 space, to try to forget the past situations and look forward to the future with illusion.

NOTE BY THE SPACE-OFFICE CO-DESIGNER (Marta García Iglesias)

After having seen some photos of the office selected by Dennis and Luis, on the first visit, I was surprised how much natural light there was, we already had the best "material" that exists to create spaces, half of the walls are floor to ceiling windows giving an open space with vegetation.

The idea was to generate a workspace, but after so much time working at home with the pros and cons that entails, we looked for an office where you feel at home, something warmer and more pleasant than a cold and functional office. We chose thus warm colors and materials such as mustard, which is also one of the colors of CNOOD, and wood. We also placed natural plants in different parts of the office.

A rest area as if it were the living room of a house and few more elements make a space where everyone can feel as comfortable as possible.

We are already walking. We may stumble like any child, but we will rise again with more strength and illusion.

我们公司将很快迎来成长期和青春期，因此，我们必须相互扶持，并和有能力将创意变成现实的成员组建团队，每个成员都必须贡献自己的创意，必须具有创造力以及专注且有条理的想象力。

在此，以一句我一直践行的并且对我非常有帮助的话结束这次沟通，并希望能有机会在马德里与 Dennis 一起分享。

"前行、思考、讨论和改进。"

我们邀请所有人来马德里，到我们的办公室，去生活、去享受、去建设、去进步。

无论你从哪里来，只要你想来，我们随时欢迎。

这里就是家！

重要的是抵达目标的道路。

The growth and adolescence of the company will come soon. For this, it will have to be supported and form a group with members who are able to bring to a successful conclusion the creative ideas that everyone has to provide. Creativity and imagination are needed day by day, focused and managed.

I finish with an activity I usually practice and that helps me. I had the opportunity to share with Dennis some moments in Madrid.

"Walking, thinking, discussing and improving."

We are all invited to Madrid, to your office, to live, to enjoy, to build, to progress.

It doesn't matter where you come from, but please come when you can.

This is your home!

What matters is the way to reach the goal.

▶ 原文（西班牙语）

Animado por aquel amigo que tan buenas sensaciones me había producido, con ganas de ayudar y de embarcarme en una nueva aventura, comenzó el proceso de gestar la empresa en Madrid.

La primera idea era no limitarse a España, tener ramificaciones a Europa, norte de África, el mercado natural por cultura y lengua de Latino América y servir como un punto de conexión entre Asia y el resto de localizaciones por su posición estratégica.

Mucha ilusión y mucho trabajo por delante, en una época difícil debido al COVID-19 y las restricciones, un gran reto, una aventura, un viaje excitante que emprender y disfrutar, con una meta... no muy bien definida al principio, con una visión pequeña por mi parte, Dennis poco a poco me ayudó a ampliar mis perspectivas y continúa animándome a pensar en grande.

Los recursos y formación que tengo están basados principalmente en la creatividad y la imaginación, por ello , debía rodearme en un principio de personas con gran capacidad de gestión que ayudaron a encauzar estas ideas, quiero hacer una mención especial a Javier Tabernero y a Alberto Croso, compañeros de viaje al inicio de esta aventura, asistiendo el nacimiento del "bebé":(CNOOD EUROPA) , se había gestado en Octubre de 2020 y después de un embarazo de 5 meses , había nacido en Madrid en Marzo de 2021.

Todo ello, mediante la asistencia y el apoyo de toda la familia, la madre CNOOD ASIA, todos sus componentes habían asistido en todo momento para que este alumbramiento fuera posible.

El camino se inició desde casa, con proceso creativo, mucho trabajo, imaginación, conferencias, intentando diseñar el día a día, semana a semana, imaginando grandes y pequeños planes, conociendo en la media de lo posible mediante conferencia, llamadas, chats, a muchos de los componentes de la familia CNOOD con intención de ayudar, siempre disponibles: Dennis, Johnson, Lu, David, Danni, Ahuan, Loreen, William, Peter, Fay, Sonia, Aurora, Belinda, Pat, Ben, … y tantos otros que no quiero olvidar, así como nuestros hermanos de Latam, Nicolás, Mario etc…

En todo momento disfrutando del camino que es más importante el objetivo final. Comenzada la andadura y habiendo estado en casa protegido, el "bebé" debe empezar a caminar, a dar sus primeros pasos, justo un año después, en Marzo de 2022 , con la visita de Denis, se produce la elección de la oficina en Madrid, estando actualmente involucrado en el proceso creativo del diseño del espacio adecuado, confortable, atractivo, equilibrado, identificado con CNOOD, un espacio para toda la familia CNOOD, para cualquier miembro que venga a Madrid, un espacio post COVID-19, para intentar olvidar las situaciones pasadas y mirar hacia el futuro con ilusión.

NOTA DE LA COODISEÑADORA DEL ESPACIO-OFICINA (Marta García Iglesias)

Después de haber visto algunas fotos de la oficina seleccionada por Dennis y Luis, al realizar la primera visita, me sorprendió la enorme cantidad de luz natural, ya teníamos el mejor "material" que existe para crear espacios, la mitad de las paredes son ventanas de suelo a techo y dan a un espacio abierto con vegetación.

La idea era generar un espacio de trabajo, pero después de tanto tiempo trabajando en casa con los pros y contras que eso conlleva, buscamos una oficina donde la sensación fuera como si estuvieras en esa casa, algo más cálido y agradable que una oficina fría y funcional. Así elegimos colores y materiales cálidos como la madera y la mostaza, que además es uno de los colores de Cnood y dispusimos plantas naturales en distintos puntos de la oficina.

Una zona de descanso como si fuera el salón de una vivienda y pocos elementos más, conforman un espacio donde todos se puedan sentir lo más confortable posible.

Estamos ya caminando, podemos tropezar como cualquier niño, pero nos volveremos a levantar con más fuerza e ilusión.

Pronto vendrá el crecimiento y la adolescencia de la empresa, para ello habrá que apoyarse y formar un grupo con componentes que tengan la capacidad de llevar a buen puerto las ideas creativas, las ideas que todos deben aportar, la creatividad, la imaginación día a día, enfocada y gestionada.

Acabo con una actividad que suelo practicar y que me sirve de ayuda, tuve la oportunidad de compartir con Dennis en algunos momentos en Madrid.

"Walking, thinking, discussing and improving."

Estamos todos invitados a Madrid, a su oficina, a vivir, a disfrutar, a construir, a progresar.

Vengan de donde vengan, pero vengan cuando puedan por favor.

¡Esta es su casa.!

Lo importante es el camino para llegar a la meta.

路易斯
Luis Camacho Cherp

已婚，有两个女儿和一个儿子，喜欢旅行、阅读、家庭生活、乡村生活、烹饪、音乐、运动，认为最重要的是和朋友聚会。

Married, with two daughters and a son, he enjoys traveling, reading, family life, the countryside, cooking, music, sports and above all meetings with friends.

以人为本，吾心所向
Focusing on People Makes CNOOD the Best Place to Work

■ Nicolas Kipreos Almallotis

合适的人，合适的地方，合适的时间，总是可遇而不可求；而"以人为本"使CNOOD成了员工心目中最适合工作的地方。

"人力资源管理"一词有一个明确的定义，这不仅存在于几乎所有的教科书中，也存在于许多公司的人力资源战略中。数百万学生已经熟记了这个定义，已成为了大多数人力资源部门员工的核心词。人力资源管理的目的是确保合适的人员处于组织中合适的时间、合适的地点。

这就是为什么我们要接触、挑选和聘用合适的人。他们在公司内被安置、调动和晋升。员工会根据需要得到发展，这也是员工定期接受评估的原因之一。我们与员工一起完成这项工作，这样一个由杰出的创造者设计的公司就可以完美地组织起来，像机械一样有序运作。

Right people, right place, right time is not always a good approach; focusing on people makes CNOOD the best place to work

There is a specific definition for the term "human resources management" which is found not only in almost all textbooks but also in the human resources strategies of many companies. Millions of students have learned this definition by heart. Today it is the core understanding of the majority of staff working in HR departments. "The purpose of human resources management is to ensure the right people are in the right place at the right time in the organization."

That is why the right people are approached selected and hired. They are placed, transferred and promoted within the company. Employees get developed as needed, which is one reason that employees are being regularly evaluated. We do all this with the staff, so that the

对任何不在人力资源部工作的员工来说，这种想法都是非常令人不安的。从战略角度来看，我认为这种观点极其危险。这种方法对于越来越多的公司来说是完全错误的。原因很简单。不在人力资源部工作的员工不会在合适的时间在合适的地点对合适的人提出问题。因为他们有完全不同的问题。

这里有一个小的选择：我的下一个挑战是什么，我的下一个项目是什么？我该如何协调职业和私人生活？我如何给予和接受反馈？我如何才能为公司的成功做出贡献？其他人对我有什么期望？我的优势是什么？我该如何培养？有什么其他的任务适合我？

甚至像这样简单的事情：谁能接替我的工作？如何找到并且预订培训？谁有我现在需要的信息？我如何推荐一个朋友来这里工作？我如何分享我的知识？

应聘者也有疑问：我为什么要在这个行业工作？我该如何申请？我的申请状态如何？这家公司适合我吗？

一味关注"合适的时间、合适的地点、合适的人"必然会导致人们更多地关注公司的要求，而不是员工。在数字化的

organization which was designed by a brilliant creator is perfectly organized and runs like clockwork.

This understanding must be quite disturbing to any employee who does not work in the HR department. From a strategic perspective, I find this viewpoint to be extremely dangerous. This approach is totally wrong for an increasing number of companies. The reason is simple. Employees who do not work in HR do not raise questions about the right people in the right place at the right time. They have completely different questions.

Here is a small selection: What is my next challenge, my next project? How can I reconcile professional and private life? How can I give and receive feedback? How can I contribute to the success of the company? What do others expect of me? What is my advantage and how can I develop it? What alternate tasks could suit me?

It can also be a simple question such as: Who can take over my shift? How do I find and book training? Who has the knowledge that I need now? How do I recommend a friend to work here? How can I share my knowledge?

Applicants also have questions: Why should I work in this particular business? How can I apply? What is the status of my application? Is this company suitable for me?

A focus on "the right people in the right place at the right time" inevitably results in more attention being given

时代，这是一种危险的战略。如果一个公司的人力资源管理方法是基于员工的需求而不是公司的要求，那么这家公司的人力资源管理将大为不同。只有这样，员工才会成为人们关注的焦点，并被视为"最重要的资产"。围绕业务需求进行定位基本上是可以的。但公司必须能够负担得起这个代价。有多少公司考虑过？

我在CNOOD工作了将近10年，我一直在想：是什么让CNOOD成为一个很棒的工作场所？一个像CNOOD一样的好的工作场所，关心和支持员工，同时也给他们设置挑战，让他们与公司一起成长，就像一个大家庭。管理者和员工相互信任和尊重，共同致力于个人和公司的成功。CNOOD努力满足员工的财务、心理、身体和情感需求。因此，我们的工作效率更高，更满意，也更愿意长期留在CNOOD。

CNOOD的企业文化强调着员工共同的价值观、态度和行为。公司的核心价值观包括诚实、自我完善和沟通，但最重要的是信任，这就是为什么我们更敬业、更满意、更富有成效的原因。CNOOD围绕其员工形成一个社区，对每个人的目标都有共同的愿景和支持，当员工作为一个整体工作时，他们会分享美好时光和挑战。

to the company's needs rather than the employees'. This is a strategy that can be dangerous in times of digitalization and demographic and social change. If your HR approach is based on the needs of the staff rather than corporate requirements, your human resources management will be quite different. Only then will your staff be at the center of attention and treated as "your most important asset." Orienting around your business requirements is basically fine. But you have to be able to afford it. How many companies have thought about this?

I have worked for almost 10 years at CNOOD, and I always wonder: what makes CNOOD a great place to work? Such a place, like CNOOD, cares about and supports its employees while also challenging them to grow with the company, Just as a big family. Managers and the employees trust and respect each other and have a shared commitment to both individual and company success. CNOOD tries to meet employees' financial, mental, physical and emotional needs. As a result, we are often more productive, satisfied and willing to stay at CNOOD in the long term.

CNOOD culture emphasizes that an organization and its employees share values, attitudes and behaviors. A company's core values include honesty, self-improvement and communication, but most of all TRUST. That is why we are more engaged, satisfied and productive. CNOOD forms a community around their employees, with a common vision and support for everyone's

在CNOOD，我们有一个健康的工作环境，因为老板（Dennis）和他的主要管理人员信任他们的员工，所以我们努力工作，并在他们的支持和指导下做出正确的决策。CNOOD的员工更有可能作为一个团队来工作，因为该公司对我们一视同仁。

当然，在CNOOD，人力资源是一个关键，这就是为什么CNOOD是一个很好的工作单位，拥有各种经验水平、背景和信仰的员工。CNOOD了解多元化团队的价值，并努力雇佣各种各样的人。拥有多种视角的员工更有可能产生令人兴奋的想法和创造性的解决方案。多样化的工作场所也欢迎新员工，并支持他们。

我在CNOOD工作得很快乐，这是一个最好的工作场所。

一个热爱CNOOD的人

goals, and when employees work as a community, they share the good times as well as the challenging ones.

At CNOOD, we have a healthy work environment because our boss (Dennis) and his main managing staff trust their employees, so as a result we work hard and make good decisions, supported and guided by them. Employees in CNOOD are more likely to work as a team because the company treats us equally and fairly.

Definitely, at CNOOD, the human resources is key. That is why CNOOD is a great place to work. It embraces employees of all experience levels, backgrounds and beliefs. CNOOD understands the value of a diverse team and makes efforts to hire a variety of people. A workforce with many perspectives is more likely to produce exciting ideas and creative solutions. A diverse workplace is also welcoming to new hires and supportive of its people.

I am happy to work at CNOOD, the best place to work.

A CNOOD lover

尼古拉斯
Nicolas Kipreos
Almallotis

尼古拉斯出生于一个希腊裔家庭，当初他们为谋求更好机遇而举家徙居智利时，可谓身无长物，唯有成功之渴望、自由之身心，以及他们的爱心和对天主计划的信德。此后，他与兄弟和两个姐妹在极为清晰的原则指引下长大成人，受到过良好的教育和道德的熏陶，养成了简朴的生活方式，心中充满无尽之爱。几家声誉卓著的机构培养陶冶了他，帮助他实现远大理想。1993年，他与帕特里夏结为伉俪，育有四个儿女（玛丽亚·赫苏斯、比森特、本哈明、华金），一家人其乐融融。他信仰虔诚，日进日新，对待同事，真诚友善，但对自己认定正确之事抑或更佳之策，则必为之争辩，不轻言放弃。恒守敬人之道，临事唯以信、爱、真。一以贯之者，宽以待人、严以求实。

他不怕犯错，但若因自己未做分内之事、未能恪尽职守而累及他人，则必心怀畏惧。在施璐德，他受到热情欢迎，颇感自在裕如。自觉有义务为公司服务，期待不久即可回报。

他的座右铭是："正面思考，积极主动，充满自信，信仰坚定，生活必将更为稳定，更多实干行动，留下更丰富的经历和成果。"

Nicolas was born to a Greek family who moved to Chile looking for better opportunities. They brought with them nothing but their desire to succeed, their mental and physical freedom, their love and their faith in God's designs. Thus, he was raised with his brother and two sisters with very clear principles, good education and morals, simplicity in the way of living and infinite love. He was molded in several institutions of great reputation that have allowed him to reach great ideals. He married Patricia in 1993 and has four children (Maria Jesus, Vicente, Benjamin and Joaquin), forming a happy family. He lives his faith piously, tries to improve every day and is honest and kind to his colleagues, but he also always defends what he believes to be right or better, never giving up easily. He always treats people with respect and deals with affairs with integrity, love and sincerity. He is always soft on the person and hard on the issue.

He is not afraid of making mistakes, but he feels ashamed if others are affected because he didn't fulfill his responsibilities. He feels very comfortable at CNOOD where he has been generously welcomed. He feels a debt to the company and hopes to pay it off soon.

His maxim is "think positively and actively, with confidence and faith, and life will become more secure, more fraught with actions and richer in experience and achievement."

改善工作表现的方法
Ways to Improve Work Performance

■ Nicolas Kipreos Almallotis

如果你是一个只有在遇到困难、工作结果不如意或者被要求专注的时候，才会考虑改善你工作表现的人，你绝不孤单，大多数人都如此。目前，我们大多数人更喜欢保持沉默，让别人指出我们工作中可能的改进之处。其中的原因是什么？这是一个更简单的选择。然而，让我们仔细考虑一下——如果你不专注于提升自己，你怎么能成长为有才华、有效率，并且擅长这份工作的人呢？

不管你有多熟练，多高效，总有可能把工作做得比以前更好。关注提高你的技能，探索学习新东西的方法，这是成为更好的自己的第一步。这不仅有助于提高你的工作表现，也为你的专业发展创造了潜在的机会。

If the only time you think about improving your work performance is when you have encountered difficulties, or the results are not satisfactory, or when you have been called to attention, you are not alone. Most of us today prefer to stay quiet and let someone else point out possible improvements in our work. The reason? Well, it's a simpler choice. However, let's think about this carefully — you want to be talented, productive and good at your job, but how can you achieve this goal if you are not focusing on improving yourself.

No matter how skilled or productive you are, there's always a possibility to do a job better than before. Keeping an eye on enhancing your skill set and exploring ways to learn something new is the initial step towards becoming a better version of yourself. It not only helps increase your work performance but also creates potential opportunities for your

1. 设定清晰的里程碑

在个人生活和职业生涯中，设定明确的里程碑都很重要。作为人类，我们总是追求卓越，这也反映在我们设定的目标上。现在，稍微大胆一点是可以的，但在"目标"这个问题上，还是要想清楚，实事求是。

专业技巧：

设定目标通常是一个让人不知所措的过程。所以你需要做的是把你的个人和职业大项目分成小块，并设定相应的目标。这样做会帮助你在工作中保持动力，保持精力充沛。此外，设定明确的目标会让你更容易跟踪自己的进步。让你庆祝你取得的每一个小胜利。在设定里程碑的时候，请记住以下几点。

（1）时刻关注最后期限。
（2）把所有重要的日程保存在一个电子日历上。
（3）提高你的项目评估技能。
（4）把每一个里程碑都当作一次学习经验。

2. 计划和优先级

组织、计划和确定优先级是我们日常生活中至关重要的一部分。事实上，这应该是一种正常的职场习惯，它会帮助你及

professional development.

1. Set clear milestones

Setting clear milestones is important in both personal and professional life. As human beings, we have a habit of shooting for the stars, and the same reflects in the goals we set. Now, it's ok to be a little bold but when it comes to "goals," it's much better to think clearly and be realistic.

Pro tips:

Setting goals is often an overwhelming process. So what you need to do is to break your big personal and professional projects into smaller chunks and set your goals accordingly. Doing this will help you stay motivated and keep your energy levels up throughout the journey. Further, setting clear goals will make it easier for you to keep track of your progress, allowing you to celebrate every small victory you achieve. While setting milestones, keep the following tips in mind.

(1) Keep your eye on the deadline.
(2) Save all the important dates on an online calendar.
(3) Improve your project evaluation skills.
(4) Treat every milestone as a learning experience.

2. Plan and Prioritize

Organizing, planning, and prioritizing are a crucial part of our daily routine. In fact, it should be a normal workplace habit

时完成工作，提高你的整体工作表现。

专业技巧：

在你开始新的一天之前，浏览一下你当天计划的任务或活动清单。下面这些小建议可能会对你有所帮助。

（1）理解"紧急"和"重要"之间的区别。总是专注于需要立即关注的任务。

（2）试着根据估计的工作量来安排你的任务。

（3）不确定性是现实。所以，保持灵活性和适应性——但要记住优先级。

3. 做好会议计划

会议很重要，但却被广泛误解。计划和安排会议几乎是每个公司的常见做法。这就是为什么仔细计划每一次会议以使其"最有效"是很重要的。

专业技巧：

花点时间计划会议，但要简短。确保会议开始前所有要素都准备就绪。为会议制定一个清晰的议程，并与所有与会者进行沟通，这样他们就能更好地准备会议。此外，还有一些小技巧，能够帮助你更好地理解会议。

（1）在发送会议邀请之前，问问自己是否真的需要。

that will support you to get things done in time and improve your overall work performance.

Pro tips:

Before you start your day, go through the list of tasks or activities you have planned for the day. Some tips that may help you along the way.

(1) Understand the difference between "urgent" and "important". Always focus on tasks that need immediate attention.

(2) Try ordering your tasks by estimated effort.

(3) Uncertainty is a reality. So, be flexible and adaptable — but keep priorities in mind.

3. Plan your meetings well

Meetings are powerful, but they are widely misunderstood. Planning and scheduling meetings is a common practice in almost every workplace. That's why it is important to carefully plan each meeting in order to make it "most effective."

Pro tips:

Take your time to plan your meetings, but keep them short. Make sure that all the necessary elements are in place before the meeting starts. Set a clear agenda for the meeting and communicate the same to all the participants so that they can come better prepared. Additionally, some tips for your better understanding:

(1) Before sending invitations for the meeting, ask yourself if it's really needed.

（2）检查每个人的时间安排，选择会议的最佳时间。

（3）为准备工作提供尽可能多的细节。

（4）为会议留出时间，并在规定的时间内总结会议内容。

4. 更好地交流

沟通是双向的。有效的沟通是一种实践，可以让你在工作中确定事情，学习新的方法来取得更好的结果，最后，提高整体的工作表现。记住，每个意见都很重要，它肯定能帮助你把你的工作表现提升到一个新的水平。

专业技巧：

（1）不要只是开始评估可用的选项，首先要制定适当的合作策略。

（2）考虑哪种工具将满足您的长期业务需求。

（3）分析以前使用过你首选工具的客户的反馈。

5. 先克服困难的任务

这一点与我们上面提到的"计划和优先级"直接相关。显然，你不可能同时做每一项任务或活动。这就是为什么弄清楚哪些任务应该先完成，哪些任务可以推迟或委托给别人是很重要的。

(2) Check everyone's availability and pick the best time for the meeting.

(3) Provide as much detail as you can for pre-preparation.

(4) Save a time slot for meeting and sum it up in the given time frame.

4. Communicate better

Communication is a two-way street. Effective communication is a practice that makes you certain about things at work, learn new and improved ways to achieve better results, and finally, improve overall work performance. Remember, every opinion matters, and it can certainly help you take your work performance to a new level.

Pro tips:

(1) Don't just start evaluating the available option. Put a proper collaboration strategy in place first.

(2) Consider which tool will meet your long-term business requirement.

(3) Analyze feedback from customers who have previously used your preferred tool.

5. Conquer difficult tasks first

This point is directly related to our above-mentioned point "plan and prioritize." Obviously, you can't do every task or activity at the same time. That's why it is important that you figure out what tasks should be completed first and what tasks can be postponed or delegated.

专业技巧：

试着根据任务的重要性和迫切性对待办事项进行排序。把"最重要的任务"放在最上面，然后从上到下检查清单上的任务。这条建议背后的想法很简单——如果一项任务对你来说有点折磨，通过尽快摆脱它来放松你的大脑。

6. 不要失去焦点

重要的是你如何避免工作中的干扰，提高你的工作表现。干扰会让你失去注意力，浪费时间，最后还会扰乱你的工作管理，导致工作和项目的延误。

专业技巧：

专注于成功地完成手头的任务。此外，在必要的时候学会说"不"。请遵循以下几个简单的习惯，帮助你在工作中保持专注。

（1）在工作时间关掉让你分心的东西（智能手机、社交网站、办公室闲聊等）。

（2）在工作间隙休息一下——听听你最喜欢的歌或者出去散个步，"保持专注"！

7. 承认自己的优缺点

"完美"这个词好得让人难以置信。你不可能每件事都做到完美。我们都有弱点，认识到它们是很重要的，这样才

Pro tips:

Try ranking each task in your to-do list according to its specific importance and urgency. Keep the "most important tasks" at the top and start checking off items in your list from top-down. The idea behind this tip is very easy — if a task seems somewhat torturous to you, ease off your mind by getting rid of it as soon as possible.

6. Don't lose focus

What matters is how you avoid workplace interruptions and improve your work performance. Interruptions make you lose focus, waste time, and in the end, disrupt your work management and cause a delay in work and projects.

Pro tips:

Keep your eyes on successfully completing the tasks at hand. Also, learn to say "no" when necessary. Please follow some easy habits that will help you stay focused at work.

(1) Turn off distractions during work hours (smartphones, social media sites, office chit chats, and more).

(2) Take short breaks between work — listen to your favorite song or go for a short walk.

7. Acknowledge your strengths and weaknesses

The word "perfect" is too good to be true. There's no way for you to be perfect in everything. We all have weak

能找到改进的机会。此外，每个人都有他/她自己的长处，也就是他们特别擅长的事情。现在，为了提高你的日常工作表现，你需要珍惜你的优点，同时克服你的缺点。

专业技巧：

做自己的批评者，不断评估自己的表现以寻求潜在的改进。如果你非常擅长某件事，那就尽你所能做到最好。想知道如何找出自己的长处和短处，这里有一些你可能想要尝试的想法。

（1）在你的表现中找到规律。

（2）确定你在工作中最喜欢的是什么。

（3）记录下你如何应对需要行动、思考和洞察力的情况。

8. 要意识到自己的局限性

不断寻找方法来完善你做得不太好的领域当然很重要，但意识到自己的局限性也很重要。一次只做一项工作，尽量减少压力，减少出错或返工的可能性。在你的头脑中保持事情清晰，你就能比预期完成得更多、更快。

spots and it's important to acknowledge them in order to identify improvement opportunities. Additionally, every individual has his/her own strengths, i.e. something that they are exceptionally good at. Now, in order to bring improvement to your everyday work performance, you need to cherish your strengths and overcome your weaknesses at the same time.

Pro tips:

Be your own critic and keep evaluating your performance for potential improvements. If you're pretty good at something, then do whatever you can to be the best at it. On how to figure out your strengths and weaknesses, here are a few ideas that you may want to try.

(1) Find patterns in your performance.

(2) Decide what you enjoy the most at work.

(3) Make a note of how you respond to situations that require action, thought, and insight.

8. Be aware of your limitations

While it's certainly important to constantly find a way to polish the areas you are not doing so well, it is also important to be aware of your own limitations. Work on one task at a time, and do everything to keep it less stressful so that you are less prone to mistakes or rework. Keep things clear in your head, and you will be able to accomplish much more than expected, much faster.

专业技巧：

了解自己的局限并不容易。事实上，除非你超越它们，否则你永远无法理解它们。简而言之，你必须在工作效率和工作压力之间划清界限。你将如何做到这一点？这里有一些你可以尝试的事情。

（1）当事情变得无情的时候，后退。
（2）不要太有野心，要现实一点。
（3）发现你的最佳状态，避免精疲力竭。

9. 有始有终

另一件可能会影响你工作效率和表现的事情是没有完成的事情。你还记得有多少次你开始做一件事，然后很快就放弃了吗？如果这种情况经常发生在你身上，那么是时候改变了。不要养成把事情做一半的习惯。如果你已经开始了一个项目或任务，确保它以最高的质量完成。

专业技巧：

为自己设定奖励。养成庆祝成功的习惯，每当你成功完成一个项目或任务时奖励自己。这样做可以提升你的工作表现，你在工作中总会有盼头。

Pro tips:

Understanding your limitations isn't easy. In fact, you will never be able to understand them until you go beyond them. In simple words, you have to draw a line between being productive at work and being stressed at work. How can you do that? Well, here are a few things you can try.

(1) Back off when things get relentless.
(2) Don't be too ambitious, be realistic.
(3) Discover your sweet spot and avoid burnout.

9. Finish what you start

Another thing that is likely to affect your productivity and performance at work is leaving things unfinished. Do you remember how many times you've started working on something and then abandon it shortly after? If this often happens to you, then it's time to change. Don't make it a habit to leave things in between. If you've started a project or task, make sure that it reaches the last, final stage with utmost quality.

Pro tips:

Set rewards for yourself. Make it a habit to celebrate success and reward yourself whenever you successfully complete a project or task. Doing this boost your work performance, and you will always have something to look forward to at your work.

10. 使用正确的工具

事实证明，当你提供了合适的工具，你的团队的整体表现就会突飞猛进。最近的研究清楚地反映出，大多数组织正在转向基于云的工具和技术，以利用他们的许多好处。据预测，在未来几年，IT 行业将成为现代企业的战略推动者——81% 的组织都同意这一点。

专业技巧：

让你自己和你的团队使用最新的工具和技术。以下是一些基本的问题，可以让你更好地了解如何为你的企业和团队找到合适的工具。

（1）你的企业的关键流程是什么，以及如何使用在线工具和应用程序来改进它们？

（2）你已经在使用商业工具了吗？如果是，那么它是否达到了你的期望？

（3）你期望得到什么样的培训或支持服务？

CNOOD 是我们的公司，我们承受着其恩惠，为此我们必须展翅高飞努力发展，做好我们的任务，当然要相互支持，努力提高我们的工作效率。只有这样，才能让 CNOOD 走得更远，让所有人无一例外地享受到公司为我们带来的美好前途。

10. Use the right tools

It's a proven fact that when you provide the right kind of tools, your team's overall performance improves by leaps. Recent research and studies clearly reflect that the majority of organizations are shifting to cloud-based tools and technology to leverage their many benefits. It has also been predicted that in the coming years IT will be a strategic enabler of modern businesses — and 81% of organizations are agreeing to it.

Pro tips:

Keep yourself and your team up-to-date with the latest tools and technology. Here are some basic questions that will give you a better idea of how you can find the right tool for your business and your team.

(1) What are your business's key processes and how they can be improved using online tools and apps?

(2) Are you already using a business tool? If yes, then is it delivering results as per your expectations?

(3) What kind of training or support services do you expect?

CNOOD is our company, we enjoy the welfare it provides, and for that we must fly high, doing our tasks well, certainly supporting each other, but also making the effort to improve our work performance. This is the only way to take CNOOD far and where ALL, without exception, can enjoy the better future it brings.

尼古拉斯出生于一个希腊裔家庭，当初他们为谋求更好机遇而举家徙居智利时，可谓身无长物，唯有成功之渴望、自由之身心，以及他们的爱心和对天主计划的信德。此后，他与兄弟和两个姐妹在极为清晰的原则指引下长大成人，受到过良好的教育和道德的熏陶，养成了简朴的生活方式，心中充满无尽之爱。几家声誉卓著的机构培养陶冶了他，帮助他实现远大理想。1993年，他与帕特里夏结为伉俪，育有四个儿女（玛丽亚·赫苏斯、比森特、本哈明、华金），一家人其乐融融。他信仰虔诚，日进日新，对待同事，真诚友善，但对自己认定正确之事抑或更佳之策，则必为之争辩，不轻言放弃。恒守敬人之道，临事唯以信、爱、真。一以贯之者，宽以待人、严以求实。

他不怕犯错，但若因自己未做分内之事、未能恪尽职守而累及他人，则必心怀畏惧。在施璐德，他受到热情欢迎，颇感自在裕如。自觉有义务为公司服务，期待不久即可回报。

他的座右铭是："正面思考，积极主动，充满自信，信仰坚定，生活必将更为稳定，更多实干行动，留下更丰富的经历和成果。"

尼古拉斯
Nicolas Kipreos
Almallotis

Nicolas was born to a Greek family who moved to Chile looking for better opportunities. They brought with them nothing but their desire to succeed, their mental and physical freedom, their love and their faith in God's designs. Thus, he was raised with his brother and two sisters with very clear principles, good education and morals, simplicity in the way of living and infinite love. He was molded in several institutions of great reputation that have allowed him to reach great ideals. He married Patricia in 1993 and has four children (Maria Jesus, Vicente, Benjamin and Joaquin), forming a happy family. He lives his faith piously, tries to improve every day and is honest and kind to his colleagues, but he also always defends what he believes to be right or better, never giving up easily. He always treats people with respect and deals with affairs with integrity, love and sincerity. He is always soft on the person and hard on the issue.

He is not afraid of making mistakes, but he feels ashamed if others are affected because he didn't fulfill his responsibilities. He feels very comfortable at CNOOD where he has been generously welcomed. He feels a debt to the company and hopes to pay it off soon.

His maxim is "think positively and actively, with confidence and faith, and life will become more secure, more fraught with actions and richer in experience and achievement."

谢谢你，选择我们
Thank You, for Choosing Us

■ Raven Song

2022年3月24日，儿子出生。

回顾他出生前后的历程，只能用上天眷顾，一波三折来形容。经历了小区封闭、同楼栋确诊、120送发热隔离病房产检、一妇婴急诊收治、上海静默等，最终在预产期9天后，他来到了这个世界。

也许是基因中带来的本能，也许是天然的纽带在空气中形成了磁场，当我看到他的第一面，抑制不住地惊喜、激动、诧异、好奇。

初为人父，一切都是小心翼翼、手忙脚乱。疲惫却乐在其中。2个多月，自己瘦了11斤，减掉的体重竟然和儿子的体重一致，让我不得不怀疑：孩子也是爸爸身上掉下的一块肉？

On March 24, 2022, my son was born.

His arrival was full of twists and turns. I could say he's really a lucky guy. At first, our community was locked down; then there were positive cases in the same building where we live; then my pregnant wife was sent to the hospital by an ambulance to an isolated ward for prenatal examinations and stayed in hospital waiting for the due date. Soon after that, Shanghai was locked down. Finally, 9 days after the due date, my son came to this world. What a timing!

It might be for the instinct hidden in our genes or the natural bond between us that the first time I saw him, I was overjoyed, thrilled and curious.

It's my first time to be a father, I was very cautious, and I acted with confusion. Tired as I was, I felt so happy. I lost 5.5 kg during 2 months—my son weighed 5.5 kg too. I couldn't help suspecting: do the kids come from their fathers?

常说养育之恩，父母的爱是伟大的、无私的。但是做了爸爸后，我发现父母之爱这种感情是自私的，即在陪伴孩子成长的过程中，会获得远远超出想象的幸福感满足感，这都是来自孩子的。感恩父母，同样，也要感恩孩子。

皮克斯有个动画《心灵奇旅》，其中的设定非常有趣。每一个孩子在初生之前，都会在"生之来处"里学习、体验各种活动、技能、兴趣，随机获得性格、属性，最终找到属于自己的"火花"，取得"地球通行证"，最终"投胎"到地球成为父母的孩子。

We always stress parental love, because the love parents have for us is great and selfless. But after I became a father, I find this love sometimes selfish—while taking care of my son, I gain a lot of happiness, making me want to accompany him more. Since this pleasant feeling comes from my son, I should be grateful for him.

There was an animation called *Soul* produced by Pixar, which is very interesting. Every child, before born into this world, would go to a place to study various kinds of skills, develop all kinds of hobbies and experience different activities. Here they will form their personalities and attributes; then finally they'll find their sparks. After getting the

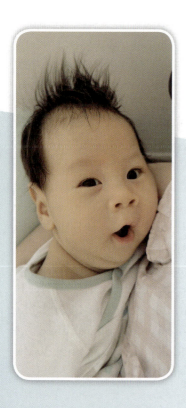

我相信存在这么一个"生之来处"。每一个孩子都是独一无二的，都拥有唯一的"火花"。

谢谢你，选择我们。

"Passport to Earth", they'll come to the world to meet their parents.

I think such place exists. Every kid is unique, and every kid sparks in his own way.

Thank you my baby, for choosing us.

宋瑞文
Raven Song

2018年加入施璐德，硕士毕业于中国石油大学（北京）。三十而立，初为人父，重担在肩，心向未来！

I joined CNOOD in 2018, and I received my master's degree from China University of Petroleum (Beijing). I have just stepped into my thirties, and I am a new father. With heavy responsibilities on my shoulders, I am longing for a bright future!

我的成长回忆及"古董"奖状

Memories of the Past and My Certificates of Honor

■ Zhengyu Ding

我一直有个愿望，想写一篇关于自己从懂事起到现在的回忆文章，当然这和名人所著的回忆录不是一回事，因为这个题目真的太大了，不好写。今天就找个小主题试写一下"我的成长回忆及'古董'奖状"。

人的一生都在成长和回忆中，有快乐，有烦恼，更有收获。人生在世，每时每刻都在成长着，从出生到幼儿园，到小学，到初中，到高中，再到大学，踏上社会，成长始终伴随着我们，恰似脚下的路，绵延不断，一直走向未来。我们一定要乐观地、快乐地成长，努力让自己成为对社会有用的人。

在我的记忆中，去幼儿园的日子现在回忆起来有点记不清了，好像是断断续续

I've always had this idea that one day I will write an essay about my life, from my childhood to my adult years. Surely it'll be different from the memoirs written by famous people. Since the scope of this topic is too big, here I will just find one aspect and share with you my precious memories of the past and my old trophies.

Human life is about growing and creating memories, in which there are happiness, sorrow, and harvests. We have never ceased to grow since the minute we were born: from kindergarten, to primary school, middle school, high school, and to university... Then, we step into society. During this whole time, we have been growing, just like the road beneath our feet, which keeps winding and leading us to the future. We have to be optimistic and make ourselves useful to the society.

My memories about my kindergarten years are vague. I only remember going

去过，后来应该是由于母亲不去上班，可以有时间在家照料我和弟弟，这样我也就不需要去幼儿园了。

在我的记忆中，小学的生活是幸福的，无忧无虑，也是轻松的。当时都是就地划区域读小学，我被划区去了一家民办小学——延西小学，因为那时正值特殊时期，学习任务基本上也不是太重。那时我们每天上学都是自己走去来回，也没有家长接送，记忆最深的是课桌上贴着一个剪纸"忠"字，这是那个时代的象征，另外还有记忆最深的是冬天在教室上课，坐在课桌椅上听老师讲课，双脚冻得冰冷，因为我们的教室在底楼，那时的生活条件也没有现在这么好，穿的鞋子也很单薄简陋，不像现在这样子都可以穿上健身鞋。

there on and off, and finally I didn't have to go there any more because my mom had more free time to take care of my younger brother and I.

The memories about my primary school life are full of happiness and pure innocence. My school was assigned according to the district where we lived. I was assigned to a private primary school—Yanxi Primary School. At that time, we did not have much homework, nor did we have to focus on our study. We went to school by foot every day. Our parents never came to pick us from school. There's a chinese character meaning "loyalty" attached to my desk, and I still remember it clearly because it symbolized that era. Another thing I remember clearly is that we were having classes in the classroom without any heaters, making us freezing and shivering. My classroom was on the ground floor, and I could not afford a pair of warm shoes,

尽管是在那年代，对于学生来说，读书上课仍然是主要任务，各门学科还是齐全的，期中期末考试成绩大家还是要攀比的，每个学期结束，每位学生的成绩报告单也要发放和公布，另外班级里大多数同学都加入了少先队，戴上红领巾，当然学期结束后，也会有评选"三好学生"或表扬学生的称号，颁发奖状，那时发的奖状，作为我们现在看来这绝对是古董级奖状，因为已有近50年了，那时我也时常被评为"三好学生"并收到这类奖状。

在我的记忆中，我的中学生活是最精彩并值得回忆，我们那时是不分初中高中，就是四年中学。

unlike the kids now who can buy all kinds of shoes, even fitness shoes.

For us students, our main task was still about study. We were taught different subjects, and we had exams during and at the end of each semester. The results would be announced. Most of the students in my class joined the Young Pioneers and had the qualification to wear the Red Scarf proudly. At the end of each semester, merit students would be praised and granted certificates, which are absolutely antiques now. The certificates have a history of nearly 50 years now. I was often praised as a merit student and got such certificates.

My middle school life, in my memory, was the most wonderful of all, and it's well worth reliving every once in a while. There was no junior or senior middle school then. We took a four-year course.

中学是快乐的，也是辛苦的，更是有收获的，每学期经常有很多社会活动，除了上课学习，还有春游，比如脱课去学工学农、到工厂和农村去学做工人和农民。我和同学们每天都在一起学习，一起游玩交流，一起打球锻炼，互相都十分了解。好同学要做到一帮一，一对红，帮助差同学积极要求上进，提高学习成绩。在学习上我是刻苦的，每个学期期中期末考试都要争取在前10名，平时在各方面的政治表现也要好。班主任还会在期末考试结束后家访，汇报每个学期学生的表现，当然有表扬也有批评，我每次都是被班主任表扬，班主任对我和我父母最常用说的一句话就是我是"懂事、成熟快，德智体全面发展的学生"，所以每学年我都能被评为学校的"三好学生"，还有两次被评为长宁区级"三好学生"的称号，中学时代有太多的奖状。

Middle school life was happy and beneficial. There were many social activities every week besides studying, such as the spring tour. We also went out of school to learn about manufacturing and farming. I would go inside the factory to learn to be a worker and go to the countryside to learn to be a farmer. I spent my days with my classmates playing, communicating, working out and playing basketball. We knew each other very well. Good students were supposed to help the less good, in the form of groups and "one on one", so as to improve their grades. I was a good student myself. I studied hard and ranked among the top 10 in every mid-term or final exam. I behaved well, too. The headmaster would visit every family by the end of each semester, to communicate with our parents about our behaviour at school. There were praises as well scoldings. I got praises every time. I often heard my teacher say that I was

四年的中学生活，让我充满力量、充满信心，我懂得了学习的重要性，懂得了爸爸妈妈与老师的期望，懂得了未来社会需要的是栋梁之材。正巧在中学毕业前一年，国家对教育制度进行了全面改革，恢复了高考制度，我们这一届正好是全国恢复高考后的第一届考生，也叫七八级，所以我们每个学生都有机会加入到高考复习迎考之中。学校还在中学四个班级中挑选出一个毕业提高班，针对性地复习迎考，最后四个班，也只有近十人考进了大专院校。在我的记忆中，高考前，我每晚都是

considerate and smart and that I was a good student in all respects. So I was selected as the merit student every year in our school, and I was the merit student in our Changning District twice. There were too many certificates of honour during this time.

I was full of faith and confidence, and gradually I knew the importance of studying. I understood what my parents and teacher expected of me and that what the future world needed was someone excellent. One year before graduation, a major change happened in our state education system—the college entrance exam was recovered! We were the first students that took the exam, we called ourselves the 1978 grade. We all had the chance to take the exam, and our

挑灯夜战，高考在7月份，那时好像上海很少听到有人家中装空调，可能空调还没有在上海出现，大热天家里热，只能在路边的电线杆灰暗的路灯下复习迎考。最后我幸运地高过分数线几分考入一所上海没名气的院校，有机会进大学校门深造。虽然学校一般，但它为国家的冶金工业发展输送了太多的国家所急需的优质人才。我的专业是钢铁冶炼，毕业后分配在钢铁厂，这学校现已更名为上海应用技术大学。

小学中学的生活学习经历已经写了太多，就不写大学的经历了，还是来回忆一下大学毕业走上工作岗位的人生经历。20世纪80年代我从学校毕业后分配到国内特种钢生产排头兵企业——上钢五厂，因为我学的是钢铁冶炼专业，所以分配到炼钢车间，向在第一线的炼钢工人师傅学习实践知识，如何在电炉炼钢中炼出每一炉的优质钢，上班是三班倒，就是二二制工作模式。这种大学生毕业后到生产第一线生产劳动实习三班倒工作状态持续了两年多，这种辛苦劳累的程度几乎不能用一般语言所表达的，后来终于坚持下来了，又由于自己在炼钢车间各方面表现好，逐渐成为电炉炼钢工段的见习炉长、技术副工长，日后被厂部领导相中提拔去厂部工作，在总厂办公室当秘书工作，后又有机会去大学全脱产学习深造外贸进出口实务。学成回厂后被安排在厂部技术改造处

school even chose one class to give special guidance. Nearly 10 students from the four classes entered college. I remember that I used to study till late night. The exam was in June, and there were few families having air conditioners. It was so hot at home that I would study by the telegraph pole at the roadside. Finally I got admitted into an ordinary college in Shanghai, with only a few points higher than the passing score. I was lucky enough to continue my study in college. Though it was an ordinary college, many excellent people who were useful to the country graduated from it. I majored in steel smelting, and I entered a steel factory after graduation. My college is now called Shanghai Institute of Technology.

I've written too much about my primary school and middle school, so I'll spare you of my college life. Instead, I would like to share with you my life experience after I started to work. After graduating from college in the 1980s, I was assigned to the No. 5 Plant of Shanghai Steel, a pioneer in the production of special steel in China. Because I majored in steel smelting, I was assigned to the steel-making workshop to learn practical knowledge from the steel-making workers on the front line, such as how to make each furnace of high-quality steel in the electric furnace steel-making process. I work in three shifts every day, which is a two-two working mode, After graduation, I went to the first production line and worked in three shifts for more

引进科工作,开始从事全厂的引进设备改造项目的工作,经常要和外商企业代表来厂交流的团队打交道,出国担当翻译,为上钢五厂所有从国外引进的大项目顺利投产作出了一定的贡献,在职期间我还写的多篇技术论文和译文得到业内专家的好评,先后被上级单位冶金局团委评为"新长征突击手"以及被上钢五厂评为厂级"先进生产(工作)者"的光荣称号,又一次获得了宝贵的奖状。

than two years. I could hardly describe in words how hard it was to work there, but I kept on working hard. Because of my good performance in all aspects in the steel-making workshop, I gradually became the probationary furnace director and deputy technical director of the electric furnace steel-making section. Later, I had the opportunity to be promoted by the leaders of the factory to work in the factory. I worked as a secretary in the general broadcasting office, and then I had the opportunity to go to the university full-time to study foreign trade practice. After coming back, I was assigned to work in the introduction section of the technical transformation division of the plant headquarters and began to engage in the introduction of equipment transformation projects of the whole plant. I often had to deal with the teams of representatives of foreign enterprises who came to the plant to communicate with each other. I worked abroad as a translator and made some contributions to the smooth production of all the major projects introduced from abroad in the No. 5 Plant of Shanghai Steel. During my tenure, I also wrote many technical papers and conducted translations, which were highly praised by experts in the industry. I was successively rated as the new Long March Raider by the Youth League Committee of the Metallurgy Bureau, a superior unit, and as the plant level advanced individual production worker by the No. 5 Plant of

在钢厂工作12年后的1994年，当时国家政策是坚持对外开放，积极引进国外先进技术装备和管理技能水平，外企也正需要懂技术又懂英文方面的人才，所以我顺势而为就离开钢厂，加入外企去开辟另一条新的业务模式。这一做就是26年，做到了退休，在这26年漫长外企工作经历中，学到了太多的东西，如何做业务，如何做好人，学习做事严谨、细致周到、为人诚实、为人处世方式等。在我工作了26年后于2020年5月退休时，德国蒂森克虏伯材料贸易的CEO是这样发邮件评价我的。

亲爱的丁先生，
希望您和您家人安全健康。

我想诚挚地感谢您多年在曼内斯曼和蒂森克虏伯的辛勤工作，您展现出了一流的品格和忠诚。

不管怎样，我的朋友，当我下一次去上海时，让我们共进晚餐，一起喝一杯。可能那要到明年了，但我一定会安排会

Shanghai Steel. Again, I won certificates of honor.

In 1994, I had worked in the steel plant for 12 years. The national policy was to adhere to the opening-up policy and actively introduce foreign advanced technology and equipment and management skills. Foreign enterprises were also in need of talents who understood both technology and English, so I took advantage of the situation and left the steel plant to join foreign enterprises to try and open up another new business model. 26 years passed, and I retired at the legal age of the country. In the 26 years of long working experience in the foreign enterprise, I had learned too many things, such as how to do business, how to be a good person, how to learn from the Germans about being rigorous, meticulous, honest, and how to behave. When I finally retired in May 2020, the CEO—Mr. W.S. of thyssenkrupp said something to me. I hereby attach the email sent by Mr. W.S.

Dear Mr. Ding,
I hope you and your family are safe and healthy.

I'd like to sincerely thank you for all your hard work, efforts and foremost integrity and loyalty to the company during the many years you had worked for Mannesmann and thyssenkrupp…

Anyhow, my friend, let us have dinner and a beer next time I am in Shanghai. Probably that is going to be next year only,

面，当面与您道别。

保重，再次非常非常感谢，老丁！！！

当然退休后的生活可以是放松心情，随心所欲，安享晚年……但对我来说，我是喜欢热闹的不太喜欢安静的人，喜欢和年轻人共处同成长，同时自己也有一些业务专长和人脉，还可以干上几年，继续与我原有熟悉业务相关的企业打交道，发挥余热，焕发我人生的第三春天。同时我也一直有一个理念：人生在世，就是要活到老，学到老，在不断工作中学习，做一个对社会有帮助的人。本着这个态度，我退休后就立马加入了我熟悉的施璐德亚洲有限公司，承蒙公司董事长池勇海博士的抬爱，任命我为公司采购中心总经理，经过一年多的运行摸索，现正在向正确的管理方向发展，前景广阔，相信经过采购中心每位成员的共同努力和坚持不懈追求，我们的采购团队一定能成为我们公司销售团队的坚实基础平台，为公司创造价值提供优质服务。

光阴似箭，日月如梭，一晃眼半世纪

however I will make sure we meet and can say good-bye in person.

Take care and many, many thanks again, Lao-Ding!!!

Of course, after my retirement, I could just relax, do whatever I want and enjoy my life. But personally, I love to be with people. I do not enjoy too much time alone. I like to live and grow with young people. At the same time, I also have some business connections, so I can still work for a few years, continue to deal with enterprises that I am familiar with, give full play to the rest of my time and glow in the third spring of my life, At the same time, I have always had an idea: It's never too old to learn. I will learn from work and be a useful person to the society. With this passion, I immediately joined CNOOD Asia which I became familiar with after retirement. Thanks for the appreciation of Dr. Chi, chairman of the company, I was appointed as the general manager of the company's procurement center. After more than a year of operation and exploration, I am now developing towards the correct management direction with broad prospects. I believe that through the joint efforts and unremitting pursuit of each member of the procurement center, our purchasing team will certainly become a solid foundation platform for our sales team to create value for the company and provide high-quality services.

Time goes by like an arrow, and

已过，人生需要回忆和追溯，每个人在自己人生成长过程中，都会有光彩夺目的一面，也会有黯然失色的不幸，我们要珍惜人生的经历和回忆。以前的奖状只能说明一个人生命历程的证明，对于我来说，即便现在是退休还在发挥余热，做自己喜欢做的事，闲暇时拿出这些古董级奖状来翻翻看看，我想也不失为很好的回忆。因为它曾经伴随着我的成长和经历，将来仍将伴随我走向更加美好的未来。

one and a half centuries have passed in a blink. Life needs to be recalled and traced. In the process of growing up, everyone has his wonderful moments, as well as misfortunes. We should cherish the experience of life and recall the memories. The old certificates can only prove a person's life course. For me, even now when I am retired, I still feel passionate to do what I like. In my spare time, I would take out these antique certificates to appreciate and to help me recall those precious years. These certificates of honor have accompanied me through the whole process of my growth and experience and will still accompany me to a better future.

丁征宇
Zhengyu Ding

1960年5月出生，浙江绍兴人，毕业于上海应用技术大学冶金工程专业。1994—2020年就职于德国蒂森克虏伯公司，2020年5月退休；同年7月加入施璐德。工作认真、做事靠谱，正直善良、热爱生活、乐于助人、善于交友，喜欢书法和运动。

Born in May 1960 in Shaoxing City in Zhejiang Province, Ding Zhengyu graduated from Shanghai Institute of Technology majoring in metallurgical engineering. He worked for Thyssenkrupp from 1994 to 2020 and retried in May 2020. In the same year, he joined CNOOD. He always works seriously with great reliability. Integrity and kindness are the essence of his personality. He attaches great importance to enjoying life and is always ready to help others and good at making friends. He is fond of calligraphy and sports.

十年之约

The Ten-Year Agreement

■ Cindy Fang

时间飞逝，一转眼加入CNOOD已近十年，至今还记得当初参加公司校招讲座、面试的场景。

而十年时间，说长不长，说短也不短。其中，有得也有失，有笑也有泪。

CNOOD是我踏出校门的第一份工作，何其幸运能够一直融入在"相互关心，创造开心"的大家庭里，与一群有爱的同事们，结伴同行，共同奋进。

而生活中在去年我也组成了自己的小家庭，现在已是8个月胖宝宝的妈妈。

从一名初入社会的稚嫩的学生，到成为一名母亲，工作的历练以及生活角色的转换使我得到了许多。

Time flies by like the running river. It has been ten years since I joined CNOOD. I could still recall those scenes of me listening to the employing lectures and accepting interviews.

Ten years of time is long to some people and short to others. There have been losses and gains, as well as tears and laughter.

This is my first work ever since I stepped out of school. I feel so lucky to be accepted in this big family where everyone cares about each other and everyone makes others happy. I am fortunate to work and march together with my colleagues.

In my life, I just had my small family last year. Now, I am a mother of a 8-month old baby.

From an innocent girl who just graduated from school, I've turned into a mature mother. Life and work have given me a lot of experiences and lessons.

但在临产之际，无法赶回东北老家，见至亲的最后一面，我也在懊悔与自责中失去。

在得与失之间，我哭过，也笑过。它教会了我成长，让我变得更强大。

这就是时间的魅力、生活的美妙之处吧。

它让我学会享受简单而真实，平淡而有爱的当下；感恩所拥有的一切。

期待下一个十年之约。

未来可期、不忘初心！

However, I wasn't able to go back to my hometown in the northeast to see my family member for the last time, because I was about to deliver the baby soon. It has become my biggest regret, and till now I am still blaming myself.

I've cried for my losses and laughed for my gains. Those moments have taught me to be strong.

This must be the power of time and the charm of life.

Life has taught me to enjoy the present time, because they are simple but true and pure but full of love. It has taught me to be grateful for all that I have.

I am full of hope for the next ten-year agreement.

The future is just ahead, and we shall remain true to the original mission.

房金凤
Cindy Fang

在施璐德从事了将近十年的单证工作。这么长时间以来,很感谢公司的培养,领导的督导,同事的帮助。也明知自己尚有许多不足之处,急需紧跟公司蒸蒸日上的步伐,不断开拓自己的视野、学识,做好公司发展的后备力量。

I am Cindy, and I have been working at CNOOD for almost ten years, handling all kinds of documents and invoices. I am very grateful for the company's cultivation, the leaders' supervision and colleagues' help. I know I am to be improved in many aspects and that I should keep up with the fast pace of the company. So I should keep broadening my horizon and arming myself with knowledge and be someone useful to the company.

2122,我已130岁

By 2122, I will be 130

■ Allen Han

我睁开眼,
看到了你。
我问你,这是不是真的。
你说,是真的。
可当我真的睁开眼,
这一切,
却不是真的。
——七月

问:你孩子还在上海吗?
答:不在,外派出差半年了。

问:近期是否有回家?
答:我儿已经两年半没回来了。

问:后面是否有返乡计划?
答:不清楚,看政策要求。

——老韩

儿行千里,

安全第一,
注意防护,

My eyes I opened,
It was you I saw
Is it true? I asked you
Yes, you replied.
But I opened my eyes again,
You were not here,
You were not for real
——July

Q: Is your child still in Shanghai?
A: No, he has been out of Shanghai for business for half a year already.

Q: Has he come back lately?
A: He has been away from home for two years already.

Q: Does he plan to come back?
A: I've no idea. It depends on the pandemic control policy.

——Han

A thousand miles away the son is from home.

Safety is always the top rule.
Stay away from the crowds,

照顾好你和七月。
家里都好，
不用挂念。
——老王

风险识别，
前置安排，
人员到位，
设备到位，
物资到位，
封闭管理，
生产监控，
保证交付。
——封控·开工

所有人员，
车子不停，
人员不歇，
通宵达旦，
抢占窗口，
完成集港。
——解封·发运

现在是2122年，
我已130岁。
回望那一年2022，
恍如隔世。
——晴·无风

And take care of July and yourself.
We are fine here.
Miss us not.
——Wang

Identify the risks.
Finish the preparations.
Human resource, ready.
Equipment, ready.
Materials, ready.
Everything in quarantine and lockdown.
Production monitored,
Delivery promised.
——Quarantine • Project Start

All the staff,
Work with our cars non-stopping,
And our staff non-resting,
Day and night.
Seize the key moments,
And complete cargo gathering.
——Quarantine finished • Products Delivery

This is in the year of 2122 now.
I am already 130 years old.
When I look back to the year of 2022,
It feels like yesterday.
——Sunny • Calm day

韩 超
Allen Han

甘肃·庆阳籍
入职五年有余
奋斗中

Qingyang City · Gansu Province
I've been working at CNOOD for five years,
And I'm still striving.

走自己的路

Be Yourself

■ Shelley Wu

当你无所畏惧时你最想做什么？永远不要忽略自己真正想做的事情，即使你可能暂时无法脱开身去做你最想做的事情，但是一定要保持与自己对话，内心里那个声音会在你遇到挫折时告诉你再坚持一下曙光就快到了，会在你稍有成绩时警醒你不要骄傲你还可以做得更好。每一个人的路都是要靠自己去走的，但是不要忘了来时的路。

光阴似箭，加入CNOOD大家庭快10年了。感叹一句，我是有多幸运才能加入到CNOOD大家庭的呢，又是有多幸运才能遇到Dennis、Fay、Tiger、Tina等人，他们是真真切切关心公司每一位成员，无论是生活还是工作都会不遗余力地给予支持和帮助；还有那么多真诚待人、富有创新、积极进取的同事们。身边优秀的人太多，常常让我焦虑不已，但是又庆幸自己身处其中，让我知道自己还有很多很多需要学习的。在CNOOD我从未担心过什么勾心斗角，尔虞我诈，因

What do you want to do most when you are fearless? Do not neglect your true desires. Even if you are not be able to do what you want right now, you have to keep communicating with yourself. The voice inside you will always tell you to carry on. When you make great achievements, the voice will remind you not to be proud and that you can always do better. You have to walk your own path, but do not forget where you come from.

Time flies by so fast, and in the blink of an eye, it has been ten years since I joined this big family of CNOOD. I always sigh how lucky I am to be here, to meet Dennis, Fay, Tiger, Tina and everyone else who care about the company. They have given me help no matter in work or life. They are so kind, creative and hardworking! They are so excellent that I am always anxious, worrying that I might fall behind one day. But with so many wonderful colleagues around me,

为 CNOOD 就是一个家，它给予我力量和敢为未来想的勇气，它和我出生的家一样重要。依然记得加入公司前两年，下班后原万航渡路办公室边上一茶一坐餐厅，Dennis 经常会请我吃饭，然后跟我聊工作，聊生活，聊我的家人，聊未来；我时常跟我爸妈和朋友提起公司老板、同事以及公司的种种，他们都感慨我很幸运地能找到一个这么好的公司，遇到一群这么好的人。我知道这是我一直以来的前进动力之一，因为我想让自己变得更好，好让自己能与这群可爱的人走得更久更远。

在 CNOOD 工作快 10 年了，可以说我见证了公司的发展，从最初二十几个人到国内有一百多个人，不断设立海外分公司，业务从货物采购到有自己的设计公司，施工公司的快速发展与全球布局。公司也见证了我的成长，从简单的订单跟踪，到组织出国参加展会，见客户，独立面对客户，做项目。生活中我在 CNOOD 的 10 年里完成了人生大事：结婚和生娃，特别感谢公司给了我一个梦幻的婚礼，在所有可敬的领导与可爱的同事们的见证下完婚，何其幸运。

I am reminded everyday that there's still a lot more to learn. I never have to worry about relationships here, as no one sets me up or gives me hard time. CNOOD is a big family from where I can always get strength and courage to face the future. It is as important as the family which I was born into. I still remember clearly that two years ago, in the CHAMATE restaurant beside our former office on Wanhang Rd, Dennis would always buy me dinners, and we talked about work, life and my family. My friends and family have heard a lot about Dennis from me, and they all feel happy for me that I can meet such a good boss and such great colleagues. My company is one of the driving forces that push me forward. I want to become a better person so that I can be with these excellent people for more years.

During my ten years here, I have witnessed the development of CNOOD which turned from a small company with twenty staff into a big enterprise of hundreds of employees. It keeps expanding and has many branches abroad. Gradually it has its own procure department and design department. Our development has become faster and faster, and we have clients all over the world. CNOOD has seen my growth too. I used to be a small clerk following orders, but I can now attend international conferences abroad, meet clients and finish projects independently. I have accomplished two major things in my

未来的路依然很长，过去的美好给予我力量，让我依然相信自己的未来可以去创造。我最想做的事情是希望自己会变得越来越好，好让自己能与 CNOOD 大家庭一起走得更久更远。

life during the 10 years: getting married and giving birth. I am very grateful for the company for a perfect wedding in which I got married with the leaders and colleagues witnessing. How lucky I am!

There's still a long way to go for me. The beautiful memories in the past have given me strength, making me believe that I can create my future with my own hands. The thing that I want to do most is that I want to be better and better so that I can be with everyone in CNOOD for longer years to come.

吴晓玲
Shelley Wu

毕业于上海对外经贸大学，2013 年 7 月正式加入施璐德，心怀感恩，脚踏实地。

Graduated from Shanghai University of International Business and Economics, and officially joined CNOOD in July 2013, always grateful and down-to-earth.

记武汉疫情与上海疫情有感
My Thoughts on Pandemic in Wuhan and Shanghai

■ Liam Wu

2020年的春节是我度过的最特别的一次。武汉整个城市仿佛一瞬间停止了运转，公交地铁停止运行，出租车也不见了身影，马路上看几乎不到一个行人，所有人都只能在家里待着。

没有走亲访友，没有外出聚餐，没有疯狂购物，更没有节日的气氛，只能宅在家里，通过电视、手机来了解最新的疫情信息。每天看着不断出现的新的感染病例和不断上升的感染数字，所有人的心里都蒙上了一层阴影，而随着封禁时间的增加，内心的焦虑也越来越强烈。

尽管疫情来势汹涌，但是也无法让武汉人民屈服，更无法让中国人民屈服。随着感染病例的增加，各地的医生护士都放弃了与家人团聚的机会，向着武汉前行，向着高危地区前行，投身到各大医院，穿着厚重的防护服，戴上几层医用口罩，争分夺秒地和死神抢夺生命、

The spring festival of 2020 is the most special one I've ever had. The whole Wuhan city was shut down: public transportation was stopped, taxis and private cars were nowhere to see, and everyone was at home.

There were no visiting family and friends, no parties or gatherings, no shopping or festival atmosphere at all. We were trapped at home, reading news about the disease everyday on TV and phone. People were so nervous and scared, seeing the growing number of infected people. The longer we were trapped at home, the more desperate we got.

Fast and fierce as the disease was, the citizens in Wuhan never gave in, nor did the whole Chinese nation. The number of infected people kept growing. Medical workers gave up their chances of being with their families; instead, they started to march to Wuhan from all directions.

和疫情抢夺时间。

与此同时，国内国外的各种各样的企业、组织都在向武汉捐款捐物，各行各业的人们也在为武汉加油打气。所有的人都在这场看不见硝烟的战场中艰苦战斗。这是一场艰巨但又必胜的"战役"，这是一场全民动员、众志成城的"战斗"。疫情带来的伤害，一张张照片让你看到心酸，酸楚的眼泪，无声的呐喊，无数次加油，最终还是相信一切都会好起来。

2022年，没想到又让我碰到了封控，这次是上海。

从2022年2月初开始，上海就陆陆续续出现了感染新冠病毒变异毒株的病例，但是基本上也都能准确防控。但是从3月开始，形势就变得严峻起来。3月中旬，各个公共场所都需要扫健康码才能进入，各地区开始核酸检测，小区也开始断断续续地进行隔离操作。到三月底直接通知要开始静默管理了。

两次特殊的经历也让我似乎从最初的"焦躁"变得渐渐"没脾气"起来。已习惯每天被小区喇叭聒噪的核酸检测通知叫醒；已习惯每天晚上抱着手机各种"我的团长我的团"；已习惯对着家里剩余的"物资"精打细算；已习惯重复日复一日没有自由的日子。

They were everywhere, in the high-risk areas and in the hospitals, wearing thick and heavy protective clothing and masks and trying their best to save lives.

At the same time, companies of different industries started to organize donations for Wuhan. Everyone was cheering Wuhan on, too. The whole country was fighting in this white war. Hard as it is, we will eventually win, with every Chinese mobilized and united. The damage that the disease has caused is enormous. Whenever we saw pictures of those impressive moments, we couldn't help shedding tears and cheering each other on. We believed that everything would eventually be OK.

But in 2022, I was put in quarantine again, this time in Shanghai.

There have been Omicron infections in Shanghai since the beginning of February, but everything was under control basically. But the situation started to get serious in March. By the middle of March, public places started to require the green code for entrance, and several communities started to organize nucleic acid tests. Some already started the quarantine policy. By the end of March, the whole city was put in quarantine.

The two special experiences have turn me from an easily agitated person into a calm one. I am now used to being waken by the broadcast that requires us to do nucleic acid tests; I am used to watching "My Chief and My Regiment" on my phone; I am used to making a

不过虽然不能随意走动,这段"没脾气"的日子倒给了我自己一个难得的"内省"机会,让我思考如何去锻炼自己的心态,一种面对生活不顺时保持钝感的"高级心态"。不如意事常八九,可与人言无二三。麻烦与快乐是孪生姐妹,只不过快乐到来时,我的心情会更高兴。因此,我在这段特殊的时间里学会了怎么把麻烦看作是生命中赖以表现自己韵律的一部分,以豁达、从容的心态而处之。

"疫"尘不染,静待"疫"散,不负阳光不负爱。愿山河无恙,祖国皆安。

careful budget for the family, facing the limited resources we have; I am used to this "freedom" at home, day after day.

Though there's no where to go, I learned to enjoy this calm period in which I can look into myself and think how I can have a better mindset. So when I am in the face of difficulties, I know how to stay "cool." There are sorrows all the time, but few can be talked about. Sorrow and happiness are like twin sisters, but I prefer to have happiness. During this time, I have learned to see sorrow as an inseparable part of life and deal with difficulties calmly.

We are protected well from the disease, and we are waiting calmly for a good result. With this deep love for life, I hope our motherland is well.

吴祖亮
Liam Wu

性别男,爱好广泛,来自鱼米之乡、体操之乡——湖北仙桃。对各种新鲜事物都充满旺盛的好奇心,喜欢体验新科技,对未来充满向往。

I am an optimistic man, and I have many hobbies. I am from Xiantao, home of fish and rice and home of gymnastics, in Hubei province. I am extremely curious about new things. I love to experience new technology, and I am looking forward to the future life.

疫情之下，团结之美

The Power of Unity in the Pandemic

■ Henry Yang

2022年4月中旬清晨，正在睡梦中的我被一阵急救车的喇叭声唤醒，我起床后打开窗户，看到一辆救护车停在小区中间，随后又有哭喊声和吵闹声传来，这已经是救护车连续第二天开进小区了。在发出长长的叹息声后，我打开冰箱，发现仅剩几个鸡蛋和西红柿，忍不住深深地吸了一口气。看着儿子焦躁地撕扯着他那长长的头发，气得我忍不住对着天爆一句粗。昔日繁花似锦，灯红酒绿的上海在疫情面前显得异常虚弱，在全国各地的援助下勉强支撑。

敲门声传来，隔壁邻居王阿姨家里有人生病过来借药，知道我家情况后又从家里拿了好多菜过来，解了我燃眉之急。打开手机微信，小区群里很多人回应了我之前上传的生活物资需求，收到了很多人的回复，看着一条条信息，恍如一道道暖流

On one early morning of April, 2022, I was waken up by the sounds of ambulances. I hurriedly got up, opened my window and saw an ambulance parked in the center of my community. Then noises of crying and arguing came—the ambulance had been here for two days in a row. I sighed and opened my fridge, only to find that there were just a few eggs and tomatoes left. I couldn't help sighing again. Seeing my son pulling his long hair with boredom, I almost lost control of my temper and almost cursed about the situation. Where had the busy streets and fancy lights gone? Shanghai is struggling, with the help from the other areas in China.

A knock on the door pulled me back from my thoughts. It was aunt Wang, my neighbor, who came to borrow some medicine because there's a patient in her house. In return, she brought me a lot of vegetables, knowing that my food was

趟过心间。手机铃声突然响起,原来是隔壁李叔叔让我儿子去他家里理发,儿子很快带上李叔叔爱抽的香烟兴高采烈地跑了过去。下午居委会通知领取抗疫保障物资,我们所有业主的集体诉求终有成果。疫情打乱了往日正常的生活,也让处于封控管理下的我们对未来感到深深忧虑和无力。但是也正是因为危机,人们不再像以前一样把自己封闭在各家各户中,而是以小区为单位组成了一个个大的家庭,团结的力量也让我们对最终战胜疫情充满信心。

由于工作性质关系,在国企和私企混迹了10多年的我常年孤身在外,单枪匹马,年轻时尚能勉强支撑。近年来渐觉吃力,体力精力专注度下降,学习能力亦在下滑,再加上正逢国内制造业升级或转移,紧迫感和危机感加剧。在2021年年中,我在即将迈入不惑之际义无反顾地加入了施璐德。

一直以来在和施璐德的接触中感受

about to run out. I had posted several messages online asking for help, and when I checked my phone, I saw that many people responded to me. Those messages made me feel so warm and so much better. Then my phone rang suddenly. It was another neighbor, uncle Lee. He offered to cut my son's hair. Then my son ran out of the door happily, with uncle Lee's favorite cigarette. In the afternoon, the Neighborhood Committee called me, asking me to get the anti-pandemic materials, at our repeated requests. The pandemic has made our life messy, and the people who are in quarantine start to worry about their future. They feel hopeless and helpless. But this time, instead of locking ourselves at home, we reached out and communicated with our neighbors, making the community a big family. Thus, we started to feel confident that the disease will finally be defeated.

I had traveled a lot for business during the ten years when I worked in state-owned companies and private companies. I did everything independently and always fought alone. But in recent years, I have started to feel tired, and I have become less energetic and less concentrated. My learning ability declined, too. What's worse, the manufacturing industry has been going through changes and updates, making me anxious and nervous. In the middle of 2021, when I just stepped into my forties, I joined CNOOD.

I have always felt the young passion

它的年轻激情富有创造力，客户至上的服务意识和合作共赢的做事理念，更重要的是施璐德团队合作之美一直深深地吸引着我。在进入施璐德后参与的首个项目摩洛哥栈桥中，亲身感受到这种团队之美。摩洛哥栈桥项目由于设计频繁修改，质量要求极高，工期紧张，场地、设备、人员不足加大施工难度，工厂也由于亏损严重濒临放弃，整个项目处于风雨飘摇。当我了解到项目情况后，内心也已严重动摇，抱着尽人事听天命的态度加入到项目团队中。然而正是在这种压力之下，年轻精英们的才华和激情在充满施璐德元素的团队中尽情释放，他们有的深入到工厂基层，和底层工人们努力克服一个又一个施工难题；有的积极和客户沟通，尽力满足客户要求的同时也努力争取到施工的最有利条件；有的积极组织各方群策群力地解决技术和质量问题；还有的积极帮助工厂联系场地设备和人员等。个人才华得以最大程度施展的同时而个人缺点则完全被团队补足。这种团队之美不仅感染了我，还感染了工厂、监理和业主。一时间我能感觉到所有人都在支持着我们前进。项目局势得以彻底扭转并顺利结束后，所有参与的人都直呼奇迹。10 个多月 2 万多吨桥梁钢结构，这个近乎不可能完成的任务，再次成为施璐德团队协作成功的磨刀石。

and creativity, as well as concepts of customer-oriented service and win-win cooperation of CNOOD during my contacts with the company. More importantly, I have been deeply attracted by the beauty of its team cooperation. In the project of Morocco, which was my first project after entering CNOOD, I personally felt the beauty of this team. The Morocco project was subject to frequent design modifications, high quality requirements, tight construction period, and insufficient site, equipment and personnel, which made it more difficult to construct. The factory was also on the verge of abandonment due to serious losses. The whole project was in a precarious situation. When I learned about the project, I was shocked. I joined the project team with the attitude of doing my best. However, under this pressure, the talent and passion of the young elites were fully released. Some of them went deep into the grassroots level of the factory and worked hard with the frontline workers to solve one construction problem after another. Some actively communicated with customers, tried their best to meet customer requirements and strove for the most favorable conditions for construction. Some actively organized all parties to work together to solve technical and quality problems. Others actively helped the factory to get access to site equipment and personnel, etc. While individual talents could be displayed to the greatest

当前国际冲突不断、供应链危机、大国走向全面对抗；国内疫情防控形势严峻、经济下行、通货膨胀；企业经营困难、失业率上升等。可以说时局艰难，形势严峻！然而危机和机遇并存，我坚信施璐德在坚持客户至上，合作共赢，以及刻在施璐德基因中的团队协作，必将逆势而上，砥砺前行，创造属于自己的奇迹！正是沧海横流，方显英雄本色；青山矗立，不坠凌云之志。

extent, individual shortcomings were completely complemented by the team. The beauty of the team inspired not only me, but also the factory, the supervisor and the owner. For a moment, I could feel that everyone was supporting us. After the situation was completely reversed and the project successfully completed, all participants were overjoyed. The nearly impossible task of erecting a bridge steel structure of nearly 20,000 tons in a bit more than 10 months once again became a test for the success of CNOOD team cooperation.

At present, international conflicts continue, supply chain crisis occurs, and major countries on the edge of comprehensive confrontation. Domestic epidemic prevention and control is strict, the economy is going down, and inflation starts. Business difficulties and the unemployment rate are rising, etc. The current situation is really difficult! However, crisis and opportunity coexist. I firmly believe that CNOOD will go against the hardships, forge ahead and create miracles by insisting on the customer-first approach, win-win cooperation and teamwork that are engraved in CNOOD's gene! It is the tough times that show the true nature of a hero. Great men shall always stand high with great ambitions.

杨 亮
Henry Yang

出生于湖北荆州，2003年毕业于武汉理工大学焊接工艺与设备专业，先后供职于上海电气集团旗下上海锅炉厂和莱茵技术（上海）有限公司。拥有10多年项目技术、质量管理和现场检验经验，2021年加入施璐德亚洲有限公司。

Born in Jingzhou City, Hubei province. I graduated from Wielding Procedure Design Department of Wuhan university of technology. I used to work in Shanghai Boiler Factory under Shanghai Electric Group, and TUV Rheinland Shanghai. I have ten years of project technology, quality control and on-site inspection experience. I joined CNOOD in 2021.

疫情下的我们

Our Life Under the Pandemic

■ Heather Zhang

来势汹汹的奥密克戎，让我们的国际大都市上海按下了暂停键。虽然我不是上海人，从在上海求学，到毕业后参加工作，在上海已经十几年了，上海就像是我的第二家乡。我想以我对上海的认识，小小的奥密克戎病毒肯定是折腾不了多久的。在3月中旬，公司就出了通知，建议大家居家办公。只是没想到，以为暂时的居家办公竟持续了2个多月，何时回归正常还不知道，只知道目前上海的形势越来越好，应该也快了。

魔幻的4月

从疫情开始那天起，有人被关在了家里，也有人穿起"铠甲"，筑起"长城"，坚持工作岗位，无论他们多么疲惫，面临多大的危险，都日夜坚守在自己的岗位，用自己的力量守护这座城市。3月26日，老公回到工作岗位，支持学校一线的抗疫

Omicron hit Shanghai so suddenly and fiercely that it put Shanghai in a "pause" status. I am not a native Shanghai citizen, but I have been studying, working and living in Shanghai for over ten years. It's like a second hometown to me. Shanghai is so invincible that, in my mind, Omicron won't last long. In the middle of March, our company suggested that we work from home. Who could have ever thought that it lasted for more than two months! We had no idea when it will be ended, but we know the situation was getting more and more optimistic. Good days should be coming soon.

The magic April

Since the start of the pandemic, some people had to stay at home because of the quarantine policy, but some other people needed to put on their "armors" and returned to their positions, because they needed to build a new "*great wall*" to

工作，4月1日开始上海封控，老公的单位一直是封闭式管理，到5月底已经2个月了。疫情下，平凡的我们，也许做着看似简单的工作，却有不凡的意义。

封控第一周，我每天元气满满，早上起来排队做核酸，一日三餐，处理工作事宜，一天天地倒也过得很充实有趣。渐渐地，封控前囤的物资也快吃完了，又紧张地投入到抢菜中，时时刻刻关注着手机消息，我在想：我一个人的口粮都这么难买，那些一家四五口人的该怎么办呢？到了4月中旬，小区衍生出"团长"角色，组织居民购买必要物资。我要感谢小区里无私奉献的志愿者们，让我们在慌乱的4月份还能有绿叶菜、水果吃，甚至有小区居民自嘲：好像吃得比平时好（大概是平时都没有时间好好地做一顿饭）。

protect the people they love. No matter how exhausted they were and no matter how big the danger they had to face, they remained where they should be and guarded this city with their power. On March 26, one of my family members returned to his position to support the schools with quarantine work. From April 1st, Shanghai started lockdown. My family member was trapped in his position, too, and it has been 2 months already. We are just ordinary people, but the things we do for each other and for the people in Shanghai make our work meaningful.

During my first week of quarantine, I woke up early everyday, energetic. I went to do the nucleic acid test first, then I prepared meals. After that, I started to work. My days were content and meaningful. Gradually, the food that I had stored ran out, so I started to use all kinds of apps to buy vegetables online. I had to stare at my phone all the time. I couldn't help thinking: How could a family have enough to eat when it was already difficult for me to buy vegetables? In the middle of April, a leader was selected from our community to make arrangements for residents to buy life necessities. I am very grateful for those volunteers who helped us selflessly, so that we could have green-leaf vegetables and fruits to eat in April. Some even joked that they ate so much better than before (they never had the time to cook a good meal before).

疫情下的我们

小小的病毒对我们的生活影响是巨大的，似乎整个上海在一瞬间失去了往日的活力和繁华。小孩子不能去学校上课，上班族不能正常到岗位上班，老年人突然不能出门遛弯儿了，身体不舒服的人也不能外出就医。但反过来想，小小的病毒对我们普通人的影响又是很小的，如果我们整天盯着手机屏幕，被网上各种负面消息淹没，让自己陷入在谣言、恐惧中，那日子大概过不下去了吧。我在想，当我们改变不了世界、改变不了别人的时候，我们可以从自己做起，把自己做好，世界才会更美好。

有人说，你怎么过好每一天，决定了你未来的样子；你成为什么样的人取决于你怎么度过你的人生。当我们每天醒来，不用急急忙忙去赶地铁通勤的时候，是不是可以更有效地利用这个时间呢？这个时代是一个需要终身学习的时代，停止学习就很容易被淘汰，因此我们需要持续地自我充电，学习语言，多读书，多思考；当我们足不出户，是不是每天多了很多时间跟家人相处？我们可以在家中设立特定的工作区域，工作时间避免家人打扰，高效完成工作之后多陪伴家人；当我们工作的节奏没有那么快的时候，我们是不是可以分出一部分时间来研究厨艺、开发新的兴趣爱好，与自己和解，向内生长，做好自己的修行；当我们居家太久，那我们更要通过自己的一些爱好来调节情绪，丰富自己的居家生活，毕竟人就像弹簧一样，持

How do we live under the pandemic

The virus has affected our life greatly. Shanghai lost its energy and prosperity overnight. Kids could not go to school, we could not go to work, the elderly could not go for a walk, and even the patients could not go to hospitals. But if we think from the other side, we'll find that the virus actually had a minor effect on us. If we keep staring at the phone and reading all kinds of depressing news, burying ourselves in rumors and fears, how can we live normally? In my opinion, when we can't change the world, we can still change ourselves. When we can't change others, we can at least change our mindset. Be a better person, and the world will be so much better.

People always say that how you live each day determines your future and that what you become depends on how you spend your life. When we no longer have to rush to catch the subway commute, can we use this time more effectively? This is an era that requires us to learn all life. We will fall behind if we stop learning. Therefore, we need to continuously recharge ourselves, learn languages, read more and think more. When we stay at home, do we spend more time with our family every day? We can set up a specific work area at home, avoid family interruptions during working hours, and spend more time with family after efficient work. When we have enough free time, can we spare some time to study

续紧绷就会失去弹力。

适应变化也是一种很重要能力，一定要积极应对，不要太轻易放松自己。疫情终将消散，一起加油，共赴春暖花开！

cooking, develop new interests, reconcile with ourselves, grow inward and improve ourselves? When we stay at home for too long, we need to adjust our emotions through some of our hobbies to enrich our home life. After all, people are like springs. If we keep tightening, we will lose our elasticity.

Adapting to changes is also a very important ability. We must actively respond to changes and not relax ourselves too much. The pandemic will eventually disappear. Let's enjoy cherry blossoms in spring!

张霄燕
Heather Zhang

中共党员，硕士毕业于上海对外经贸大学，于2014年4月加入施璐德大家庭。在施璐德的每一天都是最美好的时光，在这里一切都有可能发生，创造开心，创造奇迹。

A communist, graduated from Shanghai University of International Business and Economics with a master's degree and joined the CNOOD family in April, 2014. She enjoys her everyday here, because it's a place where miracles happen.

光阴与期望

Fading Time and Our Expectations

■ Peipei Yao

从 2013 年 3 月进入施璐德，已满九年，从 2022 年 4 月正式迈入第十个年头。十年，小婴儿可以从刚出生到小学，青少年从青春期到步入社会，刚毕业的大学生从青涩到获得满满社会经验。

十年来感觉成长很多，但感觉还是原来的自己。之前的自己不懂得人情世故，心理脆弱，现在学会宽容，不再斤斤计较。以前到一个陌生的环境会封闭自我，现在不再对新事物或陌生人战战兢兢，并勇于尝试新的东西。以前看待问题直接盲目地为事情定性，便不再更改结论，现在已学会从多方面考虑问题，慢慢了解到每个人的不易，立场不同，所看待的角度不同，结论自然不同。

It has been nine years since I became a member of CNOOD, and it will be ten years in April of 2022. In ten years, little infants could grow into a primary school student, a teenager could leave school and steps into society, and a newly graduated college student could become sophisticated in business.

I have gown a lot during the ten years, but I still stay true to myself. I was not sophisticated at all, not knowing how to handle relationships, and I was very fragile inside. But now I've learned to understand others and stay calm in face of problems. I used to protect myself from any new environment, but now I am willing to try new things. I used to jump to conclusions, but now I've learned to looked at things from different perspectives. I can now understand everyone's hardship and the position where he stands. A different angle can always lead to a different perspective.

不过同时发现，自己慢慢变得现实了，行动上可能更以利益为主。这也是社会上的"通病"。最近看了一篇文章，文中这样写道："我们身处的这个被称为后现代的时代，是一个碎片化的时代。每个人都被各种利益裹胁，人们精于计算，却没有时间反省自身。现代社会的工具理性达到了炉火纯青的地步，为了各种利益的达成，人们锱铢必较，价值理性却空前缺失。""现代人眼前的各种利益，就是海德格尔所说的遮蔽。人们在这样的遮蔽中，就像身处一座生活的迷宫。人们被这些利益遮蔽，人要走出这样的迷宫，只有建立一种思维的模式，就是不再算计眼前的利益，而是退回自我之中，回到自身的'是'之中。""在新的秩序下，人不管在怎样的环境中，都清楚晓得自己该做什么，什么是对的。这就是一种充满层次感，充满自足感，不被环境束缚的澄明之境。"对此深有感触，人易受环境影响，方向容易走偏，在此过程中，应坚持优良的品质。不要过多考虑偏利益的结果，应享受过程，享受过程中学到的事情和得到的感悟。

Gradually, I find myself more realistic. I might act more based on interests. This is a common side of the society. I read an article lately, "We are in a post-modern era, which is a fragmented era. Everyone is coerced by various interests. People are skilled in calculation, but have no time to reflect on themselves. The instrumental rationality of modern society has reached the level of perfection. In order to achieve various interests, people must compare with each other, but the value rationality is unprecedented." "The various interests in front of modern people are the shelters mentioned by Heidegger. People in such shelters are like being in mazes of life. People are covered by these interests. To get out of this maze, people can only establish a mode of thinking; that is, they no longer calculate the immediate interests, but return to themselves and their beings." "Under the new order, no matter what the environment is like, people clearly know what they should do and what is right.

在施璐德学到的东西远远不尽于此。

This is a clear stage with different layers and a sense of self-sufficiency which is not bound by the environment." I feel deeply impressed. People are easily affected by the environment and tend to deviate. In this process, we should adhere to good quality. Don't think too much about the results regarding partial interests. Instead, enjoy the process and the things learned and the insights gained.

I have learned so much more in CNOOD.

姚佩佩 / Peipei Yao

希望是种子，不知不觉长成参天大树。2013 年入职施璐德，学习成长，学习做人。

Hope is a seed which will grow into a big tree. I joined CNOOD in 2013. I am learning to grow and learning to be a better person.

志趣之路
My Way of Finding My Interest

■ Sherry Lee

大部分功成名就的人在年幼的时候已知晓自己的志趣，成年以后更加孜孜不倦地通过学习来实现自己的理想。"我的志趣是什么？"大学伊始，我开始思索这样的一个问题。我在一个坐落于山脚的学校学习化学，它远离大城市的繁华与热闹，生活只是按部就班地学习课程。学校唯有座大图书馆，排解这城市的荒凉与我内心的寂寞。同时正值播客萌芽，常常听听一些专业的自媒体人评论身边大小事，这时候我才觉得似乎自己也和他们一样身处热闹的世界。此时的我，立足于传统的通识教育，漫游于浩瀚的知识海洋，也接受一些新潮的思想，还是无法回答这个问题。

Most of the successful and famous people knew where their interests lied when they were little, and they pursue their dreams in their adult years by working and studying hard. "What are my interests?" I started to ask myself this question when I stepped into university. My university was by the foot of a mountain, where I studied and majored in chemistry. Being far away from downtown, what I could do was studying. There was a big library in the school and it became a sacred place where I could kill time and drive away the loneliness in my heart. Podcast was just emerging, and I could always hear professional We Media give remarks on things around them. Then I started to realize that I was actually in the same wonderful world with them. I was then receiving traditional education. Even though I was open to new ideas, I still could not answer that question.

在这样一个节奏缓慢的内地城市的生活让我思考，或许我缺少足够的见识和阅历去认识自己。仔细思考之下，上海是我的不二选择。怀着这样一种理念：继续提升我的专业能力，上海拥有的地域／资源优势，可以开拓我的远见。就这样，我去上海大学读研究生。那时我以为的志趣是一种对事物的强烈驱动力，可以克服一切的困难。我希望拥有这样的一种神秘的力量，能让我有所作为。

上海的读书生活没有我想象中那么精彩，与在小城市的状态并无两样。我想获得优秀的成果，这并不简单。我尽可能地付出时间和努力，结果事与愿违。当时认为我缺乏与志趣相匹配的坚韧与决心，而努力也并未落在志趣上。只得苦涩地回味"志趣"二字，我心想如果拥有明确的目标和正确的方法，还有适宜的帮助，加上努力便能事半功倍。有段时间，我徘徊于继续进修和工作两者之间，不知如何选择。高等教育中大量的学术学习和"浅尝辄止"的实习，教育与职业之间其实是割裂的关系。我站在象牙塔里面，甚至无法回答一些基本的职业问题：企业在做什么？他们需要什么样的人？我可以处于何种位置？哪些是立足于未来世界的职业素养？教科书与畅销书也无法代替我回答这个问题。回到志趣上来，或许能从工作中发现我的乐趣，是适合我能力发展的方向。基于此，我放弃了继续深造，投入工

Living in such a slow-paced inland city, I couldn't help thinking that maybe I do not have enough knowledge and experience to define who I really am. After thorough thinking, I decided that Shanghai would be my only and best choice. I had this goal in my heart: Shanghai has enough space and opportunities for me to improve my skills and broaden my mind. Therefore, I came to Shanghai to study for a master's degree. At that time, I was so innocent that I thought interest was about having a strong desire of doing something and that I could overcome any difficulties if I am interested. I hoped I could have a super power like this, so that I could make a difference one day.

Time only proved me wrong. The school life in Shanghai was not as wonderful as I thought. It was even no different from that of the small city. It's not easy to have great achievements. I tried my best to devote myself to it but the result was too frustrating. I knew I lacked the corresponding persistence and perseverance, and I was in the wrong direction. With interest, I assumed I could finally succeed if I had had a clear target, the right direction and good help. For some time, I was hesitating between further education and starting a career. It was hard to choose. The vast amount of learning and studying in higher education and limited internship have only led to a big gap between education and career. Standing in the ivory tower, I couldn't even answer the simplest questions: What are

作之中。

　　来CNOOD工作是一种偶然也是一种必然，因为这里有一群志同道合的伙伴。我对新鲜的事物抱有极强的好奇心，加上理科背景拥有的逻辑思维和分析能力，让我获得了这个工作的机会。而CNOOD就是由这样热血，接受新鲜事物，不受限定自我的一群人组成。非常幸运加入Fay的小组，Fay让我加入一个体量很大的项目组工作，系统地学习国际工程贸易。我成为Belinda的文控助理。这个项目的文件量很大，刚开始的时候，我犯了无数次错误。Belinda非常有耐心，她帮助我改正了很多的错误。工作中有一种说法，你不能在一件事情上犯两次错误。我以前不细心的坏习惯体现得尤其明显，心中着实羞愧，才逐渐养成了自查的习惯。随着熟练程度加深，我渐渐地真正分担起她的工作。以前在《富兰克林自传》里面读到类似的例子，他要求他的秘书记录下来他犯的愚蠢的错误，并一条条挑出加以改正。我有机会可以做这个训练，很可惜的是那时候没有执行。尽管如此，勤能补拙是良训，我也在工作中表现越来越好。除此之外，我喜欢思考，希望做一些创新改变现在的某一些工作模式，但是最后大部分都没有实现。现在想来，创新是奠定在丰富

companies doing? What kind of staff do they need? What position am I qualified in? What are the qualities needed in the future world? Neither textbooks nor best-sellers could answer my questions. Now we are back to the original topic-interest. I believe I could find my interest in work, and then I can find the best direction for myself. Based on this thinking, I gave up the chance for further education and got myself a job.

　　My coming to CNOOD was not incidental but inevitable, because I was deeply attracted to the colleagues here who held the same faith with me. I am extremely curious about new things, and I have strong logic thinking and analyzing ability due to my science background. That's how I got this job. Fortunately, I was accepted by this team which is made of passionate and enthusiastic people who never set boundaries for themselves. I was lucky enough to join the CEO-Fay's team. Fay assigned my to a big project with a lot of work to do, so that I could learn international engineering trade systematically. I became the assistant of Belinda, and she was very patient. She helped correct many mistakes that I made. People always say that you can't make the same mistake twice in business, but I kept making mistakes due to my carelessness and casual habits. I felt shameful so I started to examine myself regularly. My skills improved, and I got more and more sophisticated so I started to share her burden. I read a story before:

的知识和阅历的基础上的，它绝不是莽夫的跃跃欲试。在CNOOD，我度过了非常美好的近两年时光，从钢结构到喂食船，从办公室走到扬中的船厂，我觉得我的人生鲜明而丰富。在CNOOD也有遗憾的事情，这个事情也影响了我去留的决定。随着业务能力的熟练，Fay开始培训我独立进行项目现场管理。这是一个很小的订单，但心理上我莫名感到巨大的困难，心中胆怯不知道如何开始。随后这个项目，被其他同事接走。

直到现在我还能清晰地回想当初的细节，以及面对这个订单的时候内心的困境。刚开始同事Chris给我一张操作指南，让我阅读后根据实际找他讨论。里面的细则对当时的我来说太过于抽象，我无法准确理解。几天后，他问我你有什么不懂，我回答不知道。这个工作在我这里没有任何动静，因为我什么都不懂，甚至不懂得如何描述我的不懂。学会提问，不是一件简单的事情。从文件到实操中间有巨大的间隙，如果要跳过去，这需要极多的工作经验。可以转换为这样的问题，当我

Franklin asked his secretary to record the mistakes that he made and correct them one by one. I had the chance, and I could do it. Diligence redeems stupidity—it's so true. I could do better and better. I think a lot. I always come home with new ways to change the current work mode, but I did not put them into practice. After examining myself, I understood that creativity is based on rich knowledge and experience, and I was too hasty and naive. My two years at CNOOD was wonderful. From steel structure to feeding boat, from office to the boat factory, my life was full of exciting and meaningful moments. There's something I still regret today, and it's actually the reason why I decide to leave. As I got more and more sophisticated, Fay started to let me handle project site management independently. It was not a big project but I suffered huge pressure mentally. I was so afraid that I did not know where to start. Consequently, this project was taken over by other colleagues.

I could still remember the details till today and how trapped I felt when I faced the project. My colleague Chris gave me a sheet of guidance, telling me that I could discuss it with him after reading it. The details of the guidance was too abstract for me at that time, and I could not fully understand it. When he asked me several days later if I had any difficulty understanding it, I couldn't believe my answer was *I don't know*. I did not start this project at all because I knew nothing, and

还未曾拥有工作必备的素质，该如何去获取？只能眼睁睁看着机会溜走？当时我真的能从文控过渡到项目经理吗？这些疑问一直悬在心头，我一遍遍思索这个问题，一直找不到满意的答案。直到我离开CNOOD我也没有能回答：如何接洽从0到1转变？

现在的我会如何应对同一个问题？我会告诉他：直接教我如何操作每一步。而我真正要学的是：他是如何完成工作的，这个过程他又是如何思考的？每个员工分享自己最专业的东西，最简单最高效的方式让团队拥有了最强的凝聚力和竞争力。公司发展十年，我们应该站在前人的肩膀上进行思考、开拓、创新。仔细想想，这也是Dennis创办公司的理念。但是我还未注意到是同事之间思维方式的差异，这妨碍了我们之间的有效沟通。举同一个例子，讨论我和Chris之间工作风格的差异，可以归结于一个老问题：是鸡生蛋还是蛋生鸡？对于Chris来说，是蛋生鸡，可以先思考清楚了工作流程，然后便能完成工作。而对我来说，恰恰相反，我习惯先有鸡然后生蛋的方式，我能先完成工作，然后从执行过程中领悟其要义，达到熟悉业务的目的。工作风格的差异不影响结果，如果只是领进门的学问，思考在前或者思考在后都不影响结果。

it's pathetic that I didn't even know how to describe my problems! It's not that easy to raise questions. There's a big gap between documents and practice, and I still need to accumulate more experience if I want to leap over the gap. I should ask myself this question: How can I acquire the skills needed? Am I just going to let chances slip away? Could I really have become a project manager from an assistant if I had done the project well? I kept asking myself these questions but I still couldn't find the answers. I couldn't figure out these questions even when I left CNOOD: How to realize the transformation from 0 to 1?

How would I handle the same project now if I were given the chance again? I would ask Chris to teach me how to start directly. What I really need to learn include: How did he do it and in what way, with what mindset? By sharing the most professional skills of each employee, our team has acquired a strong cohesive force and competence, in the simplest but most efficient way. It has been ten years and we should think, improve and innovate by standing on the shoulders of our seniors. This is something that Dennis stuck to when he built this company. However, the differences in ways of thinking lead to the failure of effective communication, which I never realized then. For example, the differences between Chris and I could be concluded as: Egg first or chicken first? For Chris, it is egg first—make smooth the work process before starting to work.

当时的我认为这个机会白白流失是因为：一方面我没有独当一面的能力。面对前所未有的挑战，我依赖别人的帮助来完成工作。另一方面我也没有主动寻求帮助。重要的是我不知道如何请求帮助。现在回想起来，主动寻求帮助也是一种能力。这个可以说是打破自己的认知，重新认识自己，并勇敢面对困难的能力。而那个时候的我面对一个的难题，充斥着无能为力的挫败感。我对自己不敢作为惶恐不安，这个时候我发现，我无法打破我自身知识的局限，直面困难勇往直前。其次，我进行深度思考的时间不多。尽管我当时承担不少的工作，不断在接触学习新的知识，但这些都属于我原本拥有的坚持、好奇心、学习等品质的一种持续。从打破自己熟悉的领域，挑战困难，拥有决心、勇气、毅力、方法等方面仍旧非常的薄弱，从能力的角度来评价，我并没有进步。

我突然懂得大学时候认知的"志趣"实则是一种投机的本能，幻想着现实生活中挑战自己的痛苦消失。志趣分为：志向与兴趣。志向是一种理想。兴趣从心理学

But for me, it is chicken first—I tend to summarize after I finish the work, to further get to know the business. So much being said, different working styles won't affect the results. When it comes to fundamental work, it doesn't matter if you think first or do first.

I let the opportunity slip away sadly because I was not mature enough to do it independently. Facing a challenge that I had never had before, I was counting on others to help me. Furthermore, I did not ask for help. I was trapped where I was and did not even know how to ask for help. Now I know that asking for helping is also an ability. This incident taught me to break away from the old person who I was and know myself again, so that I can have the ability to face difficulties with courage. I was defeated by the obstacles in front of me, and I felt so frustrated and disappointed at myself. I was anxious and upset about not doing anything. I was still unable to step out of the limitations and face difficulties bravely. Aditionally, I did not spend much time thinking. I was occupied by too much work and eager to learn new things out of curiosity—I am used to learning all the time. I failed to break away from the old environment, face the challenges and guard myself with faith, courage, persistence and methods. I did not make any progress in improving my ability.

All of a sudden, I seemed to understand what "interest" means. It is actually the instinct of speculation, fantasizing that all the pains in life could disappear. Interest, in my

角度讲：是探索某种事物的一种心里倾向。现在看来，大学伊始，便孕育了我的兴趣——学习。只有不断地学习，探索并超越，让我的身体和精神获得无与伦比的快乐。工作一年多后，我变得很忐忑，担心自己停滞不前。那时候我希望年轻的时候，要积累尽可能多的知识和阅历，才能让自己将来游刃有余地面对困难。

在人生的每个分岔路口，尤其是青年时期，做的每一个决定，可能会影响人生的走向。读博有如在迷雾中寻找知识的出路，从而扩大自己的认知并形成科学工作方式，能沉着地面对困难与机遇。我仔细考量博士的学习与训练，吻合我目前的需求。幸运的是，我获得了深造的机会。我很感激 CNOOD 对我继续深造的理解与支持，它就像是家人一样。

现在，我与 CNOOD 告别，继续了我的求学之路，遇见更优秀的自己！

opinion, includes aspiration and amusement. Aspiration is an ambition, while amusement is the urge to explore something that you are curious about. Studying in university gives me great pleasure, and I am greatly amused. I can gain great satisfaction and happiness from studying. Even one year after working, I was still anxious, worrying that I might fall behind. I hoped to accumulate as much knowledge and experience as possible while I was young, so that I could be strong enough to face the difficulties.

Standing at the crossroads of life, every choice I make might affect my life, especially when I am young. Studying for a doctor's degree is like looking for a way out in a mist. I can extend my knowledge, form a scientific way of working and stay calm in the face of challenges. I think the studying and training course of a Ph.D. meets my demands at the moment, and luckily I got a chance for a further education. I am very grateful for the understanding ans support that CNOOD has given me when I made the decision. CNOOD is like a family to me.

Now I have to say goodbye to CNOOD and continue to study and become a better person!

李贞英
Sherry Lee

爱工作，爱读书，爱运动的超能量女孩。CNOOD 工作两年。现索邦大学物化专业博士二年级。

I love working and reading. I have super passion and energy for sports. I have been working at CNOOD for 2 years and now I am in my second year of Ph.D. of physicochemical specialty in Sorbonne Université.

随 笔

Random Thoughts

■ Tina Xu

一

不知何时，坚定的唯物主义的我变得不那么坚定了，又开始了新的思考。

恰逢复旦哲学课堂，课间休息期间的学院短片里看到王老师的寥寥数语的采访，"当下人可悲之处，把功利作为人生目标，何处安身立命"，醍醐灌顶。

开始寻找王老师的讲课内容，每一节课似乎都给混沌中的我，更多的坚定，更多向内寻找答案的方向。

三年后，终于有幸在退休后的王老师的课堂聆听他讲课。惊喜于老师除了对马克思主义哲学，对国学经典的研究造诣，对艺术哲学同样有着同样深刻的研究，对艺术于人生及创造力的意义给出了他的解读。

I

Not knowing when, as a firm-willed Marxism believer, I started to have new ideas.

It was on the philosophy class of Fudan University. During a short break, I saw the interview of Mr. Wang in a short video: "It is pathetic that people now take material wealth and honor as their life targets, but where does the true meaning of life lie?" I was deeply impressed.

I started to listen to Mr. Wang's classes online, and every class seemed to have led a bright way for me and made me believe that I should look for the answers from the inside.

Three years later, I finally had a chance to attend Mr. Wang's class in person after he retired. I admired the great insights that he had on Marxism philosophy and Chinese classics, and I was overjoyed that he also had an in-

近距离的交流，老师睿智、平和，而又富有洞察力，会让人不自觉得平静下来，沉静其中，这是一种思想碰撞的美好。我自觉老师的课也是艺术的创造，我在其中感受到了观照。"人生最有价值的是生命的淳朴和灵魂的高贵"，课间老师给我此赠言的时候，热泪盈眶。

还未有机缘听过王老师的马克思主义哲学的讲课，对老师国学经典及艺术哲学做以下摘录，用以自省。

1. 安心立命

人心的无限与人的存在现实的有限之间存在的矛盾，解决这种冲突需要超越性的方法。老师从儒释道分别给出总结，我一直认为最自洽的人生状态（以出世的精神，做入世的事情），在老师的课里也找到了更深刻的理解。

儒家的"无所为而为"，行动本身就是目的，行为本身就是发自于内心的情感体现。并不把当下所做的事情当作达到另外一个目的手段和途径，我们之所以做这件事，是因为它本应当做。所以它自己就是自己的价值，自己就是自己的目的。所以这样的人生并没有失败，在求仁的过程中，内心情感与外在行动的一致，浑然忘

depth understanding of art. He had a unique perspective of view for art, life and creativity.

Communicating with Mr. Wang face to face, I was calmed down by his wisdom, gentleness and his observing ability. I was absorbed into his thoughts and enjoyed the beautiful feeling. I think Mr. Wang's classes are art creations, and I could see the reflections of my life in it. "The most valuable thing for a human is the pureness of life and nobleness of soul," when he said this to me, I was moved to tears.

I did not have a chance to attend Mr. Wang's class on Marxism philosophy, but I took down the following note of the Chinese classics and art class for myself to abide by.

1. Settle down with an easy mind

The infinity of human heart and the limitation of reality creates a contradictory, and to deal with it, we need surmounting methods. Mr. Wang gave conclusions from Confucianism, Buddhism and Taoism respectively. I think the easiest state of life is to do practical things with a relaxing spirit, and I gained a deep understanding of it from his class.

"Acting following natural law" of Confucianism emphasizes action, and action itself is a reflection of inner feelings, without expecting anything in return. The reason we do it is that this thing have to be done. Therefore, the thing itself has its own value and becomes its own purpose. There's no such thing

我，这是儒者如何在现实中安顿自己的内心。

道家的"无为而无不为"，道即宇宙的本源和万物运行的规律，遵从道的规律，天下才能得以太平，人生才能圆满。无为不是指不做事，而是指不人为地做事。所以道家教我们做减法，减去人为的因素，减得越干净越好。"为道自损，损之又损，以至于无为。"道家论道，可是道无可言说，所以只有给人为做减法，减得彻底了，天道就看见了，顺应而为，即无不为。此为道家安顿的内心。

老师说从道家著作开始学什么呢，就是他们教我们怎么做减法的方法。要带着这样的理解去读《道德经》，去读《庄子》。这是道家的入门，后面的事情就要交给大家自己了。

佛家的"无心而为"我们带着业力而来，做事就是为了消业。做事最好没有结果，但是做事一定有结果，那么结果最好

as failure in this kind of life. While pursuing benevolence, the inner value is in accordance with the actions, and in this process, yourself is totally forgotten. This is how the Confucianism believers settle their hearts in reality.

"Do nothing and everything is done" of Taoism stresses to follow the rules of Tao, that is, the origin and rules of everything. Only in this way can the world be peaceful and the life be meaningful. It doesn't mean that you do nothing. It emphasizes that you should never do things with a purpose. Then Taoism is teaching us to do subtractions. We should discard human interference, the less the better. "The follower of knowledge learns as much as he can every day; The follower of flow forgets as much as he can every day. By attrition he reaches a state of inaction. Wherein he does nothing, but nothing remains undone." Taoism cannot be explained, and it shows people the world by doing subtractions. The heavenly Tao will reveal itself when there's nothing remained. Follow the laws, and nothing is undone. This is how the Taoists settle their hearts.

The teacher told us what to learn from Taoist books—how to do subtractions. With this in mind you will be able to understand *Tao Te Ching* and *Zhuangzi*. I've shown you the way, and I'll leave the rest for you to understand.

"Act unintentionally" of the Buddhism means that we are born guilty and we do things to release ourselves from those

和你没关系,那就不是新业了。认真做事,但是不关心事情的结果,心别上去,除心不除事。因此现实的困境不会对佛者造成困扰,此为佛者的内心安顿。

老师说:"人到四十岁还不知命,只能说此人悟性太差。"

2. 艺术哲学

"我们这个时代有一个错误,因为它是科学主义的时代。我不反对科学,但是我反对科学主义。因为科学主义是对科学的迷信,以为科学可以解决人生的所有的问题。在一个科学主义的时代,我们把真理和逻辑等同了。逻辑是重要的,因为让我们在感性视觉当中所获得的最对真理的洞察和感悟,放入了一个可普遍传达的形式当中,那叫知识。以便它 universally accessible 就普遍可通达,这就是科学所完成的他的伟大工作。但是科学的这么的一段原始发生地是伟大的想象,哲学和感悟,他不在头脑的概念思考里"。

"艺术对人类生活,包括精神活动的方方面面有多么基础的意义,所以今天我主张每一个中国大学的学生,其实在高等教育的领域中有一块一定不能忽视,并且要加强,那就是艺术的修养。这个修养不是理论的,而是实践的。"

guilt. What we do must not be the cause of something, but if something happens because of the things you do, it's better that thing has nothing to do with you, then you are not guilty for something new. Do things with a whole heart, but do not worry about the results. Just do it without thinking too much. Therefore, the dilemma in reality doesn't bother the Buddhists, and this is how they settle their hearts.

Mr. Wang said, "Know your fate when you are in your forties. If you can't, you have a troubled mind."

2. Art philosophy

"There's something wrong with the time we are in, for it's scientism. I do not object to science, but I am anti-scientism. Scientism is the superstition for science, thinking that science can settle any problems in life. In this case, we tend to confuse truth with logic. Logic is important, for it allows us to gain perception by observing what we see. It appears in a form that can be spread, and it's called knowledge. Knowledge is universally accessible, and that's what science can achieve. But science comes from great thinking, philosophy and perception, not just a single mind."

"Art plays an important and fundamental role in human life and spiritual activities. So I appeal to all the college students to cultivate the artistic mind while studying. This cannot be overlooked. We should put the idea into

"我们通过艺术的实践，它包括接受和创作两个方面，它滋养了我们的灵性，保持了我们感觉的灵性，于是我们保持了我们的想象力和创造力。"

二

2019年，砚希出生，老池寄语。

一直觉得这既是他自己的人生准则，亦是对我们的期许。

等砚希长大了，告诉她，曾经有一个自称为爷爷的叔叔，在她出生前，带着她的爸妈去参观曾国藩故居，体会家族，家风的意义，不言之教的意义。

在她出生后，准备了整套的国学经典和美学诗集，再三叮嘱，摇篮中也要给宝宝每天朗诵。

因为遇见这个叔叔，妈妈成长了，叔叔给妈妈打开了一扇窗，指了一个安心立命的方向。

以出世的精神，做入世的事情，他便是最好的榜样。

为人之格局，优雅，自信，担当，感恩，真诚，谦逊，去欲，心外无物。

做事之热情，使命，思维，能力，利他，模式，专业，极致，无问西东。

practice, not just saying it."

"Through art practices, which includes accepting and creating, our spirits are nourished, our inspirations are gained, and our imagination and creativity gets retained."

II

In 2019, my Yanxi was born. Chairman Dennis wrote to her something.

It seems to me not only his life code, but also his expectations for us.

I'll tell Yanxi when she grows up that once there was an uncle who claimed to be her grandfather. He took her parents to visit the former residence of Guofan Zeng, to feel what family, family tradition, and teaching with action means.

This grandpa also sent her a whole set of Chinese classics and poetry, asking me to read them to my baby girl everyday.

After meeting this uncle, I have grown mature. This uncle has opened a window for me and showed me the right direction.

Do practical things with a relaxing spirit—he's the best example.

To be elegant, confident, with a sense of responsibility, thankfulness, sincerity, humbleness, and be desire-free and free of distraction.

Do things with passion, a sense of mission, logical thinking, ability, benevolence, the right pattern, professionalism and perfectionism, without asking anything in return.

有一天，和飞从刘备聊到成事，刘备有梦想，有野心，有格局，有顶层设计，虚怀若谷，求贤若渴，有死心塌地地团队，可是仍不一定成功，屡败屡战。突然有点心酸地问飞，若老池未能实现他心之所愿，又可能会是什么原因呢？飞说不会的，某种意义来说，他已经成功了。

是，老池创造出来的东西，远不在于短期公司收益或者行业价值，而在于长久的理念，文化的价值，还有他带给了大家事上练的平台和机会的价值。如同打开一扇窗，如同带来的是火种和一种坚定信念，星星之火，也是璀璨的，不在于燎原与否。我们都在路上，用心为人做事，这就够了。

One day when I was chatting with Fay about Bei Liu, one of the war lords in wartime. Bei Liu was ambitious, great-minded, and he had the best consultant. He was humble and treated people well. With this strong team, he still failed though. Suddenly, I felt a bit upset. I asked if Chairman Dennis failed, what the reasons would be. Fay said Dennis wouldn't fail. To some extent, he had already succeeded.

She's right. What Dennis has created is more than a company that pursues short-term value or industry value. He created a set of long-term concepts and cultural value, as well as a platform where everyone has a chance to show their abilities. He opened a window for all of us, bringing seeds of a fire and a firm

老池说，我们终将会自己经历我们跟他争论的那些，我想是的。

于我，最重要的事，是您让我有了不管经历如何，依然心中有爱的底气。

谢谢您，Dennis。

三

"妈妈，我们想象小兔子在花园里吃草吧。"

是啊，当春天只能出现在孩子们的想象里时，才发现多怀恋我们那个物质不丰富，却也那般生动自然的童年。

这个春天，经历了太多的离别、悲伤、迷茫。

可也总有还在思考、觉醒、负重、坚持的人。唯有感恩、用心、前行，才不负这当下的时光，也许便是最好的时光。

希望明年的春天，阳光是温暖肆意，抚摸着每个人，鸟语花香是悦耳香甜，被分外珍惜的。

2022 年 4 月，上海。

faith. A single spark can shine, whether it burns the land or not. We are all on the way to doing things well and serving people. I think that'll be enough.

Chairman Dennis said that we would eventually experience the things that we once had argued with him. I think he's right.

To me, the most important thing is, you have given me the ability to love no matter what difficulties I've been through.

Thank you, Dennis.

III

"Mom, Let's imagine that a little rabbit is eating grass in the garden."

Alas! Now spring only appears in kids' imagination. How much we miss the old and happy childhood, Which was never materially rich.

This spring, Has seen too many sadness and sorrows.

But there are still many people thinking, awakening, taking responsibilities and holding on to their faiths. Only with gratefulness can we stride forward without feeling sorry for ourselves. Now might be the best and most relaxing time.

The spring next year I hope, Could be a time when sunshine touches everyone gently, Birds singing joyfully and flowers blooming fiercely, it could be a moment that everyone cherishes.

April, 2022, Shanghai

四

妈妈：砚希，要睡觉了哦，我们把眼睛闭起来吧。要不今天你来哄妈妈睡觉吧？

砚希：我还小，拍不到肩膀。等，等，等我长大了，哄妈妈睡觉。

妈妈：好的。

砚希：妈妈，你长大了吗？

妈妈：妈妈也不知道哦……

砚希：妈妈，那你还会长大吗？

妈妈：嗯，妈妈也会不断长大，和你一样。

砚希：妈妈，帮我做个北极熊，好吗？

妈妈：好的，妈妈研究下哦。

砚希：好。

妈妈：妈妈做好了，好看吗？

砚希：妈妈，这是狗狗吧？哈哈哈……

IV

Mom: Yanxi, time for bed! Let's close our eyes. What about you putting me in bed today?

Yanxi: I am still little and I can't reach your shoulders. When I grow up, I'll tuck you in.

Mom: OK then.

Yanxi: Mom, are you a grown person?

Mom: Mommy doesn't know, either...

Yanxi: Mommy, will you still grow?

Mom: Well, I'll keep growing, just like you.

Yanxi: Mommy, can you help me make a polar bear?

Mom: OK, but first let me think about how.

Yanxi: OK.

Mom: I'm done. How does it look?

Yanxi: Mommy, isn't it a dog? Ha ha ha...

妈妈：这不是北极熊吗？妈妈再研究下……

妈妈：哇，砚希，我们小区开了一个新花店哦。好漂亮的花呀，你看有好多颜色，黄色，紫色，还有粉色，好看吗？

砚希：好看。妈妈，我想去买一枝花。

妈妈：你为什么要买花呀？

砚希：我想送一枝花给我妈妈。

外婆：砚希宝宝，你披着浴巾好像新娘子呢。

Mom: Isn't this a polar bear? Wait, let me check...

Mom: Wow, Yanxi, there's a new flower shop in our community, and the flowers are so beautiful there. Look, they are yellow, purple and pink. They are beautiful, aren't they?

Yanxi: Yes mom! I want to buy a flower.

Mom: Why do you want to buy a flower?

Yanxi: I want to buy a flower for mommy.

Grandma: Darling Yanxi, you look like a bride with your bath towel on.

砚希：哈哈哈哈哈……

外婆：砚希，等你做新娘子的时候外婆就老了，就走不动路了哦……

砚希：婆婆，没关系的。你走不动路，我牵你好不好？

外婆：好……

Yanxi: Ha ha ha ha ha...

Grandma: Yanxi, by the time you become a bride, grandma will be too old to walk...

Yanxi: Grandma, don't worry. I'll take your hands if you can't walk.

Grandma: Good girl...

许秋石
Tina Xu

2014年加入CNOOD，从业15年。
我们一直在路上，不忘初心，自强，厚德。

Joined CNOOD in 2014 and has been in the industry for 15 years.
We are always on the road, and we never forget why we started. We strive to become stronger with great virtue.

施璐德实习感想
Thoughts on My Internship at CNOOD

■ Yu He

首先，特别感谢在施璐德的实习经历，感谢池总和丹妮姐的指点和关心。

初次了解施璐德是通过市场营销这门课程，第一次左老师带领我们去施璐德学习，当时是池总给我们上的这堂课，我课上印象很深的一点就是池总强调的洞察力。让我对洞察力有了更深刻的认识。其间池总给我们细致地介绍了施璐德成功的项目，遍布世界各个地方。再后来参加摩洛哥HAHA区块油气勘探项目营销策划案，有了在施璐德实习的机会。

在施璐德实习的时间不长，跟公司里面的前辈们沟通也不多，但是在我的观察和前辈们的交谈中，能够感受到施璐德独

First of all, I am very grateful for being an intern at CNOOD. I am deeply impressed by Chairman Dennis and Danni, who have given my great care and helpful guidance.

I first got to know CNOOD through my marketing course, when my teacher professor Zuo took us to visit CNOOD. Chairman Dennis was the one who gave the lecture of marketing, and I was impressed by the *insight* that he had stressed. Ever since then, I had a deeper understanding of the word insight. Chairman Dennis made a thorough introduction of the successful projects carried out by CNOOD all over the world. Later I got the chance to make the marketing plan for the Morocco HAHA oil-gas exploration and development project when I became an intern here.

I am fresh here so I haven't many chances to communicate with the seniors in the company, but I could feel its unique

有的公司文化和氛围。我深刻地感受到一种"互相尊重，彼此包容和平等对话"的公司氛围。我们在向公司的前辈请教时，他们会耐心地回答我们的问题。这种氛围是难能可贵的，在我过去工作经历中，很难碰到这种工作氛围。

在实习期间，我们主要接触的还是一些理论方面的知识。这些理论知识奠定了我们认识这个行业的基础。从方法论的角度看，首先我们要去分析市场、需求和渠道，探究项目的可行性。其次是渠道资源的整合，解决怎么做的问题。最后是优化方案的流程和方法，及时反馈交流，防止方向走偏。我们也学到了选择项目时的需要考虑因素，从宏观的地缘政治，经济周期，到微观的资源、技术、结算方式、物流、资金流、成本、单据等因素都有了一定的认识。

实习期间每次和池总的交流中，都会谈到很多话题，同时也会学到很多工作之外的东西。从学习、工作、生活和三观等方面都进行了深入的交流。我们问了很多好奇的问题，池总也耐心地为我们解答。让我印象深刻的有以下几点。首先，我们认识到如何拥有一个好的精神面貌和行为

corporate culture and atmosphere through my observation and my chats with them. Here, everyone is surrounded by the idea of mutual respect, inclusiveness and equality. When I have problems, my seniors would always explain and demonstrate to me patiently. This kind of working atmosphere is very precious, and I have never had this kind of working environment before.

It is mainly the knowledge at the theoretical level that I have learned during my internship here. Such knowledge became the basis on which we got to know this industry. From the perspective of methodology, first of all, we should analyze the market, demand and channels to explore the feasibility of the project. Second, we should analyze the integration of channel resources to know how to do it. The last is to optimize the process and methods of the scheme, facilitate timely feedback and communication and prevent the direction from going wrong. I've also learned the factors needed to be considered when selecting projects, from macro geopolitics and economic cycle to micro resources, technology, settlement methods, logistics, capital flow, cost, documents and other factors.

My conversations with Chairman Dennis involve many topics, enabling me to learn many other things besides work. We often have deep communications, covering many fields like study, work, life and values. Chairman Dennis would always answer our questions patiently

举止的重要性，一个人的气质和形象特别重要。其次，池总教会了我们认识到底层思维和方法的重要性，让我们学会如何高屋建瓴地看待问题。我们学习的东西不仅仅是为了当下的工作，在各行各业乃至生活中同样适用的底层思维和方法才更有意义。思维方式和方法论更倾向"道"这个层面，而具体的业务该如何做更倾向于"术"的层面。

在施璐德的实习期间，学到了过去很多未接触过的领域，也感受到施璐德优秀的公司文化。愿我们都奔赴美好的未来！

no matter how strange our questions are. I was impressed and I learned the following things: First, I learned the importance of having a stable mind, neat appearance and proper behavior, because one's temperament and image matter a lot. Second, Chairman Dennis taught us the importance of bottom-level thinking and methods, enabling us to see things in a more comprehensive angle. It is not only important for the work we are doing now, but also important in all industries and all walks of life. We should think in the *Taoism* way and operate our business on the *skill* level.

During my staying here, I've learned a lot of things in many fields which I have never touched before. I've been growing in the excellent corporate culture of CNOOD. There is a long and bright way ahead, and hope we all have a wonderful future!

何 禹
Yu He

上海对外经贸大学工商管理硕士在读。爱好投资理财，打羽毛球，热爱生活，不断突破自我。

Now studying for MBA in Shanghai University of International Business and Economics. I'm into investment and financing work. I'm fond of playing badminton. I love life, and I love to challenge myself.

施璐德实习总结
Summary of Internship in CNOOD

■ Xinchen Tang

2021年11月很荣幸通过了校企合作的项目获得了到施璐德实习的机会，通过实习，发现这边有着很好的工作环境以及非常和谐与融洽的同事关系。丹妮姐一直很关心着我们几位实习小朋友的日常，非常细心地和我们讲解着关于公司的各项事宜。池总也常在百忙之中抽出很多时间与我们进行深入地沟通和指导。

在进入施璐德实习的期间接触到了摩洛哥 HAHA 区块油气勘探开发项目，也尝试着自己带入到角色之中去经营这个项目，并学会了如何从社会、政治、经济和环境等各个角度去研究和分析一个项目的可行性。此外，我了解到了如何去设计并构建一个项目的实施框架，怎么去最大程度地在项目设计实施的过程之中节约成本。

It was my great honor to be chosen as an intern at CNOOD through the school-enterprise cooperation project in November, 2021. I was deeply impressed by the elegant working environment here and the harmonious atmosphere created by my friendly colleagues. Danni has provided great care for us interns in our daily lives, explaining patiently to us about our work in the company. Chairman Chi has spared a lot of time to communicate with us and give us guidance as well.

I was fortunate to be a part of the Morocco HAHA oil-gas exploration and development project, and I adapted to the role quickly and actively. Through this project, I learned how to study and analyze the feasibility of a certain project from social, political, economic and environmental perspectives. I also learned how to design and build the implementation framework of a project and how to save the costs to the greatest extent

在施璐德学习的这段时间里，给了我莫大的启发。让我更深地体悟到了，做每一件事情都需要沉下心来去对待，我们要舍得花时间、花精力，专注在我们所选择的方向之上，并朝着这个方向不断付出行动。在做事情之前要选好合作的伙伴、核心的方向，并坚持去做，这样我们就有无限的可能去做成无数伟大的事情。

在公司实习的期间，我体会到了，做人想要持续地维持吸引力，最好的做法就是保持真诚。我们在做事情之前要具备洞察力，洞察是政治与商业实践的起点与基础，市场洞察是宏观与微观的联系。我们要具备敏锐性，要敢于质疑，任何人所说的都有可能是有问题的，我们要有质疑的心。通过这一次宝贵的学习经历，让我更深刻地发现到了自身上的不足，在未来希望还有更多的机会和公司之中优秀的同事们学习到更多的东西，也希望自己在未来还能继续和大家一起工作和学习。

in the process of the implementation of the project.

I have been greatly inspired, being an intern here. I learned to handle things with a calm mindset and that we should focus our time on the things we do, go toward the direction we have chosen and keep working hard until we succeed. It is important to choose the right partner and the core direction before we act. Only in this way can we have infinitive possibilities to do great things.

It is during my internship here that I have learned that keeping a true heart is the key to maintaining individual charm. We should have the ability to observe which is the starting point and the basis of political and business practices. What's more, market observation is the bond between micro and macro economics. We should keep alerted all the time, being brave enough to question. We should have the ability of raising our doubts, as there might be problems in anything that others say. Through my internship here, I am able to know where my weaknesses lie. I hope I can have more opportunities to learn from my excellent colleagues, and I hope to still work with you and learn from you in more years to come.

汤昕晨
Xinchen Tang

本科毕业于广西财经学院，现就读上海对外经贸大学MBA。喜欢一个人听歌发呆，也喜欢走出家门打篮球、玩轮滑。愿岁月的流逝，不会给灵魂带去伤痕，即便身处喧嚣，也要明确自己的方向。

Graduated from Guangxi University of Finance and Economics with a bachelor's degree and is currently studying for MBA at Shanghai University of International Business and Economics. Xinchen Tang likes to listen to songs alone and also likes to go out to play basketball and roller skating. She hopes that the passage of time will not bring scars to the soul, and even in the hustle and bustle, She can still clarify her own direction.

莫向外求
Do Not Seek Outward

■ Tony Lau

既在佛会下，都是有缘人。

四季相续，白驹过隙。转眼我已经在 CNOOD 度过了六年的时光。人生渐往，必回思骑竹嬉游处，从我离开家乡求学在外，至今已历十三个寒暑。对于我而言，公司更像是我的另一个家，我在这里工作，在这里生活，在这里成长，回首往事，如在目前。

庚子风云，岁运并临。

天时大势，君子贞祥。

2020 年，疫情席卷全球，打乱原有的生活节奏。让人们慢下来，静下来，停下来。六年来间或有同事选择离开公司，常常让我一时感伤，不能同进退，共荣辱。将军不下马，各自奔前程。每个人都有自己的路要走，正所谓没有什么是不变

We are brought together by Buddhism, so we are bonded by fate.

Four seasons come and go, as time passes by. I have spent six years at CNOOD. When looking back, I could never forget my hometown where I spent my childhood and those years when I had fun in the bamboo forest. It has been thirteen years since I left home. To me, CNOOD is like my second home. I work here, live here and grow here. Those old times, whenever I look back, are still fresh to me.

Gengzi Rat Year, destiny and luck matter equally,

Following timing and trend, men of integrity will be blessed.

In 2020, a pandemic hit the world, and our peaceful lives were destroyed. People had to slow down, calm down and pace down. During the six years I am here, there have been colleagues leaving the company once in a while, and it made

的，只有变是不变的，从来无所谓对与错，只有选择。

于我而言，何尝不是一直居安思危，在前进中探索与思考属于自己的路。虽然说应兼听则明，见贤思齐，但是路只能自己选，也只能自己走。如果人云亦云，随波逐流，则不过是磨砖作镜，积雪为粮，或事倍功半，或徒费青春尔。

知止，《大学》言知止而后有定；定而后能静；静而后能安；安而后能虑；虑而后能得。先当停下匆忙的脚步，涤净浮躁的心灵。每逢大事有静气，不信今时无古贤。

明心，斜月三星，灵台方寸，心也。小时不懂，为何大费周章西天取经，何不使法术，挟山超海，将唐僧送至灵山。后来细品《西游记》，方才发现，唐僧也曾和我一样的疑问。行至五庄观，十停走了不到一停，唐僧问悟空你说得几时方可

me upset. How I wished we could share weal and woe together! As the old saying goes: *Generals never go off his horse, and each goes his own way*; Everyone has his own way to go. Nothing is permanent but change. Life is about making choices, regardless of being right or wrong.

To me, I am alerted all the time, being prepared for danger in times of peace. I've never stopped exploring new ways while I am marching forward. The sayings go: "Listen to both sides and you will be enlightened; heed only one side and you will be benighted." "Emulate those better than myself." But even so, I have to make my own choice and go my own way. I can't go with the flow, doing what others say, or I will be grinding bricks for mirrors and storing snow for food, wasting my precious years.

Know where you are going. As what *The Great Learning* says: know where you are going, and you'll have a clear direction; with a clear direction, you'll be able to calm down; when you are able to calm down, you'll have peace of mind; with a settled mind, you'll be able to think; when you think deeply, you'll gain. Why don't we slow down our pace and let our mind calm down? Stay cool when facing difficulties, as the old sages did.

Keep a pure heart. A leaning moon and three stars make the Chinese character 心 —the heart. The Chinese character 灵 and 寸 make the character 寻 —to find the true heart. When I was little, I did not understand why Tang

到，悟空回答，你自小时走到老，老了再小，老小千番也还难，只要你见性志诚，念念回首处，即是灵山。我也才幡然大悟，如果唐僧直接灵山授佛，其本质并未发生任何变化，佛也只是个抬头和虚名而已。而佛，并不在于灵山，在去灵山的路上，也不在路上经历的劫难，而是经历了劫难修成的心，正是佛在灵山莫远求，灵山只在汝心头，历劫明心，汝即如来。

正如我的工作与生活，想要强大，不在于名，而在于实。

如果工作上我只是夸夸其谈，名过其实，给我赋予合伙人，对我的本质没有任何改变，甚至可能适得其反，正所谓德不配位，必有灾殃。如果生活上，我只是沽名钓誉，自诩耿介，却嫉贤妒能，而常常为小事而疾言厉色，那么不过是忝列衣冠，道貌岸然，不过是活在影子中，面具

Monk went through mountains and seas for Buddhist scriptures instead of using magic directly. When I read *Journey to the West* again, I found that Tang Monk had the same question. When they arrived at the Wuzhuang Taoist Temple, after not even one-tenth of the whole journey, Tang Monk asked Monkey King when they could arrive, and Monkey King said:You started the journey when you were little, you keep going until you get old. This cycle goes round and round. But if you have a firm faith and a pure heart, wherever you go, the final destination (the Lingshan Mountain) is in your heart. I understood it all at once. If Tang Monk used magic and got the scriptures directly, he would be nothing but an ordinary monk—nothing in his nature would be changed. But Buddha exists not only in Lingshan Mountain, but also on the way to Lingshan Mountain. It does not lie in the difficulties they experience, but lies in the heart that endures the difficulties. Do not seek Buddha outward, as it's right in your heart. Keep a pure heart, and you are the Buddha yourself.

The same can be applied in my work and life: If I want to be strong, I have to be practical, regardless of fame.

If I keep bragging without doing anything practical, I will be of no value to my partners, nor will I bring any benefit to them. In this case, nothing will be changed in my nature. As the saying goes, if your virtue doesn't match your position, there will be a disaster. In

下，战战兢兢，唯唯诺诺，百害而无一利。如果我可以做到厚积薄发，积跬致远，但行好事，不问前程。可以做到多与少取，躬自厚而薄责于人，则不论外在谤誉如何，仍得心安意宁，俯仰无愧。何为取舍，一目了然。

life, if I only care about who I am in the appearance, get jealous of those who are more competent and whine about little things, I'll end up living in a fake and meaningless life. I'll live in shadow or under masks, getting too cautious and scared. But if I can accumulate my power and let it out when it's time, I'll be able to make big progresses. Just do your best, no matter what you expect. I'll give more and get less, be strict with myself and be easy on others, so that I can stay unbothered inside. It's easy to see which is the best choice.

千里之行，始于足下。适莽苍者，三餐而反，腹犹果然；适百里者，宿舂粮；适千里者，三月聚粮。

我还任重道远。

A thousand-mile journey begins with the first step.

Those who go to the suburb will take three meals with them;

Those who go a hundred miles will spend the whole night preparing for food;

And those who go a thousand miles will bring meals enough for three months.

I have my responsibilities and there's still a long way for me to go.

刘 彬
Tony Lau

自称流浪书生，2016年毕业加入CNOOD，寻梦路上从未停止脚步。

I call myself as a wandering scholar. I joined CNOOD in 2016. I've never stopped chasing my dream.

居家的第 n 天，我还剩 15g 咖啡豆
Quarantine Day n, I Have 15g Coffee Beans Left

■ Siki Wan

三月底的某一天，在我拿起咖啡袋，掂量着里面仅存的咖啡豆时，突然一股焦虑和不安涌上心头。打开物流查看海淘的咖啡豆，依然卡在海关毫无动静，面临所有快递都即将停止的尴尬时间，我打开了微信向朋友求救。直到朋友喊来闪送为我续上了大半个月的豆量，巨大的安全感又重新拥抱了我。

挑了一支日晒埃塞，磨粉烧水，一股熟悉又久违的柑橘香甜充满了我的鼻腔。坐在电脑前，喝着这杯来之不易的咖啡，回想过去的 2021 年，看似平常却又很不一样的一年。

2021 年，被疫情影响的第二年，层出不穷的零星病例，让人逐渐在害怕中麻

One day at the end of March, when I grabbed the coffee bag and saw the few coffee beans that had left, an overwhelming, anxious and upset feeling crowded in on me. The new coffee beans that I had bought online from overseas were stuck at customs. Afraid that all the delivery service would be stopped soon, I had to ask help from a friend on Wechat. I felt a sense of security again when my friend ordered the Flash Ex to send me some coffee beans, enough for me to drink for the following half month.

Choosing Ethiopia coffee, I started to grind and boil the coffee. A long lost sweet orange smell came to my nose. I sat in front of the laptop, enjoying this hard-won cup of coffee while looking back on the things that had happened in 2021, which seemed an ordinary but different year.

2021 was the second year after the pandemic took place. Cases of the disease

木。当出行受限，当口罩成为跟手机一样的必需品时，我们好像没有过多的精力去开发一项新的兴趣爱好呢。而我呢，好像很幸运地在2021年碰到了自己的新爱好。

　　快餐时代，咖啡成为必不可少的日常陪伴。从最初简简单单的提神，到现在越来越普及的咖啡文化，人们意识到咖啡不再只是杯子里的液体，而是从种子开始就被赋予了灵魂的生物。电影《美丽曼特宁》中说："生命就像一场盛宴，不懂如何享受咖啡的人，将会因饥饿而逝去。"

　　我对咖啡的感受，最初也从杯子开始，到咖啡店点单、付款、取杯。后来为

emerged in an endless stream, making people scared first then go numb. When going out became a luxury and facial masks became necessities like mobile phones, we seemed to be too exhausted to develop a new hobby. Lucky for me, I took up a new interest in 2021.

　　In the fast food era, coffee has become a daily necessity. People used to drink coffee to refresh themselves at first, but now there's something called the coffee culture. It is no longer some liquid in the cup, but something alive with a soul when it's just a seed. As is said in the movie *Mandheling*, life is like a feast, those who don't know how to enjoy coffee will die from starvation.

　　My affection for coffee began from cups. I ordered, paid and used different

了方便，开始接触速溶咖啡，再升级到挂耳，有了手动操作的空间。慢慢地，机缘巧合下了解了不少关于咖啡风味的描述。既然咖啡的品种有很多，风味又各不相同，为什么不学习自己冲煮咖啡呢？人生的意义在于体验，那我也开始体验一下"不一样"的咖啡好了。

于是我开始搜索咖啡相关的知识，系统学习；同时也参加各种各样的咖啡节，品尝各个种类的豆子，学会体会这复杂而迷人的咖啡风味。从基础入门的网红磨豆机，到信仰与颜值的天花板C40；从一只普通的咖啡壶，到冠军同款的温控壶；从V60到各式各样的滤杯，我一步一步地摸索着每一个变量对于最后咖啡风味呈现的巨大影响，直到我研究出了自己熟悉的冲煮方案，让我能够稳定地冲出一杯干净而甜感十足的咖啡，这种过程给我带来了满满的成就感。而期间的每一杯咖啡，都成了我在开启一天紧张工作前最好的调剂品。

喝一口手边的咖啡，回想这一段经历，好像所有的事物都会在到来和离去时给我们带来不一样的体验。然而事物是客观的，人是主观的，处在不同的阶段，站在不同的角度，对同一件事都会有截然不同的看法，就像咖啡一样。同一颗豆子，你可以研究不同冲煮手法带来的味道差

cups in the cafe. Then I started to drink instant coffee for convenience. Gradually, I started to operate by myself by drinking drip coffee. Exposed to all kinds of coffee, I got to know different styles by different descriptions. Since there are various types of coffee with different tastes, why can't I learn to boil coffee for myself? To me, the meaning of life lies in different experiences, so I might as well experience making different coffees.

I started to collect relevant information about coffee and studied it systematically; at the same time, I actively attended various kinds of coffee festivals and tasted different coffee beans. I was lost in the complicated and charming tastes of different kinds of coffee. I started from the basic grinding machine to the sacred and professional C40 machine; I used an ordinary coffee pot and then a temperature control kettle of the same type from the brand Champion; the filter cups varied from V60 to all other kinds of cups. I measured what huge effect each step had on the final taste and finally I had my own recipe. Now I am able to make a cup of tasty coffee and the whole process gives me a high sense of achievement. Every cup of coffee I make becomes the best starter before my work each day.

Taking a sip of the coffee at my hand and looking back on the old days, I find that things sometimes seem different when coming and going. However, this world goes around by the law of nature which is unchangable. We may have different views about different things

异，可以研究它的历史发展，品种培育，文化传播，站在不同的角度会有各种不同的收获。我想咖啡的可玩性，或者说人生的可玩性就在各种不同的感受和体验之中吧。说穿了，改变世界，抑或被世界改变，不也是一种体验吗？刚开始我们不理解，不甘心，到最后跟自己妥协，或是把不甘心贯彻到底，也是一种别样的体验。

想远了，喝口咖啡，把思绪拉回来。

2021年，还有一件很有趣的事，在朋友的带领下，发现了一家特别有意思的小咖啡店。我愿称之为在这个拥有世界上最多咖啡馆的城市之中，最有人情味的一家。

when we look from different angles. Take coffee for example, the same coffee beans could have different tastes when we boil them in different ways. We could gain much knowledge by studying their history, development and their roles in culture transmission. It is different experiences that make coffee and life so enjoyable. To be frank, changing the world or getting changed by the world is also an experience, isn't it? There are times when we are confused and discouraged, and there are times when we make a compromise. They are all special experiences to us.

I am going too far. Taking another sip of coffee, I draw myself back to reality.

Another interesting thing happened in 2021. A friend took me to a very special cafe, which I considered as the most thoughtful place in this city which has the most cafes in the world.

一个小小的店面，一场随性的分享，一位咖啡师，同时也是老板，无所谓陌不陌生，随着他的招呼加入唠嗑行列。大家围坐吧台，吧台总坐着有趣的陌生人，讲着轻快的故事。老板在给我们介绍与冲煮每一支来自不同国家，不同烘焙商的豆子，这一刻还在肯尼亚的谷地，下一秒就飞去了巴拿马的丛林，这一口你呼吸着天空之镜纯净的风，下一秒你就闻到了墨西哥阳光的甜。

老板说："一家咖啡店的主理人很重要。人情味比起咖啡品质更能留住顾客。"

是的，正如他做的这般。

当我第三次推开店门，老板已经能准确地认出我们，像朋友一样打招呼，倒上一小杯他近期最喜欢的酒与我们分享，我想这就是大家这么喜欢这家店的缘故吧。

在咖啡冷掉前，喝完了杯底最后一口咖啡。

以前我认为一个人的成长，一定是在完成一个又一个的目标。但有一天我读到一篇文章里写道，如果你过于注重目标，或许因为你在寻找幸福或成就，成为一个更圆满的自我，这时你就没有再关注当下了。当下失去了固有的价值，而沦为通向未来的踏脚石。这时，你生命的旅程不再是一场奇妙的探险，它变成了一个为了达

It was a tiny cafe where everyone could share their stories and thoughts. The boss, as well as the coffee maker, invited everyone to join his conversation. We were sitting at the bar where there were always funny strangers, telling funny stories. The boss introduced different coffee beans from different countries and companies. We were in the valley of Kenya this moment and the Amazon jungle the next. We were breathing the pure air in the Mirror of Sky this moment and smelling the sweet Mexico sunshine the next.

As the boss said: It matters a lot who manages the cafe. A friendly and comfortable atmosphere does a better job in keeping the customers than the quality of the coffee.

And that's how he managed the cafe.

When we went to the cafe for the third time, the boss could recognize who we each were and greeted us like we were his old friends. He then opened a bottle of his favorite liquor and shared with us. This was why the cafe became so popular, I assumed.

I drink the last sip of coffee before it gets cold.

A person grows when he finishes his goals one by one, as I used to think. But one day when I was reading an article, I had a new view about it. It said: If you pay too much attention to your goals, looking for your happiness or becoming a better person, you may lose the fun that the present brings to you. The

到目标、获得成就的强迫性需要。你不会再看到路边的花朵或闻到它的芬芳,也不会觉察到存在于当下的围绕着你生命的美丽和奇迹。

好的,说了这么多,也算给我之前那些或许过萃或许萃取不足而失败的咖啡,找了一个华丽的借口吧。

present then loses its value and becomes the steppingstone for you to get to the future. In this case, your life is no longer a fantastic journey but a necessity with which you achieve your goals. You will longer notice the beauty of the flowers along the road or the scent they give off, nor will you sense the beauty and wonder hidden in your life.

Well, so much being said, I think I will never regret having tried endless times to find my favorite taste of coffee, after all, experience matters most.

万诗琦
Siki Wan

2018 年加入施璐德。

Joined CNOOD in 2018.